Skeletons in the Closet

This book tackles three puzzles of pacted transitions to democracy. First, why do autocrats ever step down from power peacefully if they know that they may be held accountable for their involvement in the ancien régime? Second, when does the opposition indeed refrain from meting out punishment to the former autocrats once the transition is complete? Third, why, in some countries, does transitional justice get adopted when successors of former communists hold parliamentary majorities? Monika Nalepa argues that infiltration of the opposition with collaborators of the authoritarian regime can serve as insurance against transitional justice, making their commitments to amnesty credible. This explanation also accounts for the timing of transitional justice across East Central Europe. Nalepa supports her theory using a combination of elite interviews, archival evidence, and statistical analysis of survey experiments in Poland, Hungary, and the Czech Republic.

Monika Nalepa is Assistant Professor in the Department of Political Science at the University of Notre Dame. She is also Faculty Fellow of Notre Dame's Kellogg Institute for International Studies, the Kroc Institute for Peace Studies, and the Nanovic Institute for European Studies. In 2006–2007 and 2009, she held an appointment as Academy Scholar at the Harvard Academy for International and Area Studies. Nalepa has guest co-edited a special volume dedicated to transitional justice in the *Journal of Conflict Resolution* and has contributed articles to the *Journal of Conflict Resolution* and the *Journal of Theoretical Politics* and chapters to numerous edited volumes devoted to transitional justice, including *NOMOS: Proceedings of the American Society for Political and Legal Philosophy*.

Tadeuszowi Nalepie,
który pomógł mi zrozumieć że niczego nie muszę

Cambridge Studies in Comparative Politics

General Editor
Margaret Levi, *University of Washington, Seattle*

Assistant General Editors
Kathleen Thelen, *Massachusetts Institute of Technology*
Erik Wibbels, *Duke University*

Associate Editors
Robert H. Bates, *Harvard University*
Stephen Hanson, *University of Washington, Seattle*
Torben Iversen, *Harvard University*
Stathis Kalyvas, *Yale University*
Peter Lange, *Duke University*
Helen Milner, *Princeton University*
Frances Rosenbluth, *Yale University*
Susan Stokes, *Yale University*

Other Books in the Series

Continued after the Index.

Advance Praise for *Skeletons in the Closet*

"Monika Nalepa's *Skeletons in the Closet* offers a groundbreaking analysis of transitional justice and its role in the consolidation of new democracies. Combining rigorous theoretical analysis with an impressive array of qualitative and quantitative evidence – including interviews with elites on both sides of transitions from communist rule in Eastern Europe, as well as original surveys of citizens – this book makes a compelling case for its argument: policies that pursue transitional justice are typically not driven by the demands of voters and citizens. Instead, they must be understood as strategic choices by political elites acting in the fog of an authoritarian legacy, characterized by great uncertainty about past collaboration of resistance leaders with the former regime. This approach allows Nalepa to offer convincing explanations of puzzling aspects of the timing and the scope of transitional justice policies that have largely gone unexplained to date. This book will force scholars to rethink common conceptions about transitional justice, and it should be read not only by those who study post-communist Eastern Europe, but by anyone with an interest in transitions from authoritarianism to democracy."

Georg Vanberg, University of North Carolina at Chapel Hill

"Why weren't former communist elites immediately punished after communism fell? In this excellent book, Monika Nalepa explains why justice was delayed and, paradoxically, why in the end it was the former communists that purged themselves. Through an impressive combination of formal theory, statistical analysis, and primary research in Eastern Europe, Nalepa finds that fears of collaboration within the ranks of non-communist parties drove the timing of punishment. Where such fears were high, these parties were inhibited from enacting such legislation; where they were low, the former communists preempted the passage of harsh measures with milder ones of their own. No one who reads this carefully argued and provocative book will think about transitional justice in quite the same way again."

Jason Wittenberg, University of California at Berkeley

Skeletons in the Closet

TRANSITIONAL JUSTICE IN POST-COMMUNIST EUROPE

MONIKA NALEPA

University of Notre Dame

CAMBRIDGE
UNIVERSITY PRESS

CAMBRIDGE UNIVERSITY PRESS
Cambridge, New York, Melbourne, Madrid, Cape Town,
Singapore, São Paulo, Delhi, Mexico City

Cambridge University Press
32 Avenue of the Americas, New York, NY 10013-2473, USA

www.cambridge.org
Information on this title: www.cambridge.org/9780521735506

First published 2010
Reprinted 2012

A catalog record for this publication is available from the British Library.

Library of Congress Cataloging in Publication Data

Nalepa, Monika, 1976–
    Skeletons in the closet : transitional justice in post-Communist Europe /
Monika Nalepa.
        p.   cm. – (Cambridge studies in comparative politics)
    Includes bibliographical references and index.
    ISBN 978-0-521-51445-3 (hardback) – ISBN 978-0-521-73550-6 (pbk.)
    1. Democratization – Europe, Eastern.   2. Transitional justice – Europe,
Eastern.   3. Political purges – Europe, Eastern.   4. Post-communism – Europe,
Eastern.   I. Title.   II. Series.
    JN96.A58N35   2009
    320.947–dc22   2009012902

ISBN 978-0-521-51445-3 Hardback
ISBN 978-0-521-73550-6 Paperback

Contents

Contents

Figures

Tables

Tables

Acknowledgments

Many kind people and excellent scholars helped me write this book. Among the first were my advisers Jon Elster and John Huber. In my second year of graduate school, Jon Elster commented on a term paper I decided to share with him. We spent the entire meeting discussing a single sentence, mentioned in passing on the first page of that paper: Promises made at roundtable negotiations granting amnesty to outgoing autocrats are not credible. He tried to convince me at that time that addressing this dilemma would be a fascinating topic for a dissertation on transitional justice in post-communist Europe. Without his insistent urging, I would never have written the first part of this book. John Huber, aside from all his qualities as an outstanding comparativist, is one of the most patient people with whom I have been lucky enough to work. He read – literally – ten consecutive early versions of Chapter 7 of this book. John's advice to write a book manuscript, as opposed to a series of articles on transitional justice, was also critical for the final decision to embark on writing a manuscript in a language that is not my native tongue. Columbia University offered, for me, the ideal environment in which to earn a Ph.D. in political science. I was lucky to learn formal methods from the top scholars of the field: Chuck Cameron, David Epstein, Macartan Humphreys, and Michael Ting. I was also fortunate to work with an amazing group of political theorists including Brian Barry, Jon Elster, and David Johnston. Erik Gartzke was critical to my discovery of the literature on credible commitments in international relations. At Columbia, I was always surrounded by a fabulous group of friends. Pablo Kalmanovitz, Ozge Kemahlioglu, Georgia Kernell, Mary McCarthy, Bumba Mukherjee, and Rebecca Weitz Shapiro were eager to offer comments and, at times, tough criticism on chapter drafts, helping me to develop rough ideas into a dissertation. I was extremely fortunate to have such talented young scholars as peers. While still in graduate school at Columbia, I received both intellectual and financial support from the Center for the Study of Democracy (CSD) at the University of California in Irvine (UCI), directed at the time by Russ Dalton. The visiting researchship there helped me prepare for fieldwork in East Central Europe. I am also grateful to the CSD for providing me with numerous opportunities to present my work and for grants offered to develop other transitional justice ideas with Marek Kaminski. I also thank Bernie Groffman and Tony McGann, both faculty of the CSD. Among the students, special thanks go to Bruce Hemmer and Michael Jensen who welcomed me to the graduate student community at UCI. They not only extended their close friendship, but also took me hiking in California's state parks to remind me of the world outside of Dietrich's coffee shop.

Thanks to the National Science Foundation (SES-03–18363), the Institute for Humane Studies, the United States Institute of Peace, the Center for Conflict Resolution, and Harriman Institute at Columbia University, I was able to split nine months of fieldwork in 2003–4 among Poland, Hungary, and the Czech Republic. Many people in these three countries were incredibly helpful in setting up elite interviews and enabling my access to archives. In particular, I thank Andras Bozóki, Jan Holzer, Jan Kudrna, Grzegorz Lissowski, Wiktor Osiatyński, Filip Raciborski, and Artur Zawisza, as well as the Institute of Sociology at Warsaw University, the Helsinki Foundation in Warsaw, and the Open Society Institute in Budapest for providing me with an institutional home while I was away from Columbia.

Upon returning to the United States, I am grateful to the Columbia political science faculty for feedback on the results of my fieldwork, especially to David Epstein, Bob Ericson, Nisha Fazal, Macartan Humphreys, Jeff Lax, Sharon O'Halloran, Bob Shapiro, Jack Snyder, Michael Ting, and Greg Wawro. I also thank the political science departments of Florida State University, Rice University, and the University of Georgia; the politics departments of New York University and the University of Virginia; and the Harvard Academy at the Weatherhead Center for International Affairs and Area Studies for feedback on my dissertation research. Special thanks go to Dale Copeland and Carol Merschon at the University of Virginia, Jaroslav Gryz at the University of Georgia, Sandy Gordon and Steve Brams at New York University, Mark Souva and Jeff Staton at Florida State University, and Cliff Morgan and Rick Wilson at Rice University.

Acknowledgments

I also thank the rest of my dissertation committee – in particular, Andrzej Rapaczynski of Columbia University's Law School – who helped me realize that the way I had approached the credible commitment problem in the dissertation required significant rethinking.

Beyond graduate school, I thank Gerard Alexander, Barbara Geddes, Bob Powell, Piotr Swistak, and Georg Vanberg, who attended the Current Research Workshop sponsored by the Institute for Humane Studies in March 2006. I thank Nigel Ashford and Amanda Brand for organizing the workshop. The central model of the book was fleshed out there. I am grateful to Randy Stevenson, my senior colleague from Rice, for encouraging me to develop my idea of strategic transitional justice into a book and convincing me that I could write it quickly. I will always remain grateful to Ashley Leeds, also from Rice, for her ongoing support and for being such an inspiring role model for me to draw on as a budding assistant professor.

I was lucky to encounter the best mentors in the discipline. Anna Grzymala-Busse from the University of Michigan talked to me about framing the puzzle of delayed transitional justice into a book project in the summer of 2006. She commented on three prospectus drafts of the book and, eventually, on the entire manuscript. Another extremely important mentor was Jim Alt, who helped me develop the book prospectus in its final version in the fall of 2006 in Cambridge. Jim also read two very rough drafts of the manuscript.

Next, in chronological order, thanks go to Harvard Academy senior scholars Jorge Dominguez, Grzegorz Ekiert, and Jim Robinson, who met with me throughout the writing process to discuss specific chapters. I thank the Academy for offering me a fellowship along with the opportunity to be surrounded by such stimulating colleagues as Mary Alice Haddad, Saum Jha, Devra Moehler, Conor O'Dwyer, Kristen Roth-Ey, and Jocelyn Viterna. I am also grateful to the Senior Academy Scholars Bob Bates, Timothy Colton, and Susan Pharr for providing me with feedback on my prospectus following its presentation to the Harvard Academy. I thank the organizers of seminars in Cambridge and California, where I presented two early chapters of the book in the fall and winter of 2006–7: the Identity and Politics Workshop at the Massachusetts Institute of Technology (MIT), the Comparative Politics Workshop at Harvard, the Post-communist Politics and Economics Workshop at Harvard's Davis Center, and the Political Science Departmental Colloquium at UCI. In particular, I thank for feedback at these seminars Nathan Cisneros, Kristin

Fabbe, and Roger Petersen from the MIT Political Science Department; Meg Ryan and Elina Treger from Harvard's Government Department; and Gerald Easter from Boston College. I also wish to thank Marek Kaminski of UCI and Yoi Herrera of the University of Wisconsin in Madison for written comments on work I presented at their workshops.

My deepest thanks for their hard work go to Kathleen Hoover and Lawrence Winnie for organizing a book seminar following the completion of the first draft of the manuscript in May 2007. I am deeply grateful to the attendees of that day-long workshop: James Alt, Scott Desposato, Jorge Dominguez, Grzegorz Ekiert, Barbara Geddes, Anna Grzymała-Busse, Joshua Tucker, and Jason Wittenberg.

When, after revising the manuscript in the fall of 2007, I returned to Rice, my colleagues extended to me the warmest welcome but also organized another book workshop to offer more, but still much needed, comments. Royce Carroll, Lanny Martin, Cliff Morgan, Randy Stevenson, and Rick Wilson read the manuscript in its entirety and offered valuable comments and ideas for further revisions. Rice University also funded the research assistance of some of its best graduate students: Iliya Atanasov, Stephanie Burchard, and Carla Martinez.

I thank my new colleagues at the University of Notre Dame: Darren Davis, Michael Desch, Debra Javeline, Mary Keys, Scott Mainwaring, Sebastian Rosato, Christina Wolbrecht, and Michael Zuckert. I particularly thank Michael Coppedge for answering endless questions about manuscript preparation. I also thank the Russian and Eastern European Studies reading group at Notre Dame, in particular David Gasparetti, Alyssa Gillespie, and Mikołaj Kunicki for comments on Chapter 7. An article version of that chapter was presented at the American Political Science Association meeting in September 2008, where I received very valuable feedback from Jae-Jae Spoon. Alexandre Debs read and corrected my mathematical proofs to Chapter 3 after the Peace Science Society Meeting in October 2008. I also thank Milan Svolik and Scott Gehlbach for their comments on the model in Chapter 3.

I thank the two anonymous referees for their valuable feedback and for pointing out to me areas of the literature that I had overlooked and for helping me see the book from different angles. I also thank Rick Wilson, the chair of Rice's Political Science Department, for providing me with office space at Rice over the summer of 2008 so that in the midst of my transition to Notre Dame I could implement revisions and comments from Cambridge's two anonymous referees.

Acknowledgments

I am extremely grateful to Lew Bateman and Margaret Levi from Cambridge University Press for helping me write a book suitable for this prestigious series. They offered their own comments on more than one version of the manuscript and sought out exceptionally competent reviewers to whom I feel indebted for feedback.

I also thank Andy Saff for meticulous copyediting and Matthew Mendham for his outstanding research assistance with final edits and the index. Matthew's work as well as the book cover design was supported by a grant from the Institute for the Scholarship in the Liberal Arts, College of Arts and Letters, University of Notre Dame Interim Miscellaneous Research and Material Grant.

Although political scientists were critical in developing this project, it would not have been nearly as enjoyable without the help and presence of Suyash Agrawal. An immigrant like myself, he has the deepest understanding of challenges facing someone striving to adapt to the American way of life while scaling the ivory tower of U.S. academia. He has been the most intellectually inspiring and passionate person an academic could fall in love with. I admire him for challenging my most established convictions, initiating debates in the middle of the most casual activities. Suyash read and edited the manuscript in its entirety. I feel indebted to him for discussing the manuscript with me at every stage of the writing process.

At bottom, this work is the product of countless supporters who encouraged and challenged me and contributed to it from its inception. But I, alone, remain responsible for any shortcomings or deficiencies.

East Central European Political Organizations

Poland

Akcja Wyborcza Solidarność (AWS): Electoral Action Solidarity
Grupa Krakowska: Kraków Group
Komitet Obrony Robotników (KOR): Laborers' Defense Committee
Konfederacja Polski Niepodległej (KPN): Confederacy for Independent Poland
Kongres Liberalno-Demokratyczny (KLD): Liberal Democratic Congress
Liga Polskich Rodzin (LPR): League of Polish Families
Niezależny Związek Studentów (NZS): Independent Student Union
Niezależny Związek Zawodowy "Solidarność": Independent Trade Union "Solidarity"
Obywatelski Komitet (Koło) Poselski(e) (OKP): Civic Parliamentary Committee
Platforma Obywatelska (PO): Civic Platform
Polska Zjednoczona Partia Robotnicza (PZPR): Polish United Workers' Party
Polskie Stronnictwo Ludowe (PSL): Polish Peoples' Party
Prawo i Sprawiedliwość (PiS): Law and Justice
Ruch Obrony Rzeczpospolitej (RdR): Movement for the Republic
Ruch Odbudowy Polski (ROP): Movement for the Reconstruction of Poland
Ruch Wolność i Pokój (RWP): Movement for Freedom and Peace
Samoobrona (S): Self-Defense
Socjaldemokracja Rzeczpospolitej Polski (SdRP): Social Democracy of the Republic of Poland
Sojusz Lewicy Demokratycznej (SLD): Democratic Left Alliance

Solidarność '80 (S'80): Solidarity '80
Solidarność Walcząca (SW): Fighting Solidarity
Studencki Komitet Solidarności (SKS): Student Committee of Solidarity
Tymczasowa Komisja Koordynacyjna (TKK): Temporary Coordinating
  Committee
Unia Demokratyczna (UD): Democratic Union
Unia Pracy (UP): Labor Union
Unia Wolności (UW): Freedom Union
Wojskowa Rada Ocalenia Narodowego (WRON): Military Council of
  National Salvation

Czechoslovakia, Czech Republic, and Slovakia

Česká Strana Sociálně Demokratická (ČSSD): Czech Social Democratic
  Party
Charta 77: Charter 77
Demokratické Levice (DL): Democratic Left (Czech)
Demokratická Strana (DS): Democratic Party (Slovak)
Demokratická Únia (DÚDÚ): Democratic Union (Slovak)
Hnutie za Demokratické Slovensko (HZDS): Movement for a Democratic
  Slovakia (Slovak)
Hnutí za samosprávnou demokracii – Společnost pro Moravu a Slezsko
  (HSDSMS): Movement for Autonomous Democracy – Party for
  Moravia and Silesia
Komunistická Strana Čech a Moravy (KSČM): Communist Party of
  Bohemia and Moravia
Komunistická Strana Československa (KSČ): Communist Party of
  Czechoslovakia
Krestanská a demokratická Unie-Česka Strana Lidová (KDÚ-ČSL):
  Christian Democratic Union–Czech People's Party
Kresťanskodemokratické Hnutie (KDH): Christian Democratic Move-
  ment (Slovak)
Levý Blok (LB): Left Bloc (Czech)
Liberálně sociální unie (LSU): Liberal Social Union (Czech)
Občanská Demokratická Strana (ODS): Civic Democratic Party (Czech)
Občanské Forum (OF): Civic Forum (Czech)
Sdružení pro Republiku – Republikánská strana Československa (REP):
  Union for Republic – Republicans' Party of Czechoslovakia
Slovenská Demokratická Koalícia (SDK): Slovak Democratic Coalition

Slovenská Národná Strana (SNS): Slovak National Party
Strana Demokratickej L'avice (SDĽ): Party of the Democratic Left
  (Slovak)
Strana Občanského Porozumění (SOP): Party of Civic Understanding
  (Slovak)
Strana Zelených na Slovensku (SZS): Green Party of Slovakia
Unie Svobody (US): Freedom Union (Czech)
Združenie Robotníkov Slovenska (ZRS): Association of Slovak Workers

Hungary

Bajcsy Zsilinszky Endre Baráti Társaság (BZSBT): Bajcsy-Zsilinszky
  Friends' Association
Ellenzéki Kerekasztal (EKA): Opposition Roundtable
Fiatal Demokraták Szövetsége (FiDeSz): Alliance of Young Democrats
Fidesz-Magyar Polgári Párt (Fidesz-MPP): Fidesz-Hungarian Civic Party
Független Jógasz Fórum (FJF): Independent Lawyers' Forum
Független Kisgazdapárt (FKgP): Party of Independent Smallholders
Kereszténydemokrata Néppárt (KDNP): Christian Democratic People's
  Party
Magyar Demokrata Fórum (MDF): Hungarian Democratic Forum
Magyar Igazság és Élet Pártja (MIÉP): Hungarian Justice and Life Party
Magyar Szocialista Munkás Párt (MSzMP): Hungarian Socialist Workers'
  Party
Magyar Szocialista Párt (MSzP): Hungarian Socialist Party
Szabad Demokraták Szövetsége (SzDSz): Alliance of Free Democrats

1

Introduction

The major was dragged over to a tree by several fighters. His ankles were tied and he was strapped to one of the lowest branches. He kicked at the rope and paper forints fell from his pockets. In a few seconds the winds scattered more money than a worker could have saved in years. His body was only three feet from the ground. The revolutionists gathered leaves and paper and piled them under the suspended major. He screamed and pleaded for mercy. He cried out that he would cooperate with us and would tell us all the AVH names we wanted. But the students and workers just laughed at him. They brought the other AVH police over at gunpoint to watch. They lit the fire. As the flames licked at his hair, the AVH men turned white at the sight. They were led away to be locked up. (Beke 1957, 50)[1]

Laszlo Beke wrote this in "A Student Diary: Budapest October 16–November 1, 1956." Beke participated in the Hungarian Uprising, by far the bloodiest of the anticommunist protests in the history of communist rule in Europe (Beke 1957). The revolution ended with the Red Army effecting a massive crackdown on anticommunist forces followed by widespread repercussions against the revolution's organizers. The revolutionists' casualties vastly outnumbered those for the Soviet-backed regime.

The Budapest insurgents did not realize their main goal of returning democracy to Hungary until 1989, when a wave of democratic transitions transformed East Central Europe. The most surprising and still under-researched aspect of these transitions was their peaceful nature. In a little

---

[1] The AVH was the Hungarian secret political police. After the uprising, the tasks of the AVH were transferred to a new agency within the Ministry of Interior. Popularly referred to as the III/3 agency, it recruited most of its personnel from the former AVH and essentially followed the same operational tactics.

over a year, single-party communist regimes fell in twenty-seven countries – almost without bloodshed.

Beke's account from the 1956 Hungarian Uprising reflects the retribution that fallen dictators face. The ripest moment for such retribution is in the immediate aftermath of the transition, when memories of the ancien régime are vivid and demand for settling accounts is most pressing. Despite urgently needed political and economic reforms, little can stop the former opposition from bringing the former autocrats to justice.

Surely the communist rulers must have contemplated such scenarios and anticipated falling victim to political revenge. Consequently, they should have resisted stepping down as long as they could. The communist leadership had options other than negotiating with the opposition. They could have clung to their seats. But according to historical and sociological accounts (Los 2003; Zybertowicz and Los 2000), many opted for new careers as economic managers of privatized companies. Others from the top echelons of communist parties reformed their political organizations into modern social democratic parties that eventually became competitive in democratic elections (Grzymała-Busse 2002). The existence of these career options suggests that the outgoing communists maintained a deep-seated confidence that they would not be subject to retribution but would instead be permitted to keep their jobs. Polish and Hungarian dissidents themselves were surprised by the communists' willingness to initiate negotiations (Bozóki 2002; Dudek 2004; Roszkowski 2000).

Why did the communists allow free elections in their political systems? They could have anticipated that the former opposition would emerge victorious in these elections. There are normative arguments explaining why the opposition refrained from transitional justice (Ackerman 1992; Holmes 1994). But such normative desirability cannot constrain strategic politicians from pursuing policies that are popular. This is particularly true when such policies allow politicians to win office more easily and hold it for longer, and may even be a source of rents. The transitional justice policy featured in this book – "lustration" – fits this description perfectly because it denies public office to members and collaborators of the ancien régime. Lustration as a transitional justice policy pales in comparison with Laszlo Beke's dramatic description of the AVH officer being torched alive. Yet contrary to what one would expect, the departing communists in

Table 1.1. *Lustration and declassification in post-communist Europe: the first fifteen years after the transition.*

	1990	'91	'92	'93	'94	'95	'96	'97	'98	'99	2000	'01	'02	'03	'04
Bulgaria	░	░	L↑ C↓	L↑	░L↓	░	░L↑			C↓ L↑					
Czech Republic		L↑ P↑	C↑		L↑ P↑							L↑	C↑		C↑
Estonia					L↑										
Hungary				L↑ C↓	░	░	░L↑	L↑				░L↑	░	░	░
Lithuania	░	░L↑	░	░	░	░									
Latvia		L↑													
Poland			L↑ C↓		░	░	░L↓	L↑ C↓	L↑ C↓			░P↓ C↑	░	░	
Romania	░	░	░	░L↑						░	░L↑	░			
Slovakia														L↑	

Notes: L represents the passage of lustration laws by legislatures; a downward arrow represents a law struck down by the president (P), by the Constitutional Court (C), or by the legislature (L); an upward sloping arrow represents that the law was made harsher or upheld – again, by the president (P), by the Constitutional Court (C) or by the parliament in a subsequent term (L). The shaded cells represent the periods in which a lustration law was in force. The diagonal striped cells indicate periods in which the successor parties of the communist autocrats (who I refer to throughout the book as post-communists) held parliamentary majorities.

Poland, Hungary, Slovakia, Latvia, and Romania did not face even mild retribution in the form of lustration.

On the other hand, with other East Central European countries, the peaceful pattern of regime turnover did not shield members and collaborators of the ancien régime from lustration. In fact, no country in post-communist Europe avoided lustration indefinitely. The variation in post-transition lustration is depicted in Table 1.1, which shows when lustration went into effect in nine East Central European countries over the first fifteen years following the transition.

Czechoslovakia (later the Czech Republic) and Lithuania stand out as the region's "eager lustrants," while Poland, Hungary, and in particular Slovakia appear to be the lustration laggards. However, neither Poland, Hungary, nor Slovakia refrained from lustration altogether. Instead, these countries, as well Romania and Estonia, experienced significant delays before lustration was adopted and archived secret police files became

3

public. A further distinctive feature of implementing lustration in Poland, Hungary, Bulgaria, Romania, and Lithuania is that these laws were adopted when the former communist regimes' successor parties actually held parliamentary majorities. The puzzling phenomena of Table 1.1 set the agenda for this book:

- Why did opposition parties keep their promises of amnesty?
- Why and when were those promises broken?
- Why did the successors of former autocrats break them?

My explanation distinguishes three critical moments:

- The pre-transition stage, when the communist party is in charge and various dissident groups start getting organized
- The transition stage, during which the communists sit together with the opposition at roundtables to negotiate transitions to democracy based on an exchange: the amnesty for outgoing autocrats for free or semifree democratic elections
- The post-transition stage, during which the deals struck at the roundtable are enforced or broken

1.1. Why Lustration?

This book is about who decides to lustrate, when these choices are made, and why. In general, lustration laws can be described by three parameters: All persons in set X are screened for committing action y in the past, and if the screening procedure finds a person in X responsible for engaging in action y, he or she faces sanction z. The range of the first parameter, set X, is usually defined in terms of currently held political offices or social positions. This can include members of parliament (MPs), senators, teachers, doctors, or even priests. The second parameter, y, describes the type of collaboration that constitutes the subject of screening. Types of collaboration can range from membership in the authoritarian party, to leadership in that party, to working as an informer of the authoritarian security apparatus or working as a professional undercover agent of the secret political police. The third parameter, z, describes the sanction meted out to targets who have been found responsible for the targeted activity. The sanction ranges from merely revealing the target's past activity to the public to shaming combined with a prohibition on holding public office.

Lustration and declassification have usually been considered types of "transitional justice" procedures. Transitional justice, in its most general sense, encompasses legal institutions designed to settle scores with members and collaborators of an ancien régime (Alivizatos and Diamanouros 1997; Cassel 1998; Choi and David 2006; Elster 2004; González Enríquez, Brito, and Aguilar Fernández 2001; Kaminski and Nalepa 2006; Kritz 1995; McAdams 1997, 2001; Offe and Poppe 1999; Posner and Vermuele 2004; Roht-Arriaza and Mariezcurrena 2006; Schwartz 1995; Teitel 2000; Tolley 1998).[2] The procedures of transitional justice fall into the following four categories: (1) trials of former perpetrators of human rights violations; (2) compensation for victims; (3) legislative acts condemning the former regime; and (4) truth revelation procedures. The first category includes trials as well as lifting the controlling statutes of limitations that may have expired for crimes committed when the ancien régime remained in power. Crimes that would otherwise have been time-barred can be prosecuted. Second, compensation to victims could range from official apologies to monetary compensation to the restitution of rights to property that was confiscated by the ancien régime. The third category covers legislative acts proclaiming the criminality of the ancien régime as well as legislation expropriating former authoritarian parties of illegitimately acquired assets. Finally, truth revelation procedures comprise lustration and declassification, which opens to the public archives of the former secret political police and truth commissions (Elster 1998, 2004). Truth commissions are temporary bodies of formal inquiry appointed to document the criminal activity of the ancien régime. Truth commissions collect and record testimony from victims and perpetrators. Some truth commissions, such as the South African Truth and Reconciliation Commission, have been accorded subpoena power as well as other investigative authority to search suspects and seize evidence (Hayner 2001, 214). Usually their operation is restricted with a sunset provision. If a commission uncovers evidence of human rights violations, it issues a public report that frequently names specific perpetrators (Hayner 2001).

Truth revelation procedures are a unique subcategory of transitional justice. First, they are empowered to assign blame to all sides of the political conflict (Gibson 2006). By uncovering information that was secret prior to the transition, such procedures can implicate former autocrats as well as their resisters. In *Overcoming the Apartheid*, James Gibson (2004) explains why the final report of the South African Truth and Reconciliation

---

[2] Throughout this book, I use the term *ancien régime* to refer to the authoritarian regime preceding the transitional negotiations.

Commission was so controversial. It cited evidence that members of the African National Congress – including Winnie Mandela (Nelson Mandela's wife) – were responsible for political violence against the authoritarian enforcement apparatus. Findings of the Peruvian Truth Commission – initially expected to assign blame only to the communist guerrillas – were similarly surprising. The commission found that not only the communist Shining Path was guilty of human rights violations but that the government enforcement apparatus was culpable too.

Likewise, lustration and declassification have the potential for exposing unexpected facts about political violence or human rights violations that took place prior to the transition. For example, in the mid-1970s, students from Krakow organized a dissident group called the Grupa Krakowska. One of its members, Stanislaw Pyjas, was continuously being harassed by the secret police. At one point, the police threatened to manufacture false evidence of Pyjas's collaboration with them and release it to Grupa Krakowska's members. He continued to refuse. In May 1977, Pyjas was captured and beaten to death. This sudden manifestation of political violence brought an upsurge of anticommunist resistance in Poland.[3] It eventually led to the establishment of the Laborers' Defense Committee (KOR). All the participants of Grupa Krakowska emerged as prominent dissidents. During the year following the transition, they assumed powerful positions in politics and the media. Yet, in 2001, a journalist of one of the leading dailies and former participant of the Grupa Krakowska revealed that Leslaw Maleszka, one of the group's participants, had informed against his colleagues in Grupa Krakowska and was indirectly responsible for Pyjas's murder.[4] The community of former dissidents was shocked to learn that a dissident from Pyjas's own circle had been indirectly responsible for his murder.

But the Grupa Krakowska example is neither surprising nor unique. Indeed, the mechanism is illustrated well in Krzysztof Kieslowski's 1981 movie *Blind Chance*. The movie is divided into three parts. In one part, the main character, Witek Długosz, plays the role of a young communist. In

---

[3] Pyjas's death was a surprise to the communist authorities as well, because the secret police had planned "only" to intimidate him with a severe beating. According to the Institute of National Remembrance (IPN) prosecutor, Michal Urbaniak, if the secret police had planned to have him murdered, they would not have abandoned him in a driveway, as they did (Danko 2008).

[4] Incidentally, Maleszka had been employed after the transition as senior writer at another of the leading daily newspapers; I return to the Pyjas story in Chapter 6 while explaining the structure of dissident organizations.

another part, he becomes a dissident. And in the last, Witek aspires to be politically neutral and to avoid actively either supporting or resisting the authoritarian regime. As postulated in the film, which of the three roles Witek assumed depended simply on whether Witek caught the train from Łódz to Warsaw – hence the title, *Blind Chance*. I think that Kieslowski intended to stress the blurry lines between Witek's different roles and the path-dependence of his choices. Surprisingly, Witek has the hardest time trying to maintain neutrality. But the saddest episode is one in which he is a member of an underground dissident printing group and ends up being expelled because his fellow co-conspirators suspect him of being a secret police agent. As the viewers learn later, a Catholic priest named Father Stefan – not Witek – informed the communist police about the location and activities of the secret printing house. Ironically, Witek turns to Father Stefan for consolation after losing his co-conspirators' trust. Father Stefan advises him, "Witek, pray – pray so that you don't hate people. This is conspiracy, so responsibility counts double: once someone suspects you of collaboration, it is impossible to shake off a suspicion."

The uncertainty about who is on which side of the ancien régime is pervasive in *Blind Chance*. Just as it was difficult to know who was a collaborator, it is equally complicated to know who would benefit or lose from lustration or declassification.

Contrast this with the way in which Italy dealt with its Fascist autocrats. In April 1945, communist partisans arrested Benito Mussolini and his lover, Claretta Petacci, at Lake Como. A few days later, they were executed by Walter Audisio, a partisan whom Mussolini had earlier pardoned from a jail sentence. It took Audisio three attempts before he finally found a gun that would fire. The next day, Mussolini's and Petacci's mutilated corpses were strung upside down in a public square in Milan to broadcast how the resistance dealt with its tyrant (Luzzatto 2005).

What distinguishes the victors' justice meted out, for example, to Mussolini from the application of transitional justice procedures such as lustration in East Central Europe is the secret information factor. Although the identities of informers were unknown in East Central Europe, in Fascist Italy it was fairly clear who the tyrant and his closest collaborators were (Luzzatto 2005). In the context of long-lived authoritarian regimes, the gray area between resisting and supporting the ancien régime is wider than in short-term authoritarian episodes. Neither amnesty nor transitional justice carries the same meaning as they do in the short-term episodes that tend to follow military coups. The longer a regime is in power, the harder it becomes to separate the guilty parties from the innocent. For one, infiltration reaches wider and wider areas of public and private life. Is someone who agrees to rent out his apartment to the secret police for recruitment purposes a collaborator? What if the collaborator is unaware of the activity transpiring in his apartment? Suppose that someone agrees to provide the secret police with information not pertaining to any dissident activity in exchange for getting a passport to go abroad. Later in this book, I use archival research to demonstrate that the secret police could make use of even seemingly irrelevant information to recruit new informants.[5] However, if someone was not aware of secret police recruitment tactics, he or she cannot be regarded as guilty of conscious collaboration.

Transitional justice in contexts where the attribution of blame is almost certain and the distribution of blame is skewed to one side of the political spectrum (like post-Fascist Italy) is different from situations in which the blame is distributed more evenly. Transitional justice in which the "winning side" metes out justice to the "losing side" is often referred to as victors' justice and likened to acts of pure revenge. The outcome of such transitional justice procedures is predictable and rewards the winners further, while making it difficult for the losers to recover losses and eventually reconcile into society.

Transitional justice includes not only the relevant legislation but also the research dealing with addressing the wrongs committed by members and collaborators of the ancien régime (Kritz 1995; Poganyi 1997). A growing literature on transitional justice associates successful democratization with achieving reconciliation between the supporters and the resisters of the former authoritarian regime; there, reconciliation is understood as the capacity for sharing common democratic institutions

---

[5] The hazards of becoming an involuntary collaborator, such as those that Witek faced, are well described in one of the samizdat publications that started circulating in the aftermath of the martial law crackdown. *The Little Conspirator* was a manual for dissidents conspiring underground. It had special sections devoted to interactions with the secret police, such as interrogation, calls to be a witness in court, searches, and others. The manual instructed dissidents of their rights, informing them when it was legal to refuse questioning. Importantly, it cautioned them against sharing even seemingly innocuous information with the secret police. Innocuous pieces of information about a person targeted by the secret police could be, for instance, lectures attended by that target, the name of his girlfriend, or his hobbies. Such information could easily be used to intimidate the target when he would be approached by the secret police officer, who would initiate the conversation by saying, "We know everything about you; we know whose lectures you attend, who you date and hang out with" (Anonymous).

(Howard-Hassmann 1995; Torpey 2003). An alienated society divided into groups and classes suspicious of one another does not pose an especially great problem for an authoritarian regime that does not legitimize itself through fair elections. In contrast, democratic institutions presuppose a consensus about obeying common "rules of the game" and rely on a culture of trust and reciprocity (Knight 1992; North 1990; Putnam, Leonardi, and Nanetti 1993). For democratic consolidation, citizens must respect and participate in shared democratic institutions. For instance, they should trust courts as the final arbiters in adjudicating disputes between one another and respect judicial decisions even if they disagree with them. They should also recognize results of elections, even if their favorite candidate loses (Przeworski 1992). Many proponents of transitional justice subscribe to the view that its goal is forward-looking reconciliation rather than backward-looking revenge. However, for many former "rank and file" oppositionists in East Central Europe, transitional justice, with its reconciliation-promoting ambitions, is like the "morning after" effect following the carnival of a revolution[6]:

In a strongly alcoholic situation with lots and lots of vodka, perhaps I could picture myself reconciled with a former supporter of the communist regime. But normally, never! But jokes aside, asking about reconciliation in Poland is like asking about the AC in a car that has no wheels with the car dealer trying to convince you that AC is the car's most important feature! (interview 2004: PA9 when asked about the conditions for reconciliation in post-communist Poland 2004).[7]

Whether transitional justice procedures, such as lustration, contribute to reconciliation is an important normative question. But it is not the issue that is the subject of this book. Other works deal at length with this problem (Appel 2005; Choi and David 2006; Horne and Levi 2004; Letki 2002; Nalepa 2007). No academic research so far, however, has dealt with the possible strategic uses of lustration. Contrary to existing trends in the transitional justice literature, which ask whether or not to engage in transitional justice, I believe that the following is an equally important question: *How do the competing demands for implementing or avoiding transitional justice*

---

[6] *Carnival of a Revolution* is the title of a historical narrative of the transitions in Central Europe by Kenney (2003).
[7] All interviews were conducted by the author in 2004 and are coded according to the following rules: The first letter of the code represents the country of the interviewed politician: P = Poland, C = Czech Republic, H = Hungary; the second letter represents the affiliation: N = neutral, L = liberal, A = anticommunist, C = post-communist.

play out to create specific policy outcomes at time x instead of time y? Whether or not one believes that transitional justice is normatively desirable, post-transitional societies have gone about dealing with their respective pasts in different and often puzzling ways. In this book, I demonstrate that lustration remains a salient political issue with politicians even when voters have no particular concern with the authoritarian past anymore. Even when voters no longer consider lustration salient enough to affect their voting decisions, politicians have good reasons to feel strongly about it. Harsh bills may and have ended the careers of politicians who had previously collaborated with the communist regimes (Appel 2005; David 2003; Horne and Levi 2004; Letki 2002). These laws may be used as tools of political manipulation that eliminate electoral competition. If politicians care about retaining office and if they care about greater representation of their parties in legislatures, they cannot ignore lustration. In advanced democracies, the analogues to lustration are transparency or anticorruption legislation that screens politicians for unethical behavior (Alt, Lassen, and Rose 2007). This feature makes lustration particularly important for political scientists because it very directly affects the careers of politicians.

The Polish presidential elections in 2000 illustrate well the consequences of lustration. According to the public opinion polls, a few months prior to the election, Andrzej Olechowski was almost tied with the incumbent Aleksander Kwasniewski. After declaring, pursuant to the Polish lustration law,[8] that he had collaborated with the former secret police, Olechowski did not even make it to the runoff. In 2002, Hungarian prime minister Peter Medgyessy narrowly avoided the collapse of his newly created cabinet after an article in a Budapest daily revealed that he had worked as an undercover agent for the military counterintelligence (BBC International Monitoring 2002). More recently, Polish deputy prime minister Zyta Gilowska was forced to resign from office after being accused of collaborating with the Polish secret police. Her resignation eventually brought down the entire cabinet (Easton 2006).

Whether we consider politicians to be office seekers or policy-oriented actors, they have a stake in lustration. For office-seeking politicians,

---

[8] The Polish lustration law requires that candidates for public office declare before elections whether they had worked for or consciously collaborated with communist secret services. Declarations of collaboration are published. The bill does not ban ex-collaborators from holding any position. The voters themselves decide whether the ex-collaborator can hold the office in question (Dziennik Ustaw 2002).

lustration has the potential to forever terminate their careers. But if a politician cares about policy outcomes, he must value the office that enables him to affect his preferred outcomes. Consequently, because lustration can influence electoral outcomes and, in turn, deny him, his supporters, or his competitors' office, the politician must remain cognizant of lustration's use and effect.

Because lustration involves secret information, it affects not only individual politicians but their parties as well. For instance, if politicians who are identified as former collaborators or informers are required to step down from office, their parties lose actual as well as potential seats in the legislature. The secretive nature of information about who was or was not a collaborator creates further problems. An individual ex-collaborator knows about his or her own past, but his or her party colleagues and leadership do not. Although collectively parties would be better off purging their ranks of former collaborators instead of paying the harsh electoral costs of such disclosure, party members who previously collaborated with the communist regime have incentives to remain silent and withhold that information from party bosses. Secret information about any individual's collaboration will remain undisclosed unless a lustration or declassification procedure exposes it.[9] Parties with comparatively fewer ex-collaborators could benefit from introducing lustration. Unfortunately for them – but fortunately for their competitors – those who could benefit from lustration are often unaware of these potential benefits.

The remainder of this chapter presents the three puzzles around which this book is organized. It includes some empirical vignettes, previewing the East Central European cases more completely presented in Chapter 4 (the immediate aftermath of the transition) and Chapters 6 and 7 (the instances of delayed lustrations). Next, I discuss various alternative approaches and theories offered by the literature on transitions and democratization and preview my argument. The chapter ends with a note on terminology.

1.2. First Puzzle: Skeletons in the Closet

Consider again the empirical patterns from Table 1.1 reflecting how few East Central European democratic governments rushed to punish the former autocrats with lustration. The events in Poland and Hungary are

---

[9] Declassification is a procedure that opens files of the secret political police to the public; it can have effects similar to those of lustration, as I show in Chapter 2 of this book.

particular examples of the following general scenario. First, successfully concluded roundtable negotiations between the communist governments and dissident organizations led to the first free elections. As a result, former dissidents replaced the communist cabinet. Next, the former dissidents were in a position to implement lustration that could restrict the access of former communists and their collaborators to office. (This must have been tempting particularly in the first months following the transition, when the electoral support for such action was high.) However, contrary to expectations, the now-empowered opposition did not exact revenge on the communists by engaging in lustration or declassification. In Poland, although the issue of lustration surfaced in 1992, a fully operational procedure was not put in place until 1998. Hungary waited until 1997 for a lustration law, which initially extended to six hundred legislators and was not amended until 2000. Slovakia did not open archives of the former secret political police until 2003. In these countries, the roundtable pacts did not shield the communists entirely from lustration, but delayed and softened it. On the other hand, the Czech Republic and some of the Baltic states were quick to implement lustration and declassification policies affecting hundreds of thousands of citizens.[10]

Why did the opposition refrain from immediate lustration in so many countries? I believe that the former dissidents delayed lustration because they feared the "skeletons in their own closet." The skeletons were informers of the secret police among the opposition's ranks. If the opposition, after coming to power, decided to expose the ghosts of the communist past, it risked also exposing the informers within its own ranks. At first, it is difficult to understand why the opposition should suffer from transitional justice, but as I argue in this book, lustration is a very specific form of transitional justice because it exposes not only the faults of former autocrats, but also those of the former opposition. It is not surprising that the opposition would include many former secret police informants. Over the years of communist rule, dissident organizations had been increasingly infiltrated by agents of the secret political police. The former opposition parties did not know the identities of these agents because admitting to collaboration

---

[10] For instance, in the Czech Republic, 420,000 persons have been affected by lustrations. This number reflects the total number of lustration certificates (positive and negative) issued by the Federal Interior Ministry (between October 1991 and December 1993) and the Czech Interior Ministry (between December 1993 and May 2004). Therefore, it includes a small proportion of certificates issued to Slovaks prior to the Velvet Divorce in 1993 (interviews 2004: CN10).

would eternally stigmatize the collaborator within dissident circles. Furthermore, harboring informers, even unknowingly, would gravely undermine the credibility of a party originating in the dissident movement. Thus, the opposition knew only that it had been infiltrated to one degree or another, but it did not know the extent of the infiltration or the identities of the individual collaborators. On the other hand, the communists possessed considerably greater information about the distribution of infiltration.

The key to convincing the opposition to refrain from lustration was to hold it hostage to skeletons in its own closet: The communists had to convince the liberal opposition that implementing lustration could be damaging to the opposition itself.[11] They could persuade the opposition about this either during the roundtable negotiations, but also in their aftermath. For instance, following the roundtable negotiations in Hungary, when the first noncommunist cabinet was being formed, outgoing communist prime minister Miklos Nemeth handed the new prime minister, Jozsef Antall of the Hungarian Democratic Forum (MDF), a list of former secret police collaborators from the top echelons of opposition parties. Evidence from elite interviews discussed in Chapters 4 and 6 indicates that, according to Nemeth's list, Antall's MDF was the most infiltrated party among the opposition parties. Imre Mecs, who chaired the committee investigating links of former cabinet ministers to the secret police, described Antall's cabinet as "the most infected by former agents" and "bitterly stated that a disclosure would threaten [the cabinet's] ability to govern the country"[12] (MTI 2002). Unsurprisingly, the first lustration proposal was scrapped by combined votes of members of the ruling coalition comprised of MDF, the Smallholders (FKgP), and the Christian Democrats (KDNP). One hypothesis explaining MDF's actions is that it was keeping promises made to the outgoing autocrats during roundtable negotiations. However, this hypothesis ignores the fact that lustration amnesty would have to be delivered only after the transition was completed and the communists were powerless. I believe that MDF's abstention from lustration proposals was related to a 1956 reform making the secret police part of the Interior Ministry. This reform gave politicians

---

[11] As I explain further in Chapter 2, "the liberal opposition" is how I refer to the dissidents who had agreed to negotiate the transition with the former communists.

[12] Lending further credibility to his severe criticism of the first cabinet, Mecs added "that in 1990, four deputies of the parliamentary group of his own party also had links with the former secret services" (MTI 2002).

controlling the government exclusive access to their political rivals' files and allowed those in power to use the files to denounce former collaborators within competing parties. And because the governing politicians retained absolute control over the files, they could simultaneously prevent competitors from using the files against them. The Hungarian Democratic Forum took advantage of its exclusive access to files for as long as its parliamentary term lasted. Only after its electoral defeat in 1994 became imminent did MDF propose a lustration law. Then, however, Hungary's Constitutional Court struck down the measure. After the Hungarian Socialist Party (MSzP) assumed power in 1994, Hungary waited until 1996 for a lustration law. But then it was only a mild version. A fully operational statute was not implemented until 2002.

Poland's history similarly contains vignettes illustrating the discovery of skeletons in the closet. A key dissident representing the opposition side at the roundtable negotiations – and one of the first candidates for prime minister in the election aftermath – recalled Aleksander Kwaśniewski (one of the most important representatives of the outgoing communist government) making the following comment:

Don't mess with those files, let them be – the agents were mostly your own people (interviews 2004: PL2).

It would have been difficult for the opposition to judge the truthfulness of Kwaśniewski's threat. On the one hand, Kwaśniewski could not actually effectuate his threat without declassifying the secret files, a measure the opposition would have wanted to avoid if it was, in fact, significantly infiltrated. On the other hand, if Kwaśniewski's threat was empty, he had an incentive to exaggerate what was contained in the secret files to discourage the opposition from enacting lustration laws in the transition aftermath. Former communists, as I will demonstrate in Chapter 4, had incentives to exaggerate the extent to which the opposition was infiltrated with secret police agents to prevent the opposition from adopting lustration. However, events that occurred within the two years after the roundtable negotiations convinced the opposition that it had considerable skeletons hidden in the closet.

On May 28, 1992, Janusz Korwin Mikke, an MP from the Union of Real Politik (UPR) – a party not represented at the roundtable talks – presented a resolution requiring the minister of interior to disclose the civil servants[13]

---

[13] The list included senators, MPs, governors, judges, and prosecutors.

who had collaborated with the communist secret police. Mikke's proposal had already been signed by 105 MPs, but few of the signatories had participated in the roundtable negotiations. Those who had participated – members of the Democratic Union (UD) and the Labor Union (UP) – were largely not present in the parliament that day. In a vote of 186 to 15 (with 32 MPs abstaining), the resolution passed. The interior minister, Antoni Macierewicz, was given twenty-one days to disclose the information. However, he was not provided any governing guidelines because the bill had been neither debated nor channeled through the relevant committee. In this limited period, because of the volume of the files, Macierewicz came up only with a list of names from the former secret police files that he was able to consult.[14] The list identified sixty-one MPs. It included members of the post-communist Social Democratic Alliance (SLD) and Polish People's Party (PSL), but it also included a number of former dissidents from UD and UP. The following day, the parliament executed a vote of no confidence, bringing down the entire cabinet (including Macierewicz).

A month later, Poland's Constitutional Tribunal declared the resolution illegal, and a special investigative committee was launched to scrutinize the procedural mistakes that the Interior Department had committed while executing the resolution. MPs who found their names on the list regretted their hasty decision and tried to undo its consequences. The list had been leaked to the press and the dissident opposition, both inside and outside of parliament. It turned out that Kwaśniewski had not been bluffing when he claimed that the opposition, rather than the communists, would be hurt by lustration. When Macierewicz's famous list was circulated in the Polish Parliament, called the Sejm, the post-communists were heard sneering, because very few of the sixty-one MPs listed as secret police agents were actually members of their party (interviews 2004: PC5, PC6, and PC2).[15]

Once the lists were publicized, the public demanded lustration. But the former dissidents were now aware of the extent of secret police collaborators within their ranks, so they pulled their transitional justice punches. After dismissing the cabinet, along with Macierewicz – the

---

[14] In 1998, Jerzy Dziewulski, an MP on the ad hoc committee for dealing with the files, estimated the total length of shelves with secret police files (if stood upright) at 12 kilometers (Dziewulski 1998). The estimate of employees from the Institute of National Remembrance (IPN) is 95 kilometers.

[15] This was the case because the resolution upon which Macierewicz was acting did not include working for the communist intelligence and counterintelligence, which recruited predominantly Polish United Workers' Party (PZPR) members.

unfortunate interior minister – the special commission appointed to investigate the execution of the resolution issued a report discrediting Macierewicz's findings. The special commission uncovered that Macierewicz had been "organizing" the files with a team of researchers called the Department of Analysis (Wydział Studiów) for three months before the resolution had been proposed in the Sejm, but the evidence he produced lacked reliability.[16] For his part, Macierewicz no longer had access to the files, so he could not defend his findings.

In the aftermath of the "Macierewicz scandal," the post-communists continued to hold the opposition hostage to the threat of skeletons in its closet.[17] Successive opposition governments refrained from lustration until 1998. In the meantime, the communists secured a political afterlife as "social democrats" (Grzymała-Busse 2002). Eventually, as in all other countries where the opposition had pulled its transitional justice punches (such as Hungary, Slovakia, and Romania), Poland adopted lustration laws. Next, I explain the puzzle of why this happened and who was responsible for this turnaround on the political scene.

1.3. Second Puzzle: Why Were the Promises of Amnesty Eventually Broken?

The short answer to this puzzle is associated with the rise of political elites who had not been infiltrated by the secret police and as a result had fewer collaborators. Virtually all democratic elections in East Central Europe since the 1990s have brought turnovers in power. In 2005, the Polish parliamentary and presidential elections were won by the Law and Justice (PiS) Party, led by the twins Lech and Jarosław Kaczyński. Even though PiS did not win an absolute majority, it emerged as sufficiently strong to lead a cabinet coalition. While Lech Kaczyński served as president, his brother, Jarosław, became prime minister. PiS made its name by promising to end the vestiges of communist rule in Poland once and for all. The party would purge former police collaborators from public offices, deprive

---

[16] Macierewicz's list was rife with false positives as well as false negatives. For details, see Nalepa (2008).

[17] Chapter 3 will use a game theoretic model to show how the communists used the opposition's fear of skeletons in its closet to prevent it from engaging in lustration in the early aftermath of transition; in Chapter 4, the post-communist choice to initiate negotiations is interpreted as a signal sent to the opposition about the extent to which it is infiltrated.

former communist military and police forces of their excessive pensions and benefits, and hold Stalinist prosecutors and judges responsible for judicial murder. Eventually, it would make public all of the documentation collected by the dreaded secret political police. PiS stood by its promise when in March 2007 it passed a lustration law requiring each of approximately seven hundred thousand persons – including journalists and academics in private institutions – to declare whether they had collaborated with the communist secret political police. When the Constitutional Tribunal struck down key provisions of the law, PiS started organizing a coalition to amend the constitution to allow the extensive lustration law to be implemented.

Most striking about this wave of reckoning with the past is that it happened more than seventeen years after the transition to democracy, a transition that occurred through peaceful negotiations between the outgoing communist governments and their former opposition. To the casual observers of East Central European politics, PiS's actions seem like overzealous "witch-hunting" (Osiatyński 2007; "Tainted Vestments" 2007). Although seeking revenge is not a rare motivation for political action (Petersen 2002), it fails to explain why such retributive activity occurred so late in the democratic process. Why did the PiS engage in lustration with such determination after so much time had passed?

The short answer is that lustration has distributive effects and PiS had all the prerequisites of a party that would benefit from lustration. The Kaczyński twins had participated in the pre-transition opposition and were even part of the dissidents' team in the roundtable negotiations. Yet they remained on the fringes of the negotiations (Dubiński, Wałęsa, and Kiszczak 1990; Garlicki 2003; Glowiński 2001; Raina 1997). In a survey conducted on the eve of the roundtable negotiations in 1988 on a representative national sample of Poles, only 7.6 percent of the respondents recognized the more popular of the twins – Lech Kaczyński – and only 4.2 percent claimed to trust him. Trust awarded to Lech Wałęsa was more than ten times greater.[18] Following the transition, the Kaczyńskis were quick to distance themselves from any dissident tainted with secret service collaboration or even from people descending from "close to the surface" underground organizations.[19] This included Solidarity trade union hero

---

[18] Badanie 336/50/88, CBOS "Rozomowy przy okrąglym stole: nadzieje i sceptycyzm."

[19] In Chapter 6, I analyze in detail the relationship between the structure of the underground movement and the likelihood of infiltration. In a nutshell, it is related to how the

Lech Wałęsa. After Wałęsa was elected president in the first democratic elections for highest executive office, the Kaczyński brothers acted as heads of his chancellery. When rumors emerged in the early 1990s that Lech Wałęsa had been recruited as an agent of the secret political police during the Gdansk strike activities in the 1970s (before Solidarity was established), the Kaczyński twins quickly dissociated themselves from Wałęsa's circles (Cenckiewicz and Gontarczyk 2008). The first political party they established – Central Alliance (PC) – was the only parliamentary group free of collaborators listed by Macierewicz.[20] This suggests that early in their political career, the Kaczyński twins knew that their party was free of secret police collaborators – at least in its top party echelons. During the period when the post-communist coalition of SLD and PSL was in power, Lech Kaczyński maintained a position as head of the Highest Auditing Office (NIK). Kaczyński was awarded the post of minister of justice for his contributions to Election Action Solidarity, the coalition that united all former right-wing dissidents under the aegis of the Solidarity trade union. According to political commentaries, while holding those two positions, Lech Kaczyński could survey files of fellow party members and locate the hidden skeletons (Paradowska 1999). Today, PiS is comprised of very young MPs who are extremely unlikely to include former agents of the communist secret police. This is either because of an MP's age or because of his or her background in student unions and underground groups that maintained very low profiles before the transition. PiS's composition and political position helps explain why the party is not afraid that lustration will uncover skeletons in its own closet: It hardly has any. On the other hand, it likely knows exactly who would be affected by lustration.

As further insurance against potential "weak links" in the ranks of their party, Lech and Jarosław Kaczyński changed their party organization four times. First, they joined Wałęsa's Nonpartisan Block Supporting Reforms (BBWR), which won parliamentary elections and helped Wałęsa broaden the powers of the presidency. But after Wałęsa was rumored to be a secret

---

group valued expansion and getting the work done compared to how much it valued certainty that there were no collaborators in its ranks. The trade-off would be that the group conspiring deep underground would need to keep a very low profile.

[20] This could be related to the fact that the cabinet in which Macierewicz was interior minister was led by PC leader Jan Olszewski and that PC had 20 percent of the portfolios in that cabinet. However, a list created prior to the 1992 lustration resolution, but not circulated until later – the so called "Milczanowski list" – did not have names of PC members on it either.

police informer himself, the Kaczyński brothers abandoned BBWR and created Center Alliance. The party came in sixth in the 1991 parliamentary elections. Yet it succeeded in obtaining the highest executive office – that of prime minister – for one of its key members, Jan Olszewski. Olszewski was a lawyer with a long history of defending dissidents prosecuted under communist rule. After his government was ousted from power in 1992 and all parties descendent from dissident groups – with the exception of the left-leaning Democratic Union (UD) and Labor Union (UP) – lost in the subsequent parliamentary elections (in 1993), the Kaczyński twins joined the Solidarity Election Action (AWS) and won the 1997 elections. In 2001, as crises plagued AWS and support levels of cabinet ministers were plummeting, Lech Kaczyński maintained the highest levels of popularity (hovering around 70 percent) as justice minister.[21] At that time, Lech and Jarosław Kaczyński abandoned AWS to create PiS. Among former dissidents, the Kaczyński brothers were probably those who most frequently terminated one party and created another. Although it is likely that these party transformations were induced by changes in the electoral laws (Kaminski 1999; Kaminski, Lissowski, and Swistak 1998; Kaminski and Nalepa 2004), each new party organization presented an opportunity to purge party ranks of known collaborators. I argue in Chapter 6 that the Kaczyński twins took liberal advantage of these opportunities.

To summarize, by belonging to low-profile underground groups prior to the transition, enjoying access to secret information about which parties were infiltrated with former secret police agents, and purging known collaborators from party ranks when reinventing party labels, the Kaczyński brothers reached a point at which they were certain they would benefit from lustration. The advancement of parties such as the PiS in other countries of East Central Europe in the late 1990s explains the adoption of lustration laws much better than a notion that these countries' electorates suddenly developed preferences for dealing with their pasts and making lustration a central voting issue. In a nutshell, noncollaborating parties eventually came to power.

However, the emergence of PiS cannot alone explain the implementation of lustration in Poland. Figure 1.1, which summarizes the information from Table 1.1, shows that the first lustration law was successfully implemented in 1997, and not under anticommunist but post-communist rule. An analogous pattern also appears in Hungary. In Slovakia, the

---

[21] CBOS (2001).

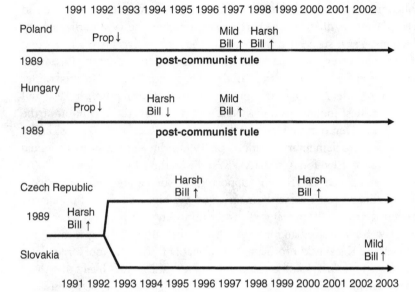

Figure 1.1. Lustration trajectories in Poland, Hungary, Czechoslovakia, the Czech Republic, and Slovakia.

opening of archives was significantly delayed, but was not implemented by post-communists.

Why do post-communists self-lustrate? To explain this paradox, one needs to look at institutional variables, such as rules of parliamentary decision making. This is the book's third puzzle.

1.4. Third Puzzle: Why Did Post-Communists Lustrate?

In Hungary and Poland, it is surprising at first that once the reinvented ex-communist parties won elections and could control legislation, they passed lustration laws. Indirectly, the post-communists were induced to action because of the rise of anticommunist parties that were impervious to the former communists' threats of exposure. If the Polish and Hungarian ex-communists anticipated losing power to anticommunist forces, under sufficiently restrictive parliamentary procedures, the post-communists could shield themselves from excessively harsh legislation by preemptively passing a less punitive version of lustration than the anticommunists would have. Stated differently, if the post-communists could appease the pivotal median with their own less penal proposal, they could try to circumvent the harsher legislation favored by hard-line anticommunists. For this explanation to work, the only requirement is that rules of procedure be closed. In other words, the legislative median should be precluded from proposing new legislation, but must instead be forced to vote up or down the legislation proposed by an agenda setter. The role of the agenda setter can be played by a committee chair – as was the case in Poland – or by a cabinet minister responsible for the requisite portfolio, as in Hungary.

The final substantive chapter of this book uses a modified agenda-setter model in a game of incomplete information to defend the following hypothesis about parliamentary rules of procedure, the proximity of general elections, and the passage of transitional justice legislation: Suppose post-communists expect to lose proposal power to anticommunists as a result of upcoming elections. In parliaments operating under closed rules, the post-communists will propose a bill that is ideal from the point of view of the party that is expected to occupy the median position after the upcoming elections. This hypothesis, like my proposed answers to the three questions identified earlier, adopts a rational choice approach. It assumes that in uncertain conditions, post-communists will act rationally to ensure their own political survival. Those uncertain conditions can be such key variables as the outcome of elections.

This approach is at odds with much of the previous research, which predicts that post-communists will avoid transitional justice at all costs. A considerable body of literature in comparative politics finds the comeback of post-communist parties in East-Central Europe surprising and attempts to explain it (Druckman and Roberts 2005; Grzymała-Busse 2002; Ishiyama 1999). It is indeed surprising that the successors of parties responsible for decades of authoritarian rule, who were so unpopular in 1989, would win elections just a couple of years later. But even more surprising is that post-communists adopted policies that scholars always considered harmful to the former communists. Why should the East Central European post-communists jeopardize their political careers by proposing legislation that would expose the exact depth of their prior involvement in the authoritarian regime? Why, in fact, would any party commit political suicide by adopting legal measures that reduce its comparative electoral prospects? The potential harm of transitional justice makes one skeptical about the very possibility of negotiated transitions. The literature on negotiated transitions predicts that autocrats concede to democratization only after they are guaranteed that the new democratic institutions will not prosecute members of the ancien régime

(Colomer 1995; O'Donnell and Schmitter 1986; Omar 1996; Przeworski 1992). Examples of such institutional guarantees include constitutions that render retroactive legislation illegal (as adopted in Hungary in 1990 or in South Africa in 1995) or electoral laws that give the outgoing regime an upper hand (such as that passed in Chile in 1984).[22] That autocrats relinquish power only after receiving some assurances of immunity is hard to reconcile with the observation that once they can do it, they try to lustrate themselves.

In the next section, I examine the relationship of lustration to other transitional justice procedures and the differences between theories explaining the passage of lustration and theories of transitional justice. I show that the timing of lustration and opening secret files cannot be explained by hypotheses traditionally used to explain the timing of transitional justice procedures.

1.5. Existing Explanations of Transitional Justice and Timing of Lustration

Existing theories of transitional justice fail to account for the specific timing of lustration in East Central Europe. A number of authors have formulated hypotheses about when one should expect transitional justice to take place. The most prevalent is Samuel Huntington's. In *The Third Wave*, he expressed the conviction that holding former autocrats accountable for their past wrongdoings should occur either in the immediate aftermath of the transition or it should not occur at all (Huntington 1991). Bruce Ackerman reaffirmed Huntington's recommendation in *The Future of Liberal Revolution* (Ackerman 1992). Carlos Nino (1996) and Jon Elster (1998, 2004) have similarly argued that public support for dealing with the past oppressors is strongest immediately after transition. These attitudes are shaped by emotions such as revenge, which are usually short-lived (Elster 1999). What may dampen transitional justice demand in the immediate aftermath of transition are other pressing issues confronting the new government (Elster 2004).

---

[22] Institutional constraints may have unanticipated adverse effects. Communist attempts to engineer electoral laws favorable to them were countersuccessful both in Hungary and Poland (Benoit and Schiemann 2001; Kaminski 1999). In South Africa, the attempt to write into the constitution a blanket amnesty for human rights violations resulted in individual amnesty granted only after testifying to the character of one's crime (Boraine 2000).

None of the hypotheses developed from the preceding theories based on notions of electoral demand can account for the variation appearing in Figure 1.1. Poland and Hungary did not adopt lustration in the immediate aftermath of their transitions. This is consistent with Huntington's urgency hypothesis: Transitional justice may get delayed if there are more pressing issues to be considered. However, the urgency hypothesis cannot explain the Czechoslovakian experience. That country confronted very similar urgent economic and political issues in the aftermath of its transition. Yet, Czechoslovakia did not delay effecting lustration and instead adopted a law early.

According to O'Donnell and Schmitter (1986), retribution is expected when former dictators no longer present a threat and citizens' fear of authoritarian backlash has dissipated. This should have led scholars of East Central Europe to expect transitional justice soon after the transition, when parliamentary representation won by post-communist parties was considerably lower than in the mid- and especially the late 1990s.

Instead, in 1994, Stephen Holmes published an article announcing the "End of Decommunization" (Holmes 1994), where he gave five possible explanations for the "startling absence of retributive politics" in East Central Europe. Among them are moral resistance to collective guilt, "skepticism towards the politization of historical memory," and economic and social problems that are more urgent and forward-looking than lustration and decommunization. While his explanations were plausible for explaining the absence of purging open collaborators of the ancien régime, they are less convincing to explain the lack of lustration that would uncover *secret* communist collaborators. Moreover, Hungary, Poland, and Slovakia's recent, yet eager, adoptions of lustration leave his verdict of "decommunization's end" premature.

Other hypotheses have also been advanced to explain the variation in the presence and stringency of transitional justice institutions. Table 1.2 summarizes expectations regarding the timing of transitional justice in East Central Europe that one would form based on the extant literature on transitional justice. Some authors postulate that where citizens have faced gross, widespread human rights abuses, the demand for prosecutions should be greater than in places where the crimes committed cost fewer lives (Elster 1998; Nino 1996). Similarly, where crimes were committed long ago, one would expect the demand for transitional justice to be lower than where they were committed more recently. Other authors have argued that the level of involvement from the international

Table 1.2. *Predictions regarding lustration timing in transitional justice literature for post-communist Europe.*

Author	Prediction	Type of Mechanism	Justification
Predictions for Post-Communist Europe			
Ackerman 1992	Absence	All transitional justice mechanisms	Normative
Elster 1996, 2004	Immediate aftermath, but not if roundtable promises made (then absence)	All transitional justice (TJ) mechanisms	Short life span of retributive emotions, impatience; new elites capitalize on popular support for TJ when it is at its highest
Holmes 1994	Absence	Decommunization	Resistance to collective responsibility, elitism, urgent economic problems competing for attention
Huntington 1991	Immediate aftermath of transition or absence	Purges, trials	Normative
Nino 1996	Immediate aftermath of transition or absence	Trials, truth commission	Popular support highest
O'Donnell and Schmitter 1986	Sooner rather than later in transition aftermath or absence	Trials, truth commissions	Fear of authoritarian backlash; lack of brutal and inhumane repressions just before the transitions
For Transitional Justice Cases in General			
Elster 1998; Nino 1996	Sooner rather than later in the transition aftermath, since time is one of the independent variables	Trials, but also truth commissions and lustration	Pressure for transitional justice where authoritarian crimes are recent and widespread
Sikkink 2004	When pressures from NGOs and INGOs are present, i.e., in the immediate aftermath rather than later	Trials and judicial procedures in particular	More NGOs and INGOs are present in the immediate aftermath or direct period preceding the transition

community – for instance, whether or not strong linkages exist between domestic nongovernmental organizations (NGOs) and international nongovernmental organizations (INGOs) (Sikkink 2004) – can strengthen the transitional justice norm.

By focusing on East Central Europe, I am in a position to use case selection to control for these effects that have been conjectured to influence the decisions to adopt transitional justice. By selecting countries with similarities in issues that compete with transitional justice for voters' attention and countries that invite similar interest from the international community, I control for the effect of urgency and INGOs. On the other hand, by selecting cases that vary in the timing and character of human rights violations prior to the transition, I can gauge the explanatory power of the timing of atrocities committed by the ancien régime and the harshness of lustration. Poland, Hungary, and the Czech Republic present remarkable variation in the timing of the most serious abuses against protesters of the communist regimes. Table 1.3 presents the most pertinent details of the major crackdowns on anticommunist protests: the aftermaths of the 1956 uprising in Hungary, the "normalization" following the Czech Prague Spring, and martial law following the eighteen months of Solidarity.

We observe variation both in the extent of the repercussions inflicted by the communist state upon those expressing their grievances toward the regime and in the timing of the protest crackdowns. Hungary's effort to end the Stalinist rule of Mátyás Rákosi and Ernő Gerő culminated in an anticommunist uprising in October 1956. The silencing of this uprising – one of the earliest in East Central Europe – was the bloodiest crackdown in the region. The numbers of dead, arrested, interned, and refugees outnumbered the casualties of Poland's martial law regime and Czechoslovakia's normalization. The most painful repercussions of the Czech normalization were the purges that took place in 1968–1969. As a result of screening procedures conducted by infamous *trojka* commissions, more than half a million people lost their jobs. In Poland, in 1981, there were relatively few deaths, but the number of those interned and those who left as refugees was the highest in the region (Ekiert 1996; Wittenberg 2006).

Despite different protest trajectories, Poland, Hungary, and the Czech Republic are similar to one another in other important respects. They transitioned to democracy around the same time after sustaining communist rule for almost half a century. Citizens in all three countries

Table 1.3. *Victims in major anticommunist protests in East Central Europe.*

Country	Date	Dead	Injured	Arrested	Interned	Sentenced	Judicial murder	Refugees	Purges
Hungary	Oct '56	4000	19,226	35,000[1]	13,000[2]	22,000	300–350[3]	193,216[4]	21,876[5]
Czechoslovakia	Aug '68	90	835	172[6]	1029[7]	N/A	N/A	100,000+[8]	500,000
Poland	Dec '81	15	36	4790[9]	15,000[10]	2580[11]	N/A	140,226[12]	12,617[13]

[1] These arrests occurred between 1956 and 1957 (Ekiert 1996).

[2] These occurred between 1957 and 1960.

[3] These murders were committed by the summer of 1961 (Ekiert 1996).

[4] Tokes (1996) reports the figure of 211,000 and writes that 45,000 returned to Hungary after the transition.

[5] These were purges from state administration.

[6] Between August 20 and September 3, 1969, 3,690 persons were arrested during demonstrations on the first anniversary of the invasion in Prague and Brno, and an additional 200 were arrested in police actions in December 1971 and in January 1972 (Ekiert 1996).

[7] On the night of April 17, 1969, 894 Czechs and 135 Slovaks were detained (and a further 2,300 searched) to prevent protests against the removal of Aleksander Dubcek and his replacement with Gustav Hussak, the conservative communist backed by Moscow.

[8] More than one hundred thousand citizens left the country before October 9, 1969, when the Czechoslovakian enforcement apparatus managed to seal the borders and ban private travel to the West. Since repressions associated with the "normalization" lasted for many years following 1968, the figure quoted by the federal Constitutional Court in its decision regarding the criminality of the communist regime (Ustavny Soud, case 1/92) – more than four hundred thousand emigrants throughout the entire communist period – may be more accurate.

[9] This reflects the total number arrested before amnesty of July 1983. There were two waves of arrests, the first associated with pacifying striking laborers (1,274 persons) and the second with arresting members of Solidarity (3,616). Data about arrests between the July 1983 and July 1984 amnesties could not be found. However, between July 1984 and the unconditional amnesty of 1986, an additional 829 persons were arrested and 296 of them sentenced. These two last figures are not accounted for in the tables (Ekiert 1996, 272).

[10] A total of 6,647 persons were interned between December 13 and February 26 alone (Ekiert 1996, 268).

[11] These sentences were given by March 1983.

[12] This figure reflects only the number of refugees who arrived at the Bavarian refugee center in West Germany in 1988 (Associated Press, January 3, 1989). It is considerably lower than the actual number of refugees.

[13] This figure includes 2,000 workers in the Lenin Shipyard, 1,500 from Warski, 2,000 from the Piast coal mine (strike participants), 440 top administrators, 200 mayors and local village administrators, and 650 top managers of industrial enterprises. Additionally, screening and verification of writers and publishers resulted in purges of 60 editors-in-chief, 20 TV directors, and 1,200 journalists. Finally, purges reached lower-rank party functionaries: 349 secretaries of local and city organizations, 307 secretaries of party committees, and 2,091 secretaries of basic organizations, and 1,800 party members were dismissed (Ekiert 1996, 268, 276).

perceive former communist rule as forcefully imposed by the Soviets. Poles, Czechs, and Hungarians consider themselves European. Therefore, in the aftermath of the transition, they all viewed joining the European Union a top priority. All three countries shared common experiences with recovering from the state socialist economy (although Czechoslovakia did not inherit as much foreign debt as Poland and Hungary did). International organizations were comparably involved in the ways in which each of these three countries dealt with its communist past. None of these countries was pressured into dealing with their perpetrators.

In summary, if it is true that more severe atrocities increase transitional justice demand regardless of the time at which they occurred, Hungarians would be expected to adopt lustration sooner or in a more stringent way than Czechs, who would in turn be expected to adopt lustration more eagerly than Poles. If it is the case that more recent atrocities trigger more intense demand for transitional justice, then one would expect Poland to adopt lustration before the Czech Republic and Hungary. And the Czech Republic would be expected to lustrate before Hungary. As it turns out, neither of these predictions are correct. Since 1991, the Czech Republic has had one of the harshest lustration laws in the region, covering over 420,000 people. Poland has had a moderately harsh law between 1997 and 2006, while Hungary had a very mild transitional justice bill between 1996 and 2001, although the bill was made harsher in 2001.[23]

Because of their similarities, these three countries form the core cases of this book. Occasionally, however, other East Central European cases are referenced as well. For instance, in Chapter 7, I devote a special empirical section not only to Poland and Hungary but also to Slovakia. Slovakia's role is quite special. Although it emerged from a peaceful transition, Slovakia inherited a lustration law from the Czech Republic, which it then chose not to implement. It turns out that one can use an agenda model, quite similar to the model of strategic pre-emption, to explain the case of delayed transitional justice in Slovakia.

---

[23] More details on the specifics of the lustration laws in the three main cases are provided in Appendix F, where I use the three parameters X, y, and z to describe the lustration laws in force.

1.6. A Roadmap of the Argument

This book is organized around the three core puzzles outlined in sections 1.2 through 1.4. The first question is why the members of the communist government were not afraid of being punished with lustration and decommunization when they considered the prospect of roundtable negotiations with the liberal opposition. Another way of asking this question is to ask: Why did the opposition, in at least some countries, refrain from transitional justice? Stated in terms of the Polish vignette discussed in the context of the first puzzle, one would ask, why did Jan Olszewski's cabinet crash when it attempted to uncover connections with the secret police in Poland? These questions are considered in Chapter 2, where I reconstruct the model of pacted transitions referenced in the literature. I show how that model is insufficient to explain peaceful democratization. In Chapter 3, I propose my own formalization of the problem in a game of transitions with secret information, which I refer to throughout the book as the skeletons in the closet model. Chapter 4 illustrates the game's equilibria with three East Central European cases: Poland, Hungary, and the Czech Republic. The illustrations build on analytic narratives, archival evidence, and aggregate data from elite interviews. These chapters comprise the first part of the book, *Skeletons in the Closet*.

The second part, "Out of the Closet," explains the yet unresolved puzzles: When and why are promises of amnesty broken? Chapter 5 explores the possibility that demands from the electorate induced politicians to embark on transitional justice. This chapter analyzes survey data from a public opinion poll I conducted in Poland, Hungary, and the Czech Republic in 2004. The results from statistical analysis show little support for the hypothesized correlation between voters' support for lustration and their willingness to elect politicians who adhere to a lustration platform. Rather, even voters who would like to see former collaborators exposed appear unwilling to make their vote depend on this preference. If voters were not a factor in the decision to lustrate, who was? The remaining explanation for lustration policies lies in the strategic choices of politicians. Chapter 6 considers the development of party systems and the structure of the pre-transition opposition to explain the emergence of parties that were undeterred by skeletons in their closet. Finally, in Chapter 7, I return once more to the findings of Table 1.1 and Figure 1.1, which illustrated not only instances of delayed lustration, but also lustration implemented by the post-communists. Why would post-communists voluntarily opt to lustrate themselves? Chapter 7 employs an agenda-setter model to explain that the post-communists' seemingly irrational behavior is, in fact, part of a preemptive strategy to avoid brutally harsh transitional justice policies. In other words, the timing of lustrations had much to do with elections; yet lustration was effected not to cater to the electorate's demands, but, instead, to eliminate electoral competition. The final chapter offers concluding remarks and possible extensions of the skeletons model to explain transitional justice in the aftermath of civil wars, such as the domestic conflict of the last forty years in Colombia.

Before moving to the main substance of the book, let me systematize my use of terminology.

1.7. *Terminology*

Following the existing literature on democratization in East and Central Europe (Bunce 1999; Grzymała-Busse 2002; Kitschelt 1999; Tucker 2006), I reserve the terms *post-communist* and East Central Europe (ECE) to describe formerly communist countries that transitioned to democracy in 1989–1990. References to *post-communist parties* describe successor communist parties, that is, party organizations built on the basis of former communist parties so that these organizations could be competitive in democratic elections after transition. Examples include Social Democracy of the Republic of Poland (SdRP) and the Hungarian Socialist Party (MSzP). I use the term *communist* in reference to parties to describe the parties in power in East and Central Europe prior to the democratic transitions, even if the term "communist" was not included in their official name. This was, for example, the case with the Polish United Workers' Party or the Hungarian Socialist Workers' Party. I employ the term *anticommunist* to describe parties created by those dissidents who were unwilling to enter into pacts with the communists. Finally, *liberal* is used to describe parties created by those former dissidents who were willing to negotiate with the outgoing communists the conditions for transition of power.

I

Skeletons in the Closet

2

Committing to Amnesty

There is a generic problem in human relationships. Consider the following situation between two sides: a dominant side (this could be an individual or a government) and a subordinate side (which I refer to as a victim).[1] Suppose the dominant side has been using repression to control the behavior of the victim, but now he decides to step down from the position that has given him control over the means of repression. To protect himself, he decides to negotiate a pact with the victim. According to this pact, the dominant side would retire from the position of authority in exchange for the victim's promise not to seek justice for the harm that was done to her. The problem is that this pact is not enforceable, since the victim is better off seeking justice than keeping her promise of amnesty. Once the dominant side retires, he has no means of protecting himself and the victim may deal with him as she desires. The dilemma features prominently in pacts concerning exchanges of amnesty for free elections. In these instances, the literature on negotiated transitions predicts that autocrats concede to democratization only after they are guaranteed immunity for past human rights violations. Examples of such institutional guarantees include constitutions that render retroactive legislation illegal or electoral laws that give the outgoing regime an upper hand (Colomer 1991; Colomer 2000; Omar 1996; Paczkowski 2000; Przeworski 1992; Sutter 1995).

2.1. A Simple Transition Game

For the sake of clarity, let us formalize this problem. Consider the Simple Transition Game (STG) in Figure 2.1, which represents the incentives

---

[1] For convenience, I will use the female pronoun to describe the victim and the male pronoun to describe the dominant side of the relationship.

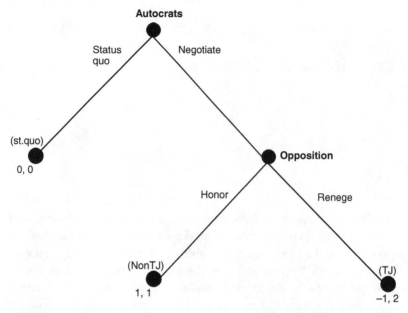

Figure 2.1. A Simple Transition Game.

that the players face while negotiating pacted transitions, assuming that such pacts involve trading amnesty for election.

There are two players, the Autocrats, *A*, and the Opposition, *O*, and two stages of the game. In the first stage, *A* decides whether to step down or not. If *A* does not step down, the game ends with the status quo payoffs of 0 to everyone. If *A* steps down, in the next stage *O* decides whether to honor the agreement about refraining from transitional justice or not. If *O* decides to keep the promise, players get a payoff of 1 each. But if *O* reneges on the agreement, it gets a payoff of 2, while *A* gets a payoff of –1. The three outcomes associated with the possibility of pacted transitions to democracy are thus:

Status quo (SQ): Autocrats do not step down.

Transition with no transitional justice (NonTJ): Autocrats step down and agreements are kept.

Transition with transitional justice (TJ): Autocrats step down and suffer from broken agreements.

SQ is the unique Nash equilibrium outcome.[2] However, in real life, one also observes NonTJ and TJ. Furthermore, note that NonTJ Pareto dominates the Nash equilibrium outcome SQ (this is why the game resembles somewhat the Prisoner's Dilemma). Both A and O prefer NonTJ to SQ. However, NonTJ fails to satisfy the conditions for Nash equilibrium, because when O's decision node is reached, O is better off reneging on the promise. Reneging is in this game a weakly dominant strategy for O.

I believe that this model adequately represents the dilemmas confronting actors engaged in pacted transitions in East Central Europe, according to scholars of transitions to democracy. As early as 1986, O'Donnell and Schmitter wrote that pacted transitions are made possible by promising the outgoing autocrats immunity from trials and prosecutions in exchange for handing down power to a democratically elected government:

> The more brutal, inhumane, and extensive were the repressive actions, the more their actual perpetrators – the institutions involved and those persons who collaborated in them and supported them – feel threatened and will tend to form a bloc opposing any transition. Where they cannot prevent the transition, they will strive to obtain iron-clad guarantees that under no circumstances will "the past be unearthed" (O'Donnell and Schmitter 1986).

This argument has been quoted repeatedly as the reason that autocrats step down peacefully. Adam Przeworski argues that East Central European communists in the late 1980s preferred a transition to a democratic regime in which they could continue their political careers to a revolution potentially depriving them of any political prospects and, possibly, lives (Przeworski 1991, 1992). A democratic transition with transitional justice is a mild equivalent of such a revolution. Note that from the perspective of Polish or Hungarian communists – especially the young and well-educated leaders such as Imre Pozgay or Aleksander Kwaśniewski – the transition to democracy offered more politically attractive prospects than embarking on a career in the outdated structures of the communist party, where advancement in the feudal ranks was not merit-based, but required patronage from senior party bureaucrats. The young technocrat communists preferred democratic transition with amnesty provided they would not be held responsible for the actions of their senior colleagues. In the event of the latter, the communists would have preferred not to have transitioned at all. Note also that the assumption of the model labeled

---

[2] The unique subgame perfect (and also Nash) equilibrium strategy profile is (SQ; Renege).

35

"status quo" need not be interpreted as the communists' ability to rule indefinitely. Instead, it can represent in reduced form the consequences of not initiating negotiations at that point in time. Eventually, with certain positive probability, this could even lead to an anticommunist revolution at some point in time, along the lines of the Romanian overthrow of Nicolai Ceausescu.[3] However, since in this part of the game tree the liberal opposition does not even get to make a move (the liberal opposition does not even get a chance to distinguish itself from the anticommunist opposition), I reduce this section of the game tree in order to focus on the interaction between the players A and O.

STG suggests that the communists' preferred scenario – a transition without transitional justice – is not feasible, because the opposition has incentives to default on any promise, using transitional justice to deprive the former autocrats of political positions. In STG, the structure of the game and payoffs are common knowledge. Thus, all players have perfect and complete information and know the payoffs of all other players. Consequently, the autocrats should anticipate the opposition's defection. How, then, can one explain with this model the actions of communists in East Central Europe, who believed the promises of amnesty? Since the delivery of amnesty is expected to take place *after* the free elections (won by the opposition), how could the communists have trusted the opposition to keep its promises? Table 1.1 shows that in many East Central European countries, the opposition honored its agreements and lustration did not take place until many years following the transition. Where lustration occurred earlier, as in Lithuania or Bulgaria, it was implemented not by the opposition but by the successor communist parties. In cases such as Poland and Hungary, lustration was delayed and the actors responsible for this implementation were not the liberal opposition participating in roundtable negotiations. Honoring the promise of amnesty is at odds with the claim that transitional justice is implemented because promises of refraining from it are not credible.

In the STG game, neither NonTJ nor TJ are Nash equilibrium outcomes. In short, the commonly observed phenomena require a theory explaining: *Why do autocrats engage in negotiations with the opposition and concede to*

---

[3] I am grateful to Barbara Geddes for suggesting to me ways of explicitly modeling such violent turnovers in the STG. For such game theoretic models, see Zielinski (1999). I decided against developing this part of the game tree – and presenting it instead in reduced form – because I wanted to focus attention on participating in negotiations.

free elections counting on amnesty and why does the opposition (sometimes) honor the agreements? The Simple Transition Game is not of much help here since one should never observe the nonequilibrium outcomes – that is, behavior in which autocrats step down and give the opposition an option to renege.

2.2. Limitations of STG

This model clearly cannot explain any of the pacted transitions. This section is devoted to understanding why. Let us start with what we know from the existing literature about authoritarian transitions. Barbara Geddes's work on the typology of authoritarian regimes (Geddes 1999, 2002) suggests that transitions from single-party authoritarian regimes, such as the East Central European communist regimes, differ from other transitions, such as those from military or personalistic dictatorships. She argues that in the case of personalistic dictatorships, their overthrow is either not accompanied by agreements, because the dictator remains in power until the bitter end, or guarantees of amnesty are ensured by third parties. On the other hand, in military regimes, the problem of credible commitments is largely irrelevant because the agreement is enforceable either by the outgoing autocrats retaining enough power or by agreements.[4]

Military regimes are defined as those wherein "a group of officers decides who will rule and exercises some influence over policy" (Geddes 1999). Pacts have been observed in countries transitioning from military rule in which the military initiates negotiations because it has already decided to return to the barracks and prefers order to the chaos of a civil war. Militaries are less concerned with lustration than with prosecution for human rights abuses, but they also trade a speedy transition for amnesty. However, the outgoing military never gives up power entirely and always remains in a position to monitor the opposition and possibly intervene. At the time of negotiations, the military does not give up its control over the enforcement apparatus and need not be so much concerned with making the promise of amnesty credible. One could model this residual "monitoring power" by adding to the STG model an additional move of the autocrats. After the opposition reneges, the autocrats could punish the opposition for reneging, and the possibility of such punishment provides the opposition with incentives to keep the promise.

---

[4] I am grateful to Geddes for this suggestion and for the comments about military and personalistic regimes that follow.

A telling example of a military dictatorship is the Chilean bargain that allowed General Augusto Pinochet to remain commander-in-chief of the army for eight years following the transition after the 1989 elections. During this period, it was unquestionable that any attempt at prosecuting human rights abuses would lead to a military intervention. Before stepping down from office, Pinochet passed a self-amnesty law. When the Christian Democrats started campaigning for transitional justice before the 1989 elections, Pinochet immediately declared that "he would end democracy if any of his men were prosecuted" (Nino 1996, 37). Trials did not start in earnest until Pinochet's retirement.

Another example comes from Argentina, where the outgoing military passed a self-amnesty law. The Peronist candidate, Italo Luder, was expected to win the elections, and his party had promised to respect the law. Unexpectedly, the Radical Party's candidate, Raul Alfonsin, won. After an electoral campaign of vows to implement retributive justice, Alfonsin took steps to overturn the amnesty law, initiating trials of the junta commanders, setting up a truth commission, and even charging the military judiciary to screen lower-level perpetrators for cases that could be considered by civilian courts. Such actions incited protests on the part of the military, culminating in three consecutive military rebellions and forcing Alfonsin to resign early. The next elections brought into power a Peronist, Carlos Menem, who respected the self-amnesty promise by almost instantly pardoning everyone who was standing trial or sentenced and stopping further transitional justice processes.

Personalistic regimes are dictatorships led by charismatic leaders, such as Ferdinand Marcos, the Shah of Iran, Benito Mussolini, or Nicolai Ceausescu. Their chances are slim of surviving a transition without being prosecuted for corruption and human rights abuses, losing their wealth, or suffering a brutal death, as the Mussolini example from the introduction of this book suggests. Hence, personalistic dictators will often be overthrown. When they do step down, it is only under extreme pressure, and they nearly always seek guarantees of amnesty from third parties. The best they can hope for is to transfer their wealth abroad and go into exile, although the recent emergence of international criminal tribunals has significantly limited these options, because there are fewer third parties willing to honor a promise of amnesty (Gilligan 2006). For instance, the first indictment issued by the Special Court for Sierra Leone against Liberia's president, Charles Taylor, collided with diplomatic efforts to coax Taylor into retirement. In exchange for stepping down, he was promised a safe haven in Nigeria. Under pressure from the international community, the Nigerian government denied Taylor protection in 2005 and he was arrested while trying to escape from Nigeria. Due to the controversies surrounding his initial indictment and under extreme pressures from the international community, the Tribunal for Sierra Leone was forced to transfer his case to a court in the Hague (Akl 2007).[5]

In sum, within the Geddes framework, one could argue that pacts following military juntas are enforceable by the military's residual control over the enforcement apparatus. Personalistic dictators are unlikely to step down unless they are under extreme pressure and can secure a promise of amnesty guaranteed by a credible third party.

Even if one accepts this argument for two types of dictatorships – personalistic and military – it cannot be adapted to explain turnovers based on pacts between communist regimes and the opposition. Geddes would classify the East Central European dictatorships as single-party authoritarianisms. In these regimes, communist parties did not control the military, nor was their rule based on the charismatic dominance of a single leader. Even in Poland, where the communists – the Polish United Workers' Party (Polska Zjednoczona Partia Robotnicza, PZPR) – were led by Wojciech Jaruzelski, a general who in 1981 had authorized and then led the martial law regime, prominent communist leaders seriously doubted whether either he or the party effectively controlled the enforcement apparatus:

After the murder of priest Jerzy Popieluszko, I became in charge of the civilian oversight of the secret police. But was civilian oversight of those forces actually possible? No. The secret police officers would talk to my men in front of their "firms." Nobody was ever invited inside. If there were no more priests murdered after Popieluszko, that was sheer coincidence – it had nothing to do with my civilian control over the Interior Ministry (interviews 2004: PC1).

Neither were communist regimes similar to personalistic dictatorships in their chances of surviving a transition, as the communists were not generally in great fear of their opposition. Particularly in Poland, Hungary, and Slovakia, the *nomenklatura* was so certain that it would continue participating in politics that it merely reformed communist party organizations, adapting them to democratic elections (Grzymała-Busse

---

[5] This development is likely to reduce the credibility of third-party agreements in the future, resulting in the hardening of personalistic regimes to the prospects of negotiated settlements.

2002).[6] A former communist leader, when commenting on the timing of the pacted transition, coined the following metaphor:

Just imagine a fort under siege where the defenders of the fort surrender and open the gates even though they could easily hold out longer. They have enough weapons and supplies. However, they decide to open up and share those supplies with others who are camping outside of the fort. They decide to use their supplies towards a common cause (interviews 2004: PC1).

Many among the communist nomenklatura engaged in economic flight and exploited their indirect control over state-owned companies. However, a considerable number of apparatchiks remained in the party, reformed it, and anticipated successful political careers free of transitional justice. They saw no immediate danger looming. Why did the Central European communists approach the negotiations so optimistically? Why were they not afraid of political revenge? Why did they open their political system to the opposition without fear that this opposition would turn against them?

In understanding why the model of trading elections for amnesty poorly explains the timing of lustration laws, the key lies in the fact that lustration and declassification are very specific forms of transitional justice in that they have a potential for harming members of the former opposition as well as the former authoritarian regime.

When former autocrats cannot compete for political office, more seats are available to their opponents. Thus, lustration can be exploited by the former opposition. But in Hungary and Poland, lustration could impact the former opposition as well as the former communists. One cannot overemphasize how this situation differs from amnesty promises in transitions from military and personalistic regimes. The rule of thumb in the latter situation seems to be, "if you are weak, you get nothing" (as in personal dictatorships without the backing of strong third parties), "and if you are strong, you get assurance of amnesty" (as in the military regimes). The only sense, however, in which the post-communists were strong was in knowing the distribution of infiltration across political parties better than the opposition that was

---

[6] According to Jakub Karpinski, the Polish word *nomenklatura* has developed a new meaning since the establishment of communist rule in Poland. Previously, as in the English language *nomenclature*, it meant "terminology" – a set of mutually related concepts. Communist rule changed the meaning to (1) a set of positions filled by decisions of officials of the communist party and (2) the activity of filling state positions through decisions made by communist party officials (Karpinski 1988).

negotiating with them. This is why the STG model proves inadequate for explaining the lack of lustration in the aftermath of pacted transitions in East Central Europe.

In this chapter, I discussed the problem of making promises of amnesty credible and contrasted the transitions from single-party regimes with military and personalistic dictatorships, showing that in the two latter cases, the problem of credible commitment can be solved in ways that are not feasible in democracies emerging from single-party authoritarian regimes. I next turn to the argument of skeletons in the closet. Chapter 3 presents my argument as an incomplete information variant of Schelling's (1980) "kidnapper's dilemma." The fourth and last chapter of this part of the book will test the theoretical argument's empirical implications with data and analytic narratives from 107 elite interviews conducted in Poland, Hungary, and the Czech Republic.

3

The Kidnapper's Dilemma

In the "kidnapper's dilemma," a kidnapper abducts a victim and demands ransom in exchange for releasing her. However, once the ransom is paid out, the kidnapper is better off doing away with the victim. After all, she may provide the police with information identifying him.[1] The victim cannot credibly commit to not revealing her abductor's identity to the police. The game has precisely the same structure as the Simple Transition Game.[2] The strategy of releasing the victim is weakly dominated by disposing of her. How can the abducted victim save her life? How can she make her promise to the kidnapper credible? A possible solution to this dilemma, suggested by Thomas Schelling (1980), runs as follows: Suppose the victim happened to have committed some heinous crime and can supply her abductor with evidence of this crime. If she were to reveal the identity of the kidnapper, he would uncover the evidence against her. Since the disutility from being held responsible for such an act outweighs the victim's utility from punishing the kidnapper, she refrains from revealing his identity and the optimal solution is ensured. The victim "has a skeleton in the kidnapper's closet," and the abductor will reveal it if he himself is revealed by the victim. This secret information makes the victim's commitment not to reveal any information to the police credible.[3]

---

[1] In this discussion, I call the victim "she" and the kidnapper "he."

[2] I am grateful to Piotr Swistak for his suggestion to use the "kidnapper's dilemma" for presenting the main intuition in the more complex model that follows.

[3] The plot of "The Albino Alligator" thriller runs along this scenario. After killing one of the co-abductees in custody of the kidnappers, the surviving victim tells the police who rescued her that the only surviving kidnapper was a victim as well (Marek Kaminski, personal communication).

3.1. The Kidnapper's Dilemma in Pacted Transitions

In the East Central European pacted transitions, the embarrassing skeletons are files of former dissidents who were secret police informers. It is useful here to explain why there would be secret police informers among dissidents. The explanation is directly linked to the long tenure of authoritarian regimes in East Central Europe. Especially toward the end of this long tenure, the communist enforcement apparatuses in East Central Europe rarely engaged in costly violence against the organized resistance. They preferred to monitor the expansion of dissident activity by infiltrating opposition organizations with a network of undercover agents. Such networks consisted of regular citizens who would report forbidden or illegal activity of their coworkers and neighbors – sometimes even family members and friends. Information supplied in this way allowed the secret enforcement apparatus to contain opposition activity without resorting to brute force.[4] While sympathizers of the communist regime were eager to become informers, the secret police valued most highly informers from within the opposition itself. The identity of such informers had to be kept secret, especially from their fellow dissidents.[5]

The files remained secret when the opposition entered the transition negotiations with the outgoing autocrats. The easiest, but also most costly, way to assess the opposition's level of infiltration would have been to adopt a lustration law. If the opposition's infiltration level were low, the opposition could gain from lustration, since the procedure would mainly target successors of the communist regime. In the opposite case, adopting lustration could hurt the opposition. Although the opposition was uncertain about the extent of its infiltration, the communists had more information about it. After all, the secret police had worked for the ancien régime. The communists could exploit this informational advantage by blocking the transition if they feared that the low levels of informers would induce the opposition to break its obligation. However, since the opposition did

---

[4] This fact helps explain why long-tenured authoritarian regimes tend to experience considerably less violence than short-lived dictatorships that have yet to develop an efficient enforcement apparatus.

[5] A telling anecdote regarding the secrecy with which opposition informers protected their identity is described by Aviezer Tucker. In his research on the Czech dissident movement, he came across three reports describing exactly the same dissident gathering. However, the most surprising discovery was not that the secret police was so well informed but that the three informers present at the same event were unaware of each other (Tucker 2000).

not know to what extent it would be implicated by a transitional justice procedure, the communists could try to convince the opposition that it was highly infiltrated. One may think of their decision to open the gates to transition as a message signaling the level of infiltration in a game of incomplete information. The signal could be noisy, since the communists had an obvious incentive to bluff (as the quote from section 1.2 attributed to Aleksander Kwaśniewski suggests). To dissuade them, the opposition could respond with ambiguity whether to adopt or refrain from transitional justice.

The preceding outlined strategic interaction helps to explain two of the puzzling phenomena illustrated in Table 1.1 and Figure 1.1, discussed in the introductory chapters: (1) that the autocrats initiate negotiations in the belief that the opposition will refrain from transitional justice; and (2) that under certain conditions, the opposition respects these promises of amnesty.

The short answers include the following. The dissident opposition may refrain from transitional justice, fearing to reveal "the skeletons in its own closet." Exploiting the opposition's uncertainty, the communists may enter negotiations leading to democratization to signal that levels of infiltration are high. However, because the communists' signal is "noisy," the opposition may respond with caution and be somewhat ambiguous about refraining from or engaging in transitional justice. The explanation sheds light onto why transitional justice will sometimes be significantly delayed or avoided all together. It also provides an alternative explanation to why the communists did not destroy the secret police files as they were stepping down from office. To put it bluntly, retaining the secret police files allowed the communists to keep the opposition in check. Assuming a positive, or explanatory, point of view allows us to understand a variety of puzzling facts associated with the secret police archives and with the timing of transitional justice.

In the next section, I use a signaling game to formalize the intuition that the communists can exploit, as a transitional justice deterrent, the opposition's uncertainty about its infiltration levels and how the opposition can learn from the communists' actions the extent of infiltration.

3.2. The Transition with Secret Information Game

In its canonical form, a signaling model has two players: a Sender and a Receiver.[6] The Sender has private information, unknown to the Receiver,

---

[6] I am grateful to Robert Powell for his modeling suggestions in developing this version of the game.

that affects the payoffs of both players. Through his choice of message, the Sender can pass on to the Receiver some originally unknown information. In response, the Receiver chooses an action. The credibility of the Sender's signal depends on how closely his preferences are aligned with those of the Receiver. Equilibria in signaling games (usually Perfect Bayesian Equilibria) have two parts: the strategy profile and the beliefs of the Receiver about the Sender's type of private information. In one important class of equilibria, separating equilibria, Senders condition their actions on the type of private information they have. In this process, some information is revealed by the Sender, and the Receiver gets to update his a priori beliefs to a posteriori status, and meaningfully conditions his actions on this information. In the other important class of equilibria, known as pooling equilibria, different types of Senders choose the same action. Such messages convey no information to the Receiver, whose a posteriori beliefs remain unchanged relative to the a priori beliefs. In such equilibria, Receivers always act the same way.

In the Transition with Secret Information (TSI) game, the autocrats *(A)* are the Sender, while the Receiver is the opposition *(O)*. The private information is the level of infiltration, $i \in [0, 1]$, where $i = 1$ represents that, relative to the autocrats, the opposition is highly infiltrated (which is best for the autocrats), while $i = 0$ represents that, relative to the opposition, the autocrats are highly infiltrated (which is least desirable for the autocrats, but most desirable for the opposition). Note that i represents relative infiltration. It reflects how collaborators are distributed across the communists and the opposition.[7] This is critical for capturing the distributive effects of lustration. A highly infiltrated opposition (with many secret police collaborators), relative to the communists, has much to lose from adopting a lustration law. If the opposition were to engage in transitional justice, it prefers less infiltration to more, while the preferences of the communists are the opposite: If the opposition were to engage in lustration, the autocrats prefer the opposition to be more infiltrated than the autocrats are. Note that because i measures relative, not absolute, infiltration, it is possible for levels of infiltration to be high for both the

---

[7] Frequently, the private information of the Sender is referred to in game theoretic models of incomplete information as the Sender's "type." I avoid this terminology here to avoid confusion as to the identity of the Sender and Receiver in this model. Although the autocrats are the Sender, the type – relative infiltration – characterizes both them *and* the opposition.

communists and the opposition or low for both. The two scenarios, though radically different in absolute numbers of collaborators, would be represented by the same value of parameter $i = 1/2$. Under these circumstances, neither side would have much to gain from a lustration law.[8] Although the model allows for infiltration to be evenly distributed across the autocrats and the opposition, information about infiltration is not equally distributed between the two players. The autocrats have private information about the exact value of i, but the opposition is uncertain about i. All the opposition knows is that the parameter i is distributed according to some probability density function, f[0,1]. To simplify the analysis, I will assume that the opposition is completely ignorant, that is, that i has a uniform distribution, $i \sim u[0,1]$. Such an assumption is not implausible, since, in reality, dissidents had very sparse information about the contents of the files. The game is shown in Figure 3.1.

In stage 1, nature determines the level of infiltration, i. The autocrats observe the exact level of i and in stage 2 they choose which message to send. The two types of messages are initiate roundtable negotiations with the opposition *(Negotiate)* or stay in power longer *(Status Quo)*. If the autocrats choose not to negotiate with the opposition, the game ends and the autocrats and the opposition receive their reversion payoffs: N_A and N_O, respectively. Initiation of negotiations is equivalent to proposing an exchange of amnesty for power sharing. In stage 3, after observing the autocrats' action, the opposition updates its beliefs regarding its infiltration level and chooses one of three actions. It can refuse to negotiate with the autocrats, in which case the game ends in a status quo with the payoffs equal to n_A and n_O for the autocrats and the opposition, respectively. This is equivalent to refusing to promise amnesty even as the price for power sharing. The opposition's acceptance of the terms of negotiation, however, is equivalent to giving a promise of amnesty. Thus, if the opposition does not refuse to participate, it can keep or renege on its negotiated promise of amnesty. In case of reneging, the game ends with the payoffs of i for the autocrats and $1-i$ for the opposition.[9] Note that in the event of transitional justice, i affects both the payoffs of the autocrats and of the opposition. The difference is that the autocrats know

---

[8] This assumes that the effects of harboring collaborators on the reputation of former communists and the former opposition are alike, which need not be the case.

[9] This implicitly assumes vNM utility functions, that is, players who are risk-neutral.

The Kidnapper's Dilemma

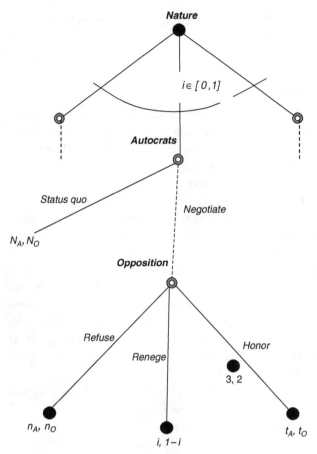

Figure 3.1. Transition with Secret Information Game.
Note: The dashed line between the Opposition's and Autocrats' node represents the Opposition's uncertainty about the value of *i*.

with certainty how *i* will affect their payoffs if the opposition reneges, whereas the opposition does not.[10] Finally, if the opposition decides to honor the agreement, the payoffs are of t_A and t_O, for the autocrats and

---

[10] I do not assume, however, that the level of infiltration affects the reversion payoff, either for the opposition or for the autocrats. This is because I am not interested in the effect that the distribution of infiltration between the autocrats and the opposition has on the successful maintenance of the authoritarian regime. I am only interested in the consequences of this distribution in the authoritarian regime aftermath. Thus, I am treating the total level of infiltration as exogenously given, which is modeled by a constant payoff normalized to 1.

the opposition, respectively. I assume the following relations between the parameters defining payoffs:

$$0 \leq n_A < N_A < t_A \leq 1$$
$$0 \leq N_O < n_O < t_O \leq 1$$

Note that there are no constraints on i, which can take up any value between 0 and 1. However, if the game ends with the opposition reneging, payoffs depend on the value of i, just as they depend on the values of the parameters. Some oppositionists may lack the organizational capacity for participating in negotiations, or they may feel that they lack the mandate – or the legitimacy – to represent citizens without having been elected. One should interpret the opposition's refusal as leading to a status quo different from the autocrat's refusal to negotiate. It is also a reduced form of what one could imagine would happen further down the game tree. In this situation, the autocrats have revealed a weakness: They have demonstrated their resolve to negotiate and the feasibility of pacting.[11] The situation where the autocrats do not initiate negotiations may represent the infeasibility of a pact. In the East Central European context, this might be caused by a strong reactionary faction within the communist party that is blocking attempts of reform-oriented members to open up the regime (Przeworski 1991, 1992; Zielinski 1999).

The justification of the remaining relations is as follows: As was explained before, if transitional justice gets adopted, the more infiltrated the opposition is, the better off the autocrats are (their payoff in such a case is i). Lustrating a relatively more infiltrated opposition makes more seats available to the autocrats and limits their political losses. At the same time, for the opposition, more infiltration among its ranks translates into fewer legislative seats, thus their payoff from lustration is decreasing in i. When infiltration is high – that is, when i is close to 1 – this outcome might even be better for autocrats than a transition with amnesty (this is why $t_A \leq 1$). The opposition prefers transitional justice when it is not implicated by the files (that is, when $t_O \leq 1-i$). In this case, the autocrats must be relatively more infiltrated and there are more seats available for the opposition. For

---

[11] This sign of weakness is similar to what Schmitter and O'Donnell (1986) describe as liberalization which typically gets introduced to increase the autocrats' legitimacy the process of Brownlee (2007) interprets allowing for free elections as a signal of the autocrats' strength, which sometimes, contrary to the autocrats intentions, reveals how fragile they are.

higher levels of infiltration (that is, i close to 1), the opposition will prefer a transition with amnesty to a transition with transitional justice. This is because lustration with a more infiltrated opposition reduces the number of seats available for the opposition and shames members of the former dissident movement. In such a case, transitioning without transitional justice is better. The worst outcome for the opposition, however, is not being invited to roundtable negotiations at all ($N_O < t_O$). Finally, reverting to the status quo after turning down an invitation to negotiate is better than not being invited to participate in negotiations at all ($N_O < n_O$).

Two informal propositions characterize the properties Perfect Bayesian Equilibria that are associated with outcomes similar to those taking place in East Central Europe.[12] The first proposition describes circumstances under which the autocrats will unconditionally choose to negotiate, irrespective of the level of infiltration. The second proposition describes the circumstances under which autocrats condition their action on the observed level of infiltration, i.

Proposition 1: If transition without transitional justice is considerably attractive for the opposition – that is, $t_o \geq 1/2$ – there exists a pooling Perfect Bayesian Equilibrium in which the autocrats step down from power irrespective of the level of infiltration and the opposition honors the promise of amnesty.

Since this is a polling equilibrium, the beliefs of the opposition supporting it are the same as the priors.[13] In the separating equilibrium described in Proposition 2, the opposition is able to learn about infiltration levels from the autocrats' action. This process of learning is referred to as "updating a priori beliefs to a posteriori beliefs."

---

[12] Appendix A contains formal versions of these statements along with information on how they were derived.

[13] A definition of PBE requires specifying the beliefs of the receiver (in our case, the opposition) that support playing equilibrium strategies. The Opposition's beliefs are given by $Pr(i \mid Negotiate) \sim u[0,1]$. This means that if the opposition observes that the autocrats negotiate, their beliefs are such that they are uniformly distributed on the [0,1] interval. We also have to specify the Opposition's beliefs off the equilibrium path, that is, what the opposition would believe, if – contrary to equilibrium behavior – it observed SQ. Since the PBE does not require beliefs to be sequentially rational, we let $Pr(i \mid SQ) \sim u(0, 1-t_O]$. Note that these beliefs are inconsequential, since the opposition does not have a chance to take an action in the event that the autocrats play status quo.

Proposition 2: If honoring amnesty promises is efficient relative to the autocrats' continuing the status quo – that is, $1-2t_O \leq N_A$ – there exists a separating Perfect Bayesian Equilibrium in which the autocrats condition their action of initiating the transition on the observed level of infiltration (that is, they negotiate only if the observed level of infiltration i is at least as high as the critical level i^*, where $i^* = 1-2t_O$). The opposition's optimal strategy is a mixed strategy, reneging on the amnesty promise with probability q and honoring the promise of amnesty with probability $1 - q$, where $q = (t_A - N_A)/(2t_O + t_A - 1)$.[14]

From Proposition 1 we learn that the fact that autocrats initiate negotiations does not mean that the opposition updates its beliefs about the extent of infiltration. The value of i^* from Proposition 2 defines the condition that needs to be satisfied for the opposition to be able to learn something about its infiltration relative to the autocrats. The condition relates the payoffs of autocrats to the payoffs of the opposition. This is because i^* represents the opposition's indifference condition $(E(i|Negotiate) = (i^*+1)/2$ or $i^* = 1-2t_O)$. In equilibrium, the autocrats' indifference condition, defined by $q = (N_A - t_A)/(i^* - t_A)$, has to be satisfied too. The two conditions can be combined into one, as I show in Appendix A, where I also specify that the opposition's beliefs supporting the Perfect Bayesian Equilibria and carry out comparative statics of the equilibrium conditions. Comparative statics on parameter q reveal that a marginal increase in the autocrats' utility from amnesty (t_A) will makes the opposition more likely to renege and that marginal increases in the opposition's utility from amnesty (t_O) or the autocrats' utility from not stepping down (N_A) will make the opposition less likely to renege. Furthermore, the more A has to gain from a transition without transitional justice relative to the authoritarian status quo, the more likely O is to renege on promises of amnesty. The opposition will be more likely to abide by its promises the more it values transition without transitional justice and the better equipped the autocrats are to hold out without democratizing. It is also straightforward to see that A's willingness to negotiate increases with O's level of infiltration.

---

[14] The opposition's posterior beliefs supporting this equilibrium are defined as $Pr(i|Negotiate) \sim u[i^*,1]$ and $Pr(i|SQ) \sim u[0, i^*)$, that is, if the opposition observes that the autocrats negotiate, it knows that their level of infiltraton is at least i^*; if it does not, it knows it's infiltration is lower than i^*.

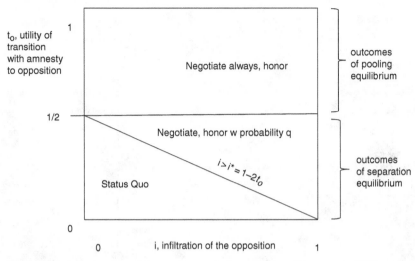

Figure 3.2. Outcomes of the pooling and separating equilibria in the TSI game. *Note:* Assume that $1-2t_O \geq N_A$.

The equilibria described in Propositions 1 and 2 are illustrated in Figure 3.2 as a function of i (infiltration observed by the autocrats) and t_O (the opposition's tolerance for amnesty).

The most important empirical implication from solving the model in Figure 3.2 is that all outcomes of the TSI game may become Perfect Bayesian Equilibria (PBE) outcomes for different parameter values. The model of TSI is a parameterized family of games with several parameters defining payoffs – that is, when one assumes specific values for these parameters, one defines a specific game. Interestingly, only three of these parameters matter for the equilibrium. In addition, for every specific set of parameters and every equilibrium, equilibrium outcomes depend on the level of infiltration. Thus, the parameters that determine which equilibrium outcome is possible are:

- How infiltrated is the opposition with secret collaborators (parameter i)?
- How attractive is transition with amnesty for the opposition (parameter t_O)?
- How attractive is holding out without initiating negotiations for the autocrats (parameter N_A)?

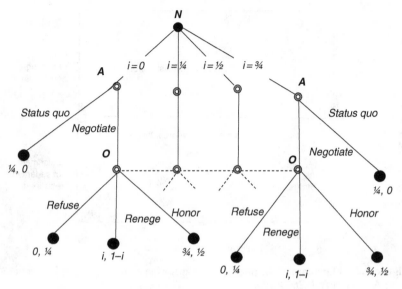

Figure 3.3. Transition with Secret Information (example).

Note that the value of i does not affect the Perfect Bayesian Equilibrium strategy profile, because its distribution is fixed. Thus i is not an internal parameter of the game, but a parameter that characterizes the decision node of the autocrats, and subsequently the decision node of the opposition; i does affect what is the equilibrium outcome, even though it does not affect the equilibrium strategy profile.

For an illustrative explanation of the TSI game, consider the game shown in Figure 3.3, in which all internal parameters have been fixed and the distribution of i has been modified to allow only for four possible levels of infiltration: 0 (the lowest level), $\frac{1}{4}$, $\frac{1}{2}$, and $\frac{3}{4}$ (the highest).

An example of a PBE in this game is the strategy profile ($q = \frac{1}{4}$, $i^* = \frac{1}{4}$) and the following set of a posteriori beliefs: $Pr(i = 0 | Neg) = 0$, $Pr(i = \frac{1}{4} | Neg) = 1/3$. $Pr(i = \frac{1}{2} | Neg) = 1/3$, $Pr(i = \frac{3}{4} | Neg) = 1/3$. In this equilibrium, the autocrats initiate the transition only if the opposition's level of infiltration is at least $\frac{1}{4}$ (thus, it is at least a third of the autocrats' own level). Having observed the autocrats' action, the opposition can update its beliefs about its level of infiltration. A priori beliefs placing the probability of $\frac{1}{4}$ on each of the four infiltration levels are updated to a posteriori beliefs that, conditional on observing "Negotiate," associate the probabilities of 0, 1/3, 1/3, and 1/3 with infiltration levels 0, $\frac{1}{4}$, $\frac{1}{2}$, and $\frac{3}{4}$, respectively.

Table 3.1. *Information and possible infiltration across types of political players.*

	Infiltration with Collaborators		Information about Infiltration
Post-communists	High	Low	Good
Liberal opposition	Low	High	Bad
Anticommunists	None		Good

Note: The double entry for post-communists and the liberal opposition stems from the fact that their relative infiltration levels are not independent. In line with our assumptions, if the post-communists are highly infiltrated, the opposition is not, and vice versa.

In this equilibrium, the opposition reneges on the amnesty promise with probability $\frac{1}{4}$ and honors the promise with a probability $\frac{3}{4}$. It is easy to understand why no separating equilibrium with the opposition playing pure strategies can be sustained. Suppose that the opposition played the pure strategy of always honoring the promise. In that case, the autocrats would have an incentive to bluff and initiate negotiations when levels of infiltration are low. But the opposition can foresee the communists' incentive to bluff. Thus, such a signal cannot be credible. Therefore, the opposition must play a mixed strategy that makes the autocrats indifferent between the status quo and initiating negotiations.

The next chapter presents the data used to estimate these parameters and validates some of the most important assumptions of the model – that is, that roundtable negotiations are equivalent to promises of amnesty and that the opposition's preferences over transitional justice were shaped by its beliefs about its degree of infiltration.

Before concluding, let me talk briefly about the nature of infiltration. As mentioned previously, infiltration is the parameter that describes how collaborators are distributed across different groups of politicians. In this book, I talk about three main groups: the post-communists (autocrats in the model), the liberal opposition (the opposition in the model), and the anticommunists. The anticommunists are parties who are not covered by the transitions model because – as described in Chapter 6 of this book – they do not appear on the political scene until much later. Groups differ not only in the extent to which they are infiltrated but also according to the information they have about who is more likely to be infiltrated. The assumptions I have made about players' infiltration and their level of information about this are represented in Table 3.1.

The anticommunists are in a privileged position, because they have no skeletons in their closet and they know about this fact. The post-communists may be highly infiltrated or they may have few collaborators, but contrary to the opposition, they *know* this is the case. Although in Chapter 6 I present a more nuanced theory of how the different opposition groups get to know whether or not they are infiltrated, it is worthwhile considering how this knowledge is related to size. One useful way to think about different types of opposition organizations and their respective infiltration is through the lens of research on the economics of religion, or religious markets (Finke et al. 1996; Finke and Stark 1998; Iannaccone et al. 1998; Stark and Bainbridge 1996; Stark and Finke 2004). This literature has been challenging the secularization hypothesis (Bruce 1992), according to which the rising opportunity costs of religious activity diminishes participation in spiritual practices (Barro and McCleary 2003; Barro and McCleary 2005; McCleary and Barro 2006a; McCleary and Barro 2006b).[15] Economic theorists have offered formal models demonstrating that religious choices can be analyzed as rational decisions (McBride 2005). Empirical studies have falsified the hypotheses about the irrationality of religious behavior (Iannaccone et al. 1998) and formulated competing hypotheses about the relationships between size, competition, participation in religious organizations, and the demands that religious movements place on their members. One of the most general theories that have received support in this literature is that smaller and more demanding religious movements tend to have higher growth potentials and lower defection rates than groups that are larger. For instance, the devotion of followers of mainline protestant churches in the twentieth century, as illustrated by the following of the Methodist churches, is contrasted with the burdens placed on worshipers of Catholic churches in Southern Europe and Latin America (Finke and Iannaccone 1993). Religious groups that place high demands on their members offer them, in exchange, selective incentives. Selective incentives are rewards that are highly valued by some but not by others (Olson 1971). In other words, the exceptional sacrifices that members of certain religious groups (such as the Moonies or Jehovah's Witnesses) make are no different from the sacrifices that

---

[15] Scholars of democratic transition and consolidation may draw analogies between the secularization hypotheses and modernization theories of democratization (Moore 1966). See also Lipset (1981).

individuals make for the pursuit of other professional or personal goals that they feel strongly about.

Because of the nature of costs and benefits offered to members of religious congregations and dissident groups, as well as the voluntary nature of participating in these organizations, it is tempting to extrapolate the solid findings from the research on religious markets to the relationship between the size of opposition groups and the demands placed on their members. If such a connection were made, demands placed on dissidents would be reflected in the extent of their infiltration. The Polish Samizdat publication *Little Conspirator* instructed first-time dissidents on how to take precautions against being recruited as collaborators. Since some of these precautions were extensively cumbersome (such as protecting calendars and address books with secret code that could be changed on a regular basis, and memorizing meeting places and dates), only those most committed to dissident activity would be willing to implement them (Anonymous). Hence, small-sized but also less infiltrated groups would typically place higher demands on their members than would larger groups, which might have relaxed or no guidelines for dealing with the secret police. This argument suggests that groups can deduce their infiltration from their size. Note that if dissident groups can infer the value of parameter i from their size, the TSI cannot be a signaling model, that is, a game with asymmetric information. I doubt, however, that the fact that larger dissident groups are easier to infiltrate than smaller ones forces us to abandon the assumption of incomplete information about the extent of infiltration. Suppose for now that the relationships between the size of a dissident organization and its infiltration do resemble the relationships between size and defection rates of religious markets. Recent, more nuanced investigations have uncovered important intervening variables that affect participation and defection rates from religious congregations. Among the most important is the presence of regulation, repression, and conflict. Stark and Finke (2004) note that religious markets clear (resulting in religious pluralism) only in the absence of regulation (Finke and Iannaccone 1993). One form of regulation – dividing areas territorially into parishes, with one denomination per parish – radically circumscribes equilibrium predictions. The occurrence of conflict is another obstructing variable. Finke and Stark (1998) specifically use Poland and Ireland as examples of places where the occupying state banishing a dominant religion mobilized higher participation than one would expect in an unrestricted religious market.

Suppose, however, that here the analogy ends and that even though religious markets do not clear under state repression, markets for dissident activity do. In this case, as I note previously, small dissident groups could well be those that place high demands on their participants, resulting in low infiltration levels.[16] Yet the fact that former dissidents could form beliefs about how easy they were to infiltrate relative to one another does not mean that they knew how infiltrated they were relative to the communists. In other words, the fact that a small and demanding dissident group had fewer collaborators than a broad and liberal group (and that both believed this was the case) has little bearing on the liberal opposition's beliefs about its infiltration relative to the communist autocrats. Most importantly, our asymmetric information setup is still valid, since the key parameter is not absolute infiltration, nor even infiltration vis-à-vis competing opposition groups, but infiltration vis-à-vis the communist party. Unfortunately, predictions from the literature on religious markets offer no direct insights on how to measure participation and resistance to infiltration in subversive versus state-sanctioned institutions.

Thus, I believe that the way I interpret infiltration in this book, as relative infiltration, cannot be derivative of opposition size or the consequence of secret police repression, although it is clearly related to the two.

Accepting the assumption of asymmetric information regarding infiltration, we are able to solve the credible commitment problem in transitions to democracy by modeling the interaction between the opposition and the autocrats as a signaling model or as a model of strategic information transmission (Crawford and Sobel 1982). In the classical, cheap talk model of Crawford and Sobel, the quality of the signal is "soft." In the TSI model, however, the autocrat's decision to initiate the negotiations has real payoff consequences. Hence the signal is not cheap talk. Note that in order for the signal to be "hard," the communists would need to have had access to lists of collaborators of some sort. However, preparing such lists would require the passage of a lustration law. Over years of secret police recruitment, the enforcement apparatus had worked with literally hundreds of thousands of informers, not all of whom became politicians. Moreover, the secret police did not keep records of informers in the form

---

[16] Note that the proliferation and diversification of dissident organizations, after the ban on Solidarity by the martial law regime in December 1981, suggest that dissident markets could indeed clear in this fashion. I develop this intuition to form the leading hypothesis in Chapter 6.

of easily accessible registers of informers, according to profession, that could be used to signal to the opposition elites the extent to which they were infiltrated. At most, the communists could demonstrate exemplary cases of the opposition's infiltration. However, because the communists always have an incentive to exaggerate the opposition's infiltration (or to "bluff"), they could neither credibly signal nor technically even extract the information for such a signal. In the model, since the deficit of information is on the opposition's side, it has a choice: Either it will risk having the extent of its infiltration revealed by adopting lustration or it will be held hostage to the threat of secret information. The next chapter describes how the former dissidents succeeding the communist government decide between the two choices.

4

Hostages and Skeletons in Poland, Hungary, and the Czech Republic

This chapter uses the main empirical implications derived from the TSI model to explain the variation in the passage of lustration laws observed in Figure 1.1. I start by explaining why I collected data in Poland, Hungary, and the Czech Republic. Next, I discuss the nature of the elite interview data. I talk of its advantages and limitations. The interviews are used in two ways to illustrate the model's results: first in analytic narratives, next in the form of aggregated responses. I illustrate the use of the qualitative data to corroborate one of the assumptions of the skeletons model: namely, that the issue of accountability for past human rights violations was salient during the roundtable negotiations. Next, I derive empirical implications from the skeletons model.

4.1. Case Selection

All three countries under investigation here share two important features: Their transitions were final and nonviolent. In fact, even though dubbed "revolutions," their actual peaceful character earned the intentionally oxymoronic adjectives of "velvet" (Czechoslovakia), "self-limiting" (Poland) (Staniszkis and Gross 1984), and "negotiated" (Hungary) (Bruszt 1990).

The lack of violence in post-communist transitions leaves little room for doubt about their contractual character and makes them suitable for applying the TSI model. The contracting sides entered roundtable pacts voluntarily, not under the threat of force. In the words of Andrzej Garlicki, the author of a famous historical account of the Polish round-table negotiations: "The roundtable negotiations are a global-scale phenomenon: Without a broken glass or any bloodshed whatsoever, a regime transition took place. Nobody, with perhaps the exception of extreme political optimists, could have foreseen such an unfolding of events" (Garlicki 2003).

4.2. The Interview Data

This chapter makes use of data from 107 elite interviews that I conducted between January and July 2004 in three East Central European countries: Poland, Hungary, and the Czech Republic.

The responding elites came from all political camps and included the president of Hungary, Laszlo Solyom; the former Czech prime minister, Petr Pithart; and the former Polish premier, Jan Olszewski. There were numerous current and former ministers, legislators, and party leaders. The sample included not only people who have given lustration laws their shape, but also journalists, academics, justices, prosecutors, and attorneys – in other words, people who have been the very targets of lustration. Finally, the set of interviewees included participants of the roundtable negotiations.

When interviewing politicians, I attempted to sample members of all three types of political parties discussed in section 1.2: post-communists (reformed successors of communist authoritarian parties), the liberal opposition (dissidents who negotiated the transition to democracy in roundtable talks with the communists), and anticommunists (dissidents who did not participate in roundtable negotiations). Anticommunists were most willing to respond to interview requests and are oversampled in the data. In the qualitative part of this research, whenever quoting from an elite, I use coding nomenclature that enables the reader to identify the identity of my respondents. The first letter stands for the country (P = Poland, H = Hungary, and C = the Czech Republic). The second letter represents affiliation (C = post-communist, L = liberal opposition, and A = anticommunist). The number is randomly assigned.[1] In this chapter, I use data from these open interviews in two ways. First, I approximate parameters of the TSI model. Second, I provide empirical support for some of the critical assumptions of the model, such as the claim that the opposition's preferences regarding transitional justice were closely linked to its beliefs over infiltration. Where possible, I present aggregated data and their interpretation. The following responses give an idea of the type

---

[1] N is used to represent ideologically neutral respondents.

of data I obtained in the interviews. They provide empirical support for the claim that the opposition's preferences regarding transitional justice were closely linked to its beliefs regarding infiltration.

It would be naïve to think that lustration hurts only communists . . . agents were everywhere. I would expect a lot more of them among the dissidents, because if you were to infiltrate anyone, why would the communists infiltrate themselves? They needed snitches in churches and dissident circles, not amongst themselves. That's where the collaborators are (interviews 2004: CN5).

They're not punishing the hunters, but their prey [with this lustration]. Most dissidents do not support lustration (interviews 2004: CL5).

When I first heard that the files contain our own [the opposition's] people, I felt offended, but at that time, I had no idea how many collaborators there were. Kozlowski knew, after he had seen the files, but he never told us anything. I never supported the ideas of Antoni Macierewicz, but it is only now [after lists of collaborators have been released] that I see how infiltrated we were (interviews 2004: PL5).[2]

The post-Solidarity left had most to lose from lustration and that's why it avoided it (interviews 2004: PN2).[3]

Whenever researchers use elite interviews, the question of corroboration arises. To what extent can we treat elite interviews as evidence? This is a good point to clarify that the elite interviews cannot directly prove that the uncertainty about the effects of lustration facilitated peaceful transitions. They offer, however, a consistent backing of the skeletons story, especially since my interviewees were not only political players. Six of my Polish interviewees took part in preparations to main roundtable negotiations, and another five of them were actual roundtable participants. Thus, more than 10 percent of interviewed Polish elites were involved in the roundtable negotiations. There is always a possibility that their answers were insincere, but frequently the elites made comments that did not place them in a very positive light. Consider, for instance, the opinion of PL12, who, when asked to interpret the meaning of "Pacta sund servanda," drew my attention to the important difference between the "Decalogue of a politician and the Decalogue of an individual" (interviews 2004: PL12). This is particularly telling given the personal experience of PL12, who found himself on the infamous

---

[2] Krzysztof Kozlowski was a member of the liberal opposition and the first noncommunist interior minister in Poland; Antoni Macierewicz was an anticommunist and interior minister in one of the first post-transition cabinets and was a proud supporter of very harsh transitional justice.

[3] The next chapter provides details about how the interviews were conducted and how the data are coded.

Macierewicz list, but due to a lack of lustration legislation had to wait years for the opportunity to clear his name in court.

Importantly, the purpose of elite interviews is to provide empirical and historical nuance to analytic narratives. Rather than verifying the model, they are to help us evaluate it and gain confidence in the infiltration story.

4.3. Empirical Implications

This section is devoted to formulating the empirical implications from the results derived from the model described in the previous chapter. First, in the equilibria where the level of infiltration does not matter in conditioning the behavior of the communists, the opposition is either enthusiastic about transition with amnesty (in which case the communists initiate negotiations as described in Proposition 1) or it is not going to accept their invitation (in which case the communists do not initiate negotiations).

Second, in the equilibrium with updating (described in Proposition 2), for the communists to step down, the level of infiltration must exceed a certain threshold. In this equilibrium, the opposition's resistance to transition with amnesty may be offset by how long the communists are willing to hold out without proceeding to transition. In other words, if the signal about infiltration is meaningful, the levels of infiltration must be high. And if the opposition is not too enthusiastic about a transition without lustration, the communists must be able to hold out without negotiations for a considerable period.

Why have I chosen the case study method to evaluate these empirical implications? Testing hypotheses about beliefs and intentions of elites with a statistical model is extremely difficult. Furthermore, it is unclear how one operationalizes the parameters of interest. When issues have low salience with the electorate (as Chapter 5 demonstrates to be the case with transitional justice), survey data are a poor proxy of the elite's preferred policy choices. Even scholars who have been using formal theory to model elite decisions have argued in favor of the case study approach:

The case study method . . . by making use of data derived from archival material or elite interviews, provides more direct access to subjective perceptions and motivations. It can paint an accurate picture of actors' perceptions of the choices available to them, and it can provide evidence of why they chose as they did (Vanberg 2000).

I approach the challenge of evaluating the empirical implications of the TSI model with two distinct strategies. In the first, analytical narratives describe how, in each of the three countries, (1) the dissident movements developed, (2) if and how they became infiltrated, and (3) how the opposition's past and infiltration became relevant for transitional justice decisions through the mid-1990s. My second strategy consists of presenting data in aggregate format, where each of the critical parameters of the model is operationalized with aggregated responses from elite interviews. Those skeptical of aggregating data are offered the case narratives, and those demanding more systematic evidence have available tables summarizing all elite responses by country. After presenting data in both formats, I locate the Polish, Hungarian, and Czech equilibrium outcomes in figures, as functions of the value of the transition with amnesty to the opposition and the level of infiltration of the opposition. The following section describes how the promises of amnesty were delivered or broken in Poland, Hungary, and the Czech Republic. The transitional justice trajectories of these three stable democracies reflect how different parameters come into play in making pacts possible and the democracies' agreements enforceable.

4.4. Hostages and Skeletons: Analytical Narratives

This section begins with Czechoslovakia, a case in which infiltration was too low to induce communists to step down and where transition with amnesty was not an attractive option for the opposition. Based on elite interview data, Poland and Hungary are classified as cases where infiltration was high enough for the opposition to engage in playing a mixed strategy that sometimes involved democratic transition with amnesty. These cases are considered in a subsequent subsection.

4.4.1. Czechoslovakia: No Skeleton, No Hostage

Asked about the nature and size of the most prominent Czech dissident organization, the Charter 77 movement, a famous dissident and one of the movement's best-known advocates abroad said:

It is relatively easy to be a hero in times of war. In no way do I want to undermine wartime heroism, but I believe that it is easier to challenge a regime which you know will end in some foreseeable future. It is extremely difficult to be a hero when you are facing a regime when you don't know how long it is going to be there. That requires a lot of personal courage. That is why there were so few heroes in communist Czechoslovakia. All in all, there were 1,500 Charter 77 signatories; out of the 1,500, at most 250 were active, less than 100 were very active. They did not represent a majority, even of Charter 77 (interviews 2004: CL2).

The small opposition described by CL2 was especially resistant to infiltration. The Czechoslovakian regime adopted extreme measures of repercussion against those who had the courage to oppose it. Therefore, resistance was rare. For example, in the aftermath of the Prague Spring, everyone suspected of revisionist activity was banned from white-collar jobs and was forced instead to work in coal mines and steel mills. Every aspect of society was permeated with the repressions that followed the Prague Spring crackdown (known as "normalization"). Petruska Sustrova may be a poster-child for this phenomenon. After participating in the Prague Spring, she was prevented from obtaining a high school diploma. When asked why the transitional justice in Czechoslovakia took such a harsh turn in roundtable negotiations and why they were brief and superficial compared to the negotiations in Poland or Hungary, Sustrova said that there was simply "no one the communists could strike a deal with" (interview 2004: PA9). Note that this does not necessarily coincide with CL2's opinion that the size of the opposition in Czechoslovakia was small. Sustrova was merely implying that there was a scarcity of oppositionists willing to negotiate. Might this mean that few oppositionists had skeletons in their closet with which they could be held hostage? In the remainder of this section, I argue that this was precisely the case.

Harsh demobilization measures were easy to implement because Czechoslovakia's resistance did not have any extraparty organization. The Prague Spring movement was created and contained within existing party structures. Grzegorz Ekiert attributes the success of demobilization policies to the "low level of popular mobilization before the intervention and the absence of independent centers of power as well as organizational foundations for autonomous political action" (Ekiert 1996, 172).

Because the Prague Spring was, to a large extent, a movement of intraparty democratization, the secret police aimed at eradicating further resistance by focusing on the Communist Party of Czechoslovakia (KSČ). First, approximately 70 percent of the party's membership was purged. Next, the party was drastically infiltrated with informers. Among the communist parties of Poland, Hungary, and Czechoslovakia, the Czechoslovak communist party was the only one in which the secret police had been recruiting informers as early as the 1960s and 1970s. Thus, because the secret police was not targeting the opposition with infiltration, dissident groups could be virtually certain that their infiltration levels were low. Consequently, the communists had no available skeletons to use as ransom in exchange for insurance from transitional justice.

The same communists who had managed the "normalization" in the aftermath of the 1968 Prague Spring remained in office for the next twenty years. Their attachment to communist ideals and methods of implementation changed little over time. Czechoslovakia's transition occurred much later than Hungary's and Poland's. For example, spontaneous student demonstrations did not break out in Prague until November 17, 1989. This was four months after the first noncommunist cabinet in the Soviet bloc had already formed in Poland, and two months after the Hungarian communists had committed themselves to the first fully democratic elections in the region. As mass protests marked the beginning of the Velvet Revolution, Gustav Husak, Czechoslovakia's president and first secretary of KSČ, responded with a call for returning to the "ideals of the Prague Spring." The regime's reaction manifested a complete misunderstanding of the situation. The Prague Spring had been a revisionist trend within the communist party, not a part of the wave of democratization sweeping across Europe. When the communists finally invited the opposition to negotiate the conditions for regime transition, hardly anything remained to negotiate (Calda 1996). Thus, in Czechoslovakia, the roundtable negotiations began extremely late and were very short, lasting only from November 26 to December 9, 1989. Most scholars of post-communism refuse to call the Czech transition a negotiated one at all, and prefer the expression "regime implosion" (Kitschelt 1999).

Nor were the offers and demands made on both sides of the table comparable to the Polish roundtable. In Poland, the communists rejected many of the Polish opposition's demands as being too far-reaching. One such example was the call for the legalization of dissident associations, such as Solidarity,[4] which the communists refused. By contrast, in Czechoslovakia, the communists insisted that the Civic Forum (OF) register as a political party, but the OF resisted this demand, afraid that to do so would hurt its mandate. Conversely, the Polish opposition would have rejected

---

[4] Both in Hungary and Czechoslovakia, it was legal to register party organizations other than the communist party even before the roundtable. In Hungary, SzDSz (Alliance of Free Democrats) had been a party since November 1988 and the MDF (Hungarian Democratic Forum) decided not to become one.

various proposals that its Czechoslovakian counterparts, OF, accepted from the KSČ. For instance, the OF was invited to participate in the transitory government.[5] Polish Solidarity resisted this kind of cooptation, afraid that the post-transition cabinet would end up dominated by communists. This would taint the newly democratized government with responsibility for communism in Poland and undermine its credibility as an advocate of democracy. Yet that appears not to have concerned the Czech opposition; it obviously felt more secure in its demands than Solidarity did.

If the Czechoslovakian autocrats had little option but to step down, were any promises about refraining from transitional justice meaningful? Clearly, the communists had no means of enforcing these promises. Their paramilitary stronghold, the People's Militia, had already been disbanded, with its equipment handed over to the army.[6]

By the ninth round of the roundtable talks, the opposition began to insist that it be given oversight of the secret police files. The new (communist) prime minister remarked that "if a non-communist became Interior Minister, mid-level bureaucrats in the ministry might offer passive or even active resistance" (Calda 1996, 159). To buttress their weak bargaining position, the communists eagerly brought up the possibility of "international repercussions," a euphemism for the threat of Soviet intervention (Calda 1996, 159). In December 1989, such threats lacked any credibility. Mikhail Gorbachev had informally conceded to German unification and had already given his famous speech in Strasbourg on a "common European home" (Quint 1997). Thus, the communists' demands were flatly unrealistic.

Issues related to the former secret police came up during the fifth round of roundtable negotiations. Václav Havel, who had been a leading figure of the Velvet Revolution, asked communist Karel Urbanek what would become of the former secret police officers. Urbanek suggested that they be employed as auditors to track down tax evaders and to combat drug trafficking (Calda 1996, 159–60). Urbanek likely did not understand the question as one of transitional justice, but as a social dilemma of providing work for tens of thousands of trained police officers. The only explicit promise that the opposition made about transitional justice was to President Husak. To

---

[5] The quota of cabinet portfolios allotted to the OF was 45 percent, with the remainder of ministries given to the KSČ and National Front.

[6] By contrast, in Hungary the disbanding of the People's Militia was discussed at the roundtable and even included on the ballot of the November 1990 referendum, held two months after the signing of the roundtable accords.

encourage Husak's resignation, the opposition promised him a pension and "respect." However, if Husak failed to resign, the opposition threatened another general strike (Calda 1996, 150). It seems, then, that even though the Czech communists attempted to negotiate the terms of transition, the opposition was not receptive to the proposals. It was becoming increasingly clear that the communists had very little bargaining power.

The first free elections in Czechoslovakia were held in June 1990. Lustration started in earnest in the spring of 1990 when the interior minister, Rychard Sacher, began to verify the files of the StB (the secret service of the communist era) on members of parliament. The vetting process had not been authorized by a specific law, nor was it circumscribed by any specific, formal guidelines. However, prior to the first free elections, all political parties consented to an internal lustration process conducted by the Interior Ministry. In that process, candidates whose files indicated that they had been collaborators would be removed from the party list. At that point, the issue of lustration was still a concern of elites only. This changed dramatically when Sacher's assistant, Jan Ruml, found that the chair of the People's Party (SL), Roman Bartoncik, had been a collaborator. SL refused to remove Bartoncik, a front runner, from the party list. The conflict escalated to the point where President Havel got involved and advised Bartoncik that if he did not withdraw his candidacy, his file would be released to the media. Bartoncik regarded this threat as a bluff and remained in the race. Havel kept his word. The first lustration scandal broke out immediately after the first election. Once the tacit agreement on internal lustration between party leaders broke down, every MP in the new parliament was suspect. The pressing need for a statute providing formal legal authority and circumscribing guidelines for lustration became apparent.

At the same time, anticommunist sentiments were radicalizing at the local level and in the provinces. In one of Prague's heavy-arms industrial plants, a newly emerging trade union formulated demands for expropriating the communist party's assets. Although such an expropriation would constitute a breach in the roundtable agreements, Prague workers' demands initiated the process of recovering the resources of the communist party. In Brno, the appointment of a communist city mayor provoked an outcry of protests calling for stringency in dealing with former collaborators and supporters of the past regime.[7]

---

[7] On the emergence of an anticommunist right in Brno, led by Petr Cybulka, see Suk (2003, 326); on the emergence of decommunization at the factory level, see Suk (2003, 351–80).

Immediately following the 1990 elections, an ad hoc committee was appointed to investigate the communist riot police use of violence against demonstrators protesting on November 17.[8] After completing its task of revealing those responsible for the use of violence, the committee's chair, Petr Toman, refused to resign. The committee had been granted access to the StB's files, so he proceeded to examine the files on MPs, cabinet members, and even local branches of government and academic institutions. The committee's investigation, just as the earlier ones of Rychard Sacher and Jan Ruml, had no legal basis whatsoever. Members of the Social Democratic Party came to call Toman's commission the "parliamentary political police" (interviews: CL1 2004). The committee's activity, particularly the ease with which it extended its jurisdiction beyond investigating the violence of November 17, made the urgency of passing a formal lustration bill even more apparent. The parliament was at the time dominated by the Civic Forum (Obcanske Forum), an umbrella organization of all political groups opposed to the communists that was created at the outset of the Velvet Revolution. Civic Forum participated in the roundtable negotiations.

Members of the Civic Forum recognized the need for lustration, but disagreed about what activity constituted "collaboration." The cabinet proposal required evidence that the targeted person had consciously collaborated with the secret police, as opposed to having inadvertently disclosed information that could later be used for recruitment purposes.[9] When the bill reached the floor of the parliament, however, it became the subject of heated debate. Scores of MPs presented dissenting opinions.[10] In the end, the bill was completely rewritten. In its final version, the criterion for "collaboration" was having one's name appear in the register of persons under the scrutiny of the StB. The bill required more than 400,000 people seeking managerial positions in the public sector to apply to the Interior Ministry for a lustration certificate.[11]

---

[8] This was the second body appointed to investigate the massacre. The first commission appointed by the communist legislature did not deliver satisfactory results.

[9] Ways in which the secret police would use such information for recruitment purposes were described in Chapter 3.

[10] The debate was seen as one of the events leading to the breakup of the Civic Forum into smaller parties. For a content analysis of speeches given during that debate, see David (2003).

[11] Oddly, the law did not cover positions filled through elections.

The preceding discussion does suggest a diversity of ideas about how to shape the lustration process. However, few political actors within the Civic Forum and parties that ultimately broke away from it considered lustration an altogether bad idea. A diversity of opinions regarding one of the first lustration bills ever drafted is not unusual. In addition, heated debates over any transitional legislation, not only transitional justice, are a fairly common characteristic of young and underinstitutionalized party systems (Kopecký 2001). The consensus around the idea that lustration, in one form or another, must be implemented (David 2003) is consistent with the Civic Forum's lack of concern for skeletons in its closet. Importantly, to all parties in the former Civic Forum, lustration presented itself as yet another opportunity for containing the development of the communist party. In Czechoslovakia, the party was far from reforming into a post-transition socialist democratic party along the lines of the Polish or Hungarian post-communists (Grzymała-Busse 2002). The lustration law was combined with a decommunization law, ensuring that both undercover as well as open collaborators would be targeted. As it turned out, such a harsh lustration procedure did implicate some dissidents. However, as I explain in this chapter, this was the result of insufficiently particularized criteria for classifying targets of the lustration procedure.

By 1994, the Interior Ministry had received around 240,000 requests for lustration certificates. Out of the 236,988 certificates issued before 1994, 4 percent (9,444) confirmed collaboration with the StB secret police. In its initial version, the law did not specify any procedures of appeal, except for those in the lowest category of collaboration – that of a candidate, that is, those who were merely *potential* targets for recruitment by the secret political police. If the target of lustration felt she had been mistakenly assigned to that category, she could seek justice before an appeals committee. By May 2, 1994, 577 requests for reexamination had been filed (CTK 1994c). However, as a result of the Constitutional Court's decision, the category of candidacy for collaboration was invalidated from the statute and, along with it, the appeals procedure (Ustavny Soud Ceske Republiky 2002, Pl. US 1/92).[12]

Some of those who felt that their certificates misrepresented their past began filing civil law suits against the Interior Ministry. This movement was initiated by Vladimir Mikule, a Czech Social Democratic Party

---

[12] The decision is available at Pl. US 1/92. Hethe Clark notes that between 1991 and 1997, a total of 316,000 requests for lustration certificates had been processed (Clark 1998).

(ČSSD) deputy who resigned from parliament after receiving an adverse certificate. By January 2005, 800 of the 3,200 people who chose to clear their names through litigation had gone to court. Members of the ČSSD viewed the lustration bill as an attempt to legalize collective guilt (interviews 2004: CL1, CL6). They argued that being mentioned in the register meant very little in terms of actual collaboration, because the register was simply an index of all persons mentioned in the files for any reason. In particular, candidates for recruitment by the secret political police were listed, often without their knowledge.

Skeptics claim that the Czech StB files are less than reliable because they were "edited" by the secret services in anticipation of the fall of communism (Tucker 2004). This contention is dubious because it assumes that the secret police would have been able to anticipate the fall of communism and predict which dissidents would strive for political careers.

When the precise composition of the interim government was discussed in round seven of the roundtables, Vasil Mohorita, one of the communist representatives, demanded that three key portfolios (Interior, Defense, and Foreign Affairs) be secured for the communists. Milosz Calda writes that "the round nine decision to put the Calfa-Komarek-Carnogorski triumvirate in charge of the Interior Ministry made it possible for the StB to manipulate the files on their agents or to destroy many of them" (Calda 1996, 113). On the other hand, corrupt StB officers had incentives to record the existence of false agents in order to boost their career prospects and their income. Recruiting an émigré dissident, for instance, gave the secret police officer a chance to accumulate quite a sum out of per diems paid in foreign currency (interviews 2004: CL2, PC2) (Kavan 2002). As a result, many innocent dissidents (such as Jan Kavan or Vaclav Mikule) were erroneously identified in the lustration process as collaborators. Thus, the register is probably neither accurate in naming actual StB collaborators nor comprehensive in identifying all of them.

In an attempt to prevent cases of false accusation such as the ones just described from recurring, the Senate passed a law in August 2001 declassifying the communist police files. The bill was proposed by the opposition Civic Democratic Party (ODS) and made all files kept by the former StB available to the wider public. The bill was implemented on March 20, 2003, when the entire register (known as the *Seznam*) appeared on the Ministry of Interior's website. The list identified 75,000 spies and informers of the StB and revealed that approximately 1 in every 130 Czechs had worked with the secret police.

The Czech Republic is clearly an outlier in East Central Europe with respect to lustration. Not only was it the first country to adopt lustration in the region, but its lustration laws also cover the greatest number of people, almost 5 percent of the population. Three grand lustration bills have been passed. Successive bills were enacted because each contained a sunset provision and therefore expired. The political actors continued to present proposals for more lustration because they felt that the political scene remained infiltrated with collaborators.

4.4.2. Refraining from Transitional Justice: Poland and Hungary

Poland and Hungary, in marked contrast to Czechoslovakia, exemplify countries with sizable opposition movements susceptible to infiltration. As the elite interview data indicate, the communists wanted to negotiate with the dissidents in Poland and Hungary. They had skeletons in their closets and could be held hostage by the communists. In other words, the existence of collaborators among the Polish and Hungarian dissidents – their skeletons – provided the communists with insurance that promises of amnesty from lustration would be kept. Stated differently, the pre-transition dissident organizations in Poland and Hungary, their structure, and the tactics that the secret police employed to combat them directly affected the resulting transitional justice decisions.

4.4.2.1. Poland A former Polish underground publisher, asked to assess the size of the secret informer network in Poland, exclaimed, "The opposition in Poland was so numerous that it must have had more secret police agents in its ranks than there were oppositionists in the remaining countries of the communist bloc all taken together!" (interview 2004: PA3).

How could the opposition become so numerous? Timothy Garton Ash provides a concise answer: "In Poland the transition lasted ten years, in Hungary ten months, in Czechoslovakia ten days" (Garton Ash 1983). Solidarity, the first independent trade union in the Soviet bloc, was legalized in 1980 after it signed the first accords with the communist government in Gdansk. Before that, it had coordinated strikes across Poland in August 1980. The consistent protest effort forced the communist government to negotiate with Solidarity representatives, legalize the independent trade union, and commit to respecting basic individual rights and freedoms. Many believed that Poland was about to become the first state in the bloc to become independent of the Soviet Union. At the height of its popularity, the trade union had 9.5 million members, nearly four times more than the communist party organization, called the Polish United Workers' Party (PZPR).[13] Furthermore, during the sixteen months in which Solidarity was a legal trade union, other civic associations proliferated. These included independent professional unions, the Farmers' Solidarity (Solidarnosc Rolnicza), student unions, and even independent unions of the police and armed forces – all comprising a few more million members.

This outburst of civil society came to a dramatic finale with the enactment of martial law on December 13, 1981, by General Wojciech Jaruzelski. Jaruzelski appointed the Military Council of National Salvation (Wojskowa Rada Ocalenia Narodowego) as an interim executive body. The Polish communist state carried out the military crackdown on Solidarity without any aid from the Warsaw Pact or Soviet armies. The introduction and implementation of martial law was a fully internally administered operation. The total number of people arrested for political offenses reached 4,790 by the time the government was forced to announce amnesty to free prison space in July 1983. There were two waves of arrests. The first was associated with pacifying striking laborers (numbering 1,274) and the second with arresting members of Solidarity (3,616). Data for arrests between the July 1983 and July 1984 amnesties could not be found. However, between July 1984 and the unconditional amnesty of 1986, a further 829 persons were arrested and 296 of them sentenced (Ekiert 1996, 272).[14] One of the interviewed academics in Poland offered the following interpretation of martial law:

In 1981 Urban[15] wrote to Kania[16] that Solidarity was becoming a force impossible to contain or control and he said that he believed that introducing martial law was necessary to destroy its network. He also planned a scenario according to which

---

[13] Membership in the communist PZPR at its peak barely touched 3 million. It declined between 1979 and 1982 from 3,091,000 to 2,327,000, mainly as a result of voluntary departure in reaction to martial law policies (Grzymała-Busse 2002). Jadwiga Staniszkis and Jan Gross (1984) have speculated that the departure of these members ensured the party's survival.

[14] This information is summarized in Table 1.3.

[15] Jerzy Urban was the press secretary of the PZPR from 1981 to 1989. In 1983, in a confidential letter to the minister of internal affairs, Czeslaw Kiszckzak, he proposed the creation of a special division for propaganda, whose aim would be to improve the public's perception of the communist, secret, riot, and regular police forces.

[16] Stanislaw Kania was general secretary of the PZPR's Central Committee from September 1980 (one month following the legalization of Solidarity), until October 1981, when merely a month before the introduction of martial law, he was replaced by martial law mastermind (and the current minister of internal affairs) General Wojciech Jarulzelski.

thousands of Solidarity members would be temporarily arrested and confronted with the secret police, which would conduct preparatory activities for recruiting them as agents. The principal purpose of the operation would be to separate potential collaborators from those who would refuse to cooperate. Persons who acted tough so that it was obvious they would not collaborate were left alone and no sanctions were ever taken against them (interviews 2004: PA12).

This response suggests how, after more than ten thousand opposition members were arrested, Solidarity could have been infested with hundreds of informers. Evidence cited in monographs published by archivists from the Institute of National Remembrance corroborates the suggestion of my respondent. A special program (termed *Jodla*) was established to target key Solidarity leaders, arrest them, and try to recruit them as collaborators (Cenckiewicz 2004, 452). One of the recruitment operations took place in the internment camp Strzembielinek. When it opened doors to interns on December 13, there were only four registered informers working for the secret police. By December 31, there were thirteen more, and by the end of the following month, the secret police had thirty collaborators in Strzembielinek. In total, in that location alone, between December 13, 1981, and November 10, 1982, the secret police conducted 306 interviews with the arrested leaders, extracting 89 commitments to collaboration (sealed with signed declarations of consent). Of those, 29 evolved into full-fledged collaboration. Throughout the Baltic Coast, between December 13, 1981, and May 15, 1982, 186 Solidarity leaders from the Baltic Coast alone consented to collaboration, of whom seven represented the national leadership of Solidarity (which was an illegal organization at the time). Two of the collaborators had served as delegates to the first Solidarity Congress (Cenckiewicz 2004, 450–1). Moreover, in January 1982, Jodla was incorporated into a larger program called Renaissance. Anticipating that the ban on Solidarity would not prevent the most committed unionists from continuing activity in conspiracy, Renaissance aimed at encouraging freshly minted collaborators recruited during martial law to infiltrate the new Solidarity cells underground. This was a reasonable assumption on the part of the secret police. The 1981 crackdown against Solidarity, as opposed to previous communist crackdowns against the Prague Spring in Czechoslovakia or the Soviet invasion on the Budapest Uprising in 1956, was accompanied by sealing the borders with the West. Dissidents unable to seek refuge abroad were trapped in the communist state with very little opportunity to continue dissident activity. Renaissance resulted in the recruitment of twenty-five collaborators in the Gdansk Shipyard alone and forty additional collaborators in the neighboring industrial plants on the Baltic Coast. The recruits were supposed to form the elite leadership of the newly reorganized movement.

Crackdowns on anticommunist strikes and demonstrations prior to 1981 had brought similar spikes in the recruitment of collaborators. For instance, Slawomir Cenckiewicz and P. Gontarczyk document that just within two weeks of the "December events" that took place in the winter of 1970 in Gdansk, the secret police recruited fifty-three persons in the Gdansk Shipyard alone, followed by a further eighty-six in January 1971 (Cenckiewicz 2004; Cenckiewicz and Gontarczyk 2008).

How common was this knowledge about the level of infiltration among dissidents? At the time of their recruitment, it was extremely low. According to archival evidence from the Institute of National Remembrance summarized by Cenckiewicz, among the 642 pieces of information supplied from the sixty-one secret collaborators who participated in the first Solidarity Congress in September 1981, 61.7 percent were of "good" or "excellent" quality. The quality of supplied information gives an idea of secret police access to the commanding heights of Solidarity. Indirectly, it shows how clueless Solidarity delegates were that they were being infiltrated. Surely they would have been more cautious if they had known at the time how closely they were being watched. The fact that the opposition had a vague idea about the extent of its infiltration is corroborated by the following quote from the president of a libertarian NGO in Poland:

Few among those who participated in the roundtable negotiations knew what was in the files. For instance, Adam Michnik, along with two historians, established the so-called "Historical Commission," which for a couple of months in 1990 surveyed the archives of the secret police. After that, Michnik became a staunch resister of opening the files in any form or of carrying out lustration, but he never said what he found in those files (interviews 2004: PN8).

An attorney and former dissident who had defended two of his colleagues in lustration court cases concurred with PN8's opinion, saying, "[Only] Kozlowski [the liberal interior minister] and the Solidarity left knew well what was in the files" (interviews 2004: PN10). Another archivist even said:

The secret police organized the roundtable negotiations. The communists promised not to come back to power in return for lack of transitional justice. The files of secret agents who had been Solidarity members were the guarantor of the promise. The contract was of the sort "we have something on you and you've got something on us" (interviews 2004: PN11).

Adam Michnik was a prominent dissident who after the transition became editor-in-chief of *Gazeta Wyborcza*, the first Polish daily that was not controlled by the communist government. Indeed, shortly after the Historical Commission had surveyed the contents of the former secret police archives, Michnik became *consistently opposed* to lustration. His newspaper started advocating restraint against transitional justice in favor of "forward-looking reconciliation." Former prominent dissidents complained that although *Wyborcza* promised to be a forum of debate about the desirable extent of lustration, it refused to publish articles calling for lustration (interviews 2004: PL16).

How did government actors respond to the signals communicated by dissidents who were allowed to consult the files? To answer this question, we have to move back a few months to the beginning of the roundtable negotiations.

The Polish roundtable negotiations were held from February 9 to April 6, 1989, between the representatives of the underground Solidarity, the representatives of communist-controlled trade union OPZZ, and the communist government. Representatives of the Catholic Church, bishops Alojzy Orszulik and Jerzy Dabrowski, were also present.[17] The most important outcome of the negotiations was the communists' concession to semi-free elections.[18] This outcome initiated an entire wave of peaceful transitions bringing to power the former dissidents of East Central Europe. As a result of Solidarity's overwhelming victory, the first noncommunist cabinet, headed by Tadeusz Mazowiecki, was appointed in 1989. Solidarity's victory was facilitated by the communists' oversight in agreeing to an institutional design that eventually made it impossible for a communist-led government to form.[19] At that point, few former communists were

---

[17] In July 2007, historians from the Institute of National Remembrance revealed that Bishop Dabrowski had been recording the meetings of the Polish bishops for the Polish secret police (Nowacki 2007).

[18] The elections were "semi-free" in the sense that only the 35 percent quota was open for free contestation to non-PZPR members (or its satellite parties), whereas PZPR and its satellite organizations were guaranteed the remaining 65 percent of the seats. MPs who were elected in the 1989 from the Solidarity mandate were united in the Civic Parliamentary Committee (OKP), which later broke up into multiple post-Solidarity parties – some more liberal, such as Democratic Union (UD) or the Liberal-Democratic Congress (KLD), and some of them more conservative, such as Center Alliance (PC) or the National-Christian Alliance (ZChN). For more details about the fragmentation of the Polish party system, see Kaminski 2001; Kaminski, Lissowski, and Swistak 1998.

[19] The "mistake" was as follows. At the roundtable, the communists secured 65 percent of the seats in the lower house for their own candidates. In addition, they had hoped to win

concerned about whether promises of amnesty would be kept (interviews 2004: PL4, PL7). Quite predictably, the first post-Solidarity government "pulled its transitional justice punches" (Elster 2004). Both the military and the foreign service, another stronghold of secret police recruitment, remained intact after the transition. Although some screening and employment cuts took place, most of the army and security apparatus remained in office. Only security service operatives in the embassies and the Interior Ministry itself, who were particularly active in tracking down Solidarity representatives abroad, were fired (Kosobudzki 1990). In 1992, Senator Zbigniew Romaszewski advanced a proposal to conduct a verification of communist army officers. He argued that army purges would serve as "a form of fending off enemy infiltration from outside, as the army is the single most sensitive point of each country." But members of the former opposition, especially the roundtable negotiators who were at that time cabinet members, advised against the proposal. President Lech Wałęsa, Solidarity's leader, admitted publicly that he was "in favor of a reasonable exchange of senior staff in the army, as a much better idea than screening" ("Senate on Screening Resolution" 1992). Ex-dissident members of the cabinet supported this policy. At a meeting of the Sejm's National Defense committee, Deputy Defense Minister Bronislaw Komorowski opposed the plan to vet army officers, claiming:

The ministry has no evidence of the purported disloyalty of army commanders and it sees no cause for suspicion. Implementing the Senate proposal would deprive the army of about 7,000 officers. From the point of view of the army and state defense, both the Senate's bill and all the other proposals in the matter must be

some of the 35 percent of seats open for free contestation to non-party members. However, part of the 65 percent was to be filled by candidates on the "national list," which contained thirty-three names of famous communist candidates. For a candidate from this list to "win" a seat in the legislature, he or she needed the support (expressed by not having his or her name crossed out) of at least 50 percent of the voters. Only two communists from the national list received the required support. To make things worse for the communists, the Solidarity candidates won the entire 35 percent quota open for free contestation. With thirty-three seats unfilled in the legislature, the communist coalition would hold only 62.2 percent of the seats instead of the planned 65 percent. The leaders of Solidarity quickly agreed to have the electoral law amended so that the unfilled seats would be allotted to communist candidates. However, with Solidarity holding ninety-nine out of one hundred seats in the Senate, the 65 percent communist majority could win the "cabinet game" in parliament (that is, approve a prime minister in an investiture vote), but was unable to pass legislation without Solidarity's consent (Solidarity had "blocking" power). The crisis of legitimacy that emerged in the aftermath of the elections was irreversible. For details, see Kaminski (1999).

considered harmful, because they are bound to decimate the commanding staff (Polish News Bulletin 1992).

All of this transpired while there were public protests in front of former communist secret police headquarters in which protesters demanded the dismantling of the authoritarian party and the public release of the secret police files (Dudek 2004, 408).[20]

In May 1992, a group of 105 MPs passed a lustration resolution. Members of the Democratic Union (UD), the party of Premier Mazowiecki, were absent. The UD's members were the first to curtail the implementation of the resolution by bringing down the cabinet who had attempted to implement it.[21]

In 1992, when six proposals of lustration were submitted to the Sejm, the UD was the only party (other than the post-communist SLD) that did not sponsor any such proposal. It also moved to reject the four harshest proposals and have the remaining two sent back for committee work. During those debates, as well as in 1993, when a special committee on lustration was created in the parliament, the UD campaigned against lustration. It argued that most of the evidence was destroyed and the remaining files could have been fabricated. In 1993, Jarosław Kaczyński said:

They [the liberal opposition] should have acted more decisively – outlawed PZPR, taken over control of the enforcement apparatus, arrested a few secret police chiefs and communist party leaders, unsealed the archives of the central committee and those of the Defense and Internal Affairs departments. That might have stopped the process of the *nomenklatura*'s appropriation (Kaczyński, Bichniewicz, and Rudnicki 1993).[22]

Mazowiecki, however, publicly dismissed such actions as unwarranted attempts to provoke "the generals." Nevertheless, when asked directly, he

---

[20] Antoni Dudek describes a protest in Poznań on January 18, 1990. The Dissident organization Solidarność Walcząca ("Fighting Solidarity") staged a protest in which the group marched from the communist party headquarters to a the building of the secret police, while chanting "Securitate," the name of the Romanian secret police; a few hundred protesters broke through the first ring of defense by riot police units and fell short of storming the building, just as three days earlier close to a hundred thousand East Germans had in Lichtenberg (Dudek 2004, 408).

[21] The introduction of this book fully described the details of how the resolution was passed in the parliament and of the ensuing crisis that followed.

[22] The term "appropriation of the *nomenklatura*" has come to signify the process by way of which former communist apparatchiks used their privileged access to economic benefits to cushion their exile from politics. A. Zybertowicz and M. Los (2000), for instance, argue that communist managers of formerly state-owned enterprises (SOEs) had an unfair advantage in acquiring SOEs that were being privatized in the early 1990s.

denied feeling personally threatened as cabinet leader with the prospect of a communist backlash (Milewicz 1999).

Mazowiecki not only failed to hold to members of the military and police collectively responsible for human rights violations committed by the communist enforcement apparatus, but he even went so far as to offer promotions to the existing personnel. The generals' promotions were regarded as "spectacular" not only because of the number of officers promoted, but also because of the particular candidates advanced to higher ranks. Seven generals were promoted to a higher rank, and twenty-two colonels (plus one from the Ministry of Internal Affairs) were promoted to generals (General Tadeusz Wilecki, chief of the General Staff of the Polish Army, in an interview with Zbigniew Lentowicz for *Rzeczpospolita*, 1990). This allowed some military officers to become so confident that they denied their role in supporting the past regime, as expressed by one of the officers awarded promotion:

Our consciences and hands are clean. I have always served the country, and I remained faithful to my oath. Today, I can find no justification which would allow certain politicians to apply the principle of collective responsibility, to put us in an ambiguous situation, and to undermine my credibility. I look at the Defense Ministry's leadership that I am a part of from the professional point of view. One needs to spend many years in the service in order to become a general. During this period, an officer's competence, his ability to supervise very large teams and, first of all, his allegiance to Poland are subject to numerous trials. I have full confidence in the people whom I promote. I have met many of them during their training. I believe that it is unfair to attach double-meaning labels to many of them. At the same time, one could attach such labels to the majority of adult Poles, including the ardent supporters of decommunization. On the other hand, it would be a tragedy to destabilize the army, considering the complex international situation. I believe that reason will win over a dogmatic approach to the screening issue (interview with Zbigniew Lentowicz for *Rzeczpospolita*, 1990).

Lustration did not appear again on the legislative agenda until 1997. Those circumstances are most fully described in Part II of this book. The passage of the new law and its aftermath are the subject of Chapters 6 and 7. Importantly, a lustration law proportional to the extent of secret police infiltration was not implemented until 2007.

4.4.2.2 Hungary Entering the University of Economics in Budapest from the Liberty Bridge (Szabadsag), one is startled by an impressive image of Karl Marx on the very left of the main gate. But before realizing that Hungary's institutional décor appears to still lag behind social and political changes, at the other end of the main gate a large marble memorial plaque catches one's eye – this one honoring Imre Nagy, a hero of the Hungarian anticommunist uprising. Young Hungarians, in particular, comment that these contrasting images serve as a good metaphor for Hungary's schizophrenic ways of dealing with the past (interviews 2004: HL2).

In Hungary, the communist regime lasted from 1948 to 1989. In the two preceding years of semidemocracy, between 1946 and 1948, the Soviets tightened their control over all institutions of the new state.[23] In late 1953, the Stalinists relaxed their control over the rule of Mátyás Rakosi, which led to the premiership of Imre Nagy. Nagy represented a promise of de-Stalinization, liberalization, and reform. But he failed to build a political base within the communist party and was ousted from his post and the party in March 1955. Rakosi was not able to purge the party of Nagy's supporters and was replaced by Ernő Gerő.[24] This shift only deepened the crisis and encouraged further criticism of party politics, culminating in the 1956 uprising of the Hungarian people against the communist state. The Hungarian army, which had been completely reorganized following World War II, was too weak to take any decisive steps against the revolutionaries.[25] Instead of supporting the communist state, the police forces joined the ranks of the revolutionaries, and some units, such as the ones in Budapest, even coordinated the distribution of firearms among the insurgents. The first response of the Soviet troops stationed either in Hungary or in close proximity to its borders failed to end the uprising. So, the Hungarian communist state collapsed. Meanwhile, the revolutionary movement was amazingly effective at developing revolutionary institutions. Over the eleven days during which the insurgents controlled Hungary, seventy parties and associations were created, eighteen of which were registered. Also, a network of workers' councils independent of the official communist trade unions emerged. It was not until the communist János Kádár asked the Soviet Union for reinforcement troops that communist rule was reinstalled on November 4, 1956.

Ekiert (1996) cites the most recent Soviet sources, disclosing that by January 15, 1957, the second Soviet intervention caused the death of about

---

[23] Even in that period, trials and purges of members of noncommunist parties were conducted under the pretext of denazification.

[24] The replacement was encouraged by the Soviet Union, which during the Twentieth Congress of the Communist Party of the Soviet Union condemned Stalinist methods.

[25] The army's reaction was largely ambiguous. For more information about the reaction of communist state institutions to the uprisings, see Ekiert (1996, ch. 3).

four thousand Hungarians and the wounding of another thirteen thousand. In addition, 193,216 refugees escaped to Austria and Yugoslavia before Hungary succeeded in resealing its borders. At the same time, 669 Soviets were killed and 1,495 wounded.

Yet, by the late 1960s, Hungary had earned a reputation as the "merriest barrack in the communist camp." Even today, some former dissidents seem to be proud of this reputation (interviews 2004: HL1). The communist party in Hungary – the Hungarian Socialist Workers' Party (MSzMP) – included over eight hundred thousand members. For a country with a population of just over 10 million, and with virtually no authoritarian violence since the 1960s, this is a remarkably high figure. R. F. Miller and F. Fehér (1984) describe how successful János Kádár's policies were in silencing the opposition: "In order for society to be crushed it also had to be bribed." After crushing what remained of the revolutionary institutions, Kádár reverted to mild Khrushchevite policies, which remained in place for years following the fall of Khrushchev himself.[26] The Hungarian regime was open to reform, increasing the wealth of Hungarians and even allowing them to travel abroad. The regime earned itself the label of "Goulash communism."

Scholars of Hungary's transitional justice have struggled to explain why Hungary delayed dealing with its past (Halmai and Scheppele 1997; Letki 2002; Marsh 1996; Okolicsanyi 1992, 1993; Sajó 1996). Most proffered theories state that avoiding violence was the principal concern on both sides. Memories of the 1956 uprising were still vivid. Under this theory, though, transitional justice should never be adopted, so it fails to account for the phenomenon of delayed lustrations.

On the other hand, few scholars identify infiltration of the opposition as a possible reason for lack of transitional justice. This may be attributed to the fact that, until the 1980s, participation in the opposition was a very elite affair (Wittenberg 2006). The opposition was concentrated in Budapest intelligentsia circles and joining required a recommendation from the inside. As a result, the opposition was fairly small and not particularly infiltrated with secret police agents. This changed when the Hungarian Democratic Forum (MDF) was created. MDF was a movement inspired by a grassroots ideology of Hungarian nationalism, known best as the "nepi" culture. MDF did not aspire to become a political party. When it registered officially, its ideology was declared as "neutral." The very fact

---

[26] For details on Hungary–Soviet relations, see ibid., 115.

that it was registered was owed largely to close ties between MDF's members and communists from the reformist circles of the MSzMP. Hungarians otherwise lacking prior political experience – such as those who became active in the MDF – were poorly aware of the presence of the secret police (Department III/3) in their lives under Kádár's communism. There is, therefore, little doubt that the MDF movement's ranks were infiltrated with secret police agents (interviews: HA5 and HA2 2004).[27] If for no other reason, it was simply more accessible in contrast to the more careful, if not elitist, SzDSz.

MDF appeared to be a natural partner with which the communist reformers could negotiate the transition. However, the Hungarian roundtable negotiations that took place between June and September 1989 turned out to be much more complicated. Essentially, they comprised two independent roundtables. First, there was the opposition table, Ellenzéki Kerekasztal (EKA), at which the opposition forces agreed on a common stance against the regime. Second, there were the national roundtable talks that brought together three teams: the opposition team, the communist government's team, and the "third side." I describe each of the three in this section.[28]

The opposition team was created upon the invitation of the Independent Lawyers' Forum and comprised eight opposition groups, including the MDF, the Alliance of Young Democrats (Fidesz), the Bajcsy-Zsilinszky Friends' Association (BZSBT), and the Alliance of Free Democrats (SzDSz). It also included a group of historic descendents of the parties present in the semidemocratic period of 1945 through 1947, such as the Smallholders (FKgP), the Social Democratic Party, and the Christian Democrats (KDNP). To a large extent, the opposition roundtable was

---

[27] III/3 was the department of the secret police that dealt with internal counterintelligence; foreign counterintelligence was the domain of department III/2; intelligence gathering was the domain of the III/1 department. The scope of lustration – that is, whether it was supposed to include agents working abroad as well as inside Hungary – became the topic of heated debate much later, similar to the 2002 debate that occurred in Poland.

[28] Although details about the roundtable negotiations are a fascinating subject of discussion, here I describe them only when they are pertinent to explaining the extent to which the opposition and the communists were infiltrated. That is why the discussion of the Polish and Czech roundtables is limited to facts most relevant for transitional justice. Readers interested in the details of the pacts are referred to the voluminous literature on the subject: For works in English and Polish, see Bozóki 2002, Calda 1996, Elster 1996, Kaminski 1991, Osiatynski 1996, and Sajó 1996; for an account in Czech, see Suk 2003; and for a Hungarian account, see Bozóki and Elbert 1999.

a reaction of these various groups to the communists' attempts to conduct separate negotiations with each individual dissident group. That strategy obviously would have weakened the opposition's bargaining power. To increase unity among members of the opposition, EKA adopted unanimity as the rule for decision making. This voting rule was the only condition under which SzDSz agreed that EKA negotiate with the communists, fearing that otherwise the opponent would exploit the party's weaker position. Fidesz – SzDSz's youth organization – agreed to talk with the MSzMP, but only as part of a united opposition (Bozóki 2002).

The communist team consisted of lawyers from the Ministry of Justice, all of whom were members of the MSzMP. Additionally, a "third side" was made up of organizations that were affiliated with the MSzMP but technically not part of it.

The existence of an official forum for debate among the numerous opposition groups did not mean that, in contrast, the communist leaders presented a unified position. Unlike the communist parties in Poland and Czechoslovakia, the MSzMP was more pluralist and involved numerous reformist circles. The most influential was led by Imre Pozgay, famous for his close ties to the MDF. Although close in policy preferences, the MDF and Pozgay's reformist circle had unequal access to secret police information. The communists, to a large extent, controlled the secret police; they used this information when strategizing at the roundtable. As I discuss in the next section, almost up until the first free elections, the III/3 division of the Hungarian secret police was monitoring the activity of the opposition through its agents. As described in the discussion of the first puzzle in Chapter 1, Miklos Nemeth used this information to intimidate the first MDF government and pressure it into avoiding transitional justice. It is plausible that the reform communists (such as Pozgay), who were in close contact with the opposition groups, inflated and exploited the divisions within the ruling camp to extract concessions from the opposition.[29] They would present the communist hard-liners as willing to call off roundtable negotiations if the reformists failed to gain some benefits for the outgoing regime. These could include a presidential appointment or an election date early enough to avoid wholesale defeat. The KDNP and MDF either

---

[29] This is consistent with the literature on pacted transitions that argues that these transitions are frequently preceded by splits within the ruling elites into hard-liners and soft-liners (O'Donnell and Schmitter 1986) or hard-liners and reformers (Przeworski 1991).

believed the communist reformers or simply acted as their advocates on the floor of EKA. They supported the idea of direct presidential elections preceding the general parliamentary elections that would ensure that Pozgay got the presidential position. In response to MDF's and KDNP's proposal, the more radical opposition groups, such as Fidesz and SzDSz, undertook steps to ensure EKA's tough stance to extract concessions from the communists.

The behavior of EKA members during roundtable negotiations provides some insights about the extent to which they were infiltrated with secret police agents. Groups succumbing to communist demands were plausibly more infiltrated than groups that took a tough stance in the opposition negotiations. Indeed, most interviewees indicated that young parties, such as Fidesz, were less infiltrated than the historical parties, such as the Smallholders and KDNP. The MDF was registered as an association as early as 1987, after having declared itself to be a neutral group.[30] Its members had decent careers in Kadar's communist state. These factors made the MDF party particularly suspect of links to the secret police. Ivan Szabo, a former MDF MP, has been quoted as saying that the reason MDF blocked the SzDSz's lustration proposals between 1990 and 1994 was that lustration would make the government lose its majority support in parliament, so extensive was its infiltration. The MDF was rumored to be the most infiltrated party. Szabo, the finance minister in Jozsef Antall's cabinet, admitted a few years later that a full disclosure of secret police agents would have threatened the MDF's ability to govern the country (Molnar 2002). On the other hand, the communist party was long believed to have escaped infiltration, since its members felt obligated to provide communist authorities with the information they required even without signing an official contract of any sort.

Not only did the MDF refrain from adopting lustration, it also actively prevented a proposal from passing. In 1990, a scandalous revelation – later dubbed the "Danubegate affair" – prompted work on the bill by two opposition MPs from SzDSz, Gabor Demszky and Peter Hack. A

---

[30] Although some members of FiDesz did have social ties with members of the reformist circles of MSzMP, these ties were severed when FiDeSz refused to sign the roundtable accords. Furthermore, as I demonstrate in Chapter 6, FiDeSz changed its ideological position between 1994 and 2002, which eventually led to its becoming an antiliberal populist movement, and this change induced many of the original members, including those who participated in the original Latiletek meetings – which preceded the roundtable negotiations – to leave FiDeSZ.

former secret police officer, Major József Végvári, contacted the SzDSz headquarters in January 1990, only three months prior to the scheduled first democratic elections. Vegvari had information that the secret police was still infiltrating the roundtable opposition (EKA). After the elections, every former dissident was under suspicion for ties with the III/3. The purpose of the Demszky-Hack law was to put an end to rumors being spread in the newly elected parliament about ties of former opposition MPs to the secret police collaborator network. Lustration would end these rumors by appointing a public body to verify them (interviews 2004: HA4).

However, in light of MDF's fear of having its skeletons exposed and given the way in which Antall, the MDF prime minister, was making private use of the files to secure support for his policies from coalition partners, it is hardly surprising that MDF blocked the Demszky-Hack proposal.

Lustration was absent from the legislative agenda until 1994. Media sources report that at that time Antall started selectively releasing dossiers damaging ex-communists' reputations prior to the 1994 elections to prevent the Hungarian Socialist Party (MSzP) from winning. Despite these efforts, in 1994 it became apparent that MSzP would win elections anyway. At that time, the MDF, along with its coalition partners, who a few years earlier had opposed any transitional justice legislation, passed a very harsh lustration law. It covered not only politicians, but also reached the media, as well as legal and academic circles – a total of twelve thousand people. To ensure that the law would affect the post-communists, the definition of a lustrable offense also included receiving summarized periodic reports from the secret political police. Thus, anyone who had held a cabinet post in one of the pre-transition communist governments would be prevented from holding office. MDF was hoping that a lustration law would lessen the communist success in the upcoming elections. Also, since Antall was about to lose exclusive access to the secret files stored in the Interior Ministry, he preferred that the post-communist leader who was to replace him in the post of prime minister would not have that same access, but rather that the contents of the files be overseen by a screening agency, independent of the government. The harshness of the law, however, backfired when the Constitutional Court ruled it illegal in December 1994. The decision came after the MSzP had won an absolute majority in parliament. As a result, Hungary waited until 2001 for a workable lustration law. How Hungary arrived at that law is described and explained in the second part of this book.

4.5. Evidence from Aggregate Data

The preceding analytic narratives are supported by the aggregate data from elite interviews. The aggregated interview data presented in the tables justified the choice of specific parameters. Among the respondents, fifty-one were interviewed in Poland, twenty-six in Hungary, and thirty in the Czech Republic. The tables shown in this section usually contain fewer respondents. This is because the interview protocol included open questions, and I did not pressure elites into responding. When talking to elites, exerting such pressure can gravely distort the qualitative data collection process. Thus, in Tables 4.1, 4.2, 4.3, and 4.4, open responses have been reported whenever they were given.

4.5.1. Operationalizing i: The Level of Infiltration

Table 4.1 summarizes answers to the following questions: "Did lustration hurt only the communists or also the opposition? How infiltrated were dissident circles by secret police collaborators?" These responses substantiate my assumption about the infiltration parameter i that greater infiltration benefited communists while the opposition's preferences were just the opposite.

These data suggest that the oppositions in Poland and Hungary were deeply infiltrated since more than half of the elite respondents believed that to be the case. In the Czech Republic, according to the respondents, the communist party was more significantly infiltrated compared to the opposition. This is consistent with the fact that the Polish opposition was much larger than that of Czechoslovakia. It also comports with the

Table 4.1. *Operationalizing "how infiltrated is the opposition with secret collaborators?" (parameter i) in Poland, Hungary, and the Czech Republic.*

Which parties were most infiltrated by secret police agents?	Poland	Hungary	Czech Republic	Number of responses
Communists – considerably	24%	15.8%	53.8%	16
Communists – somewhat	12.0%	15.8%	0%	6
Liberals – considerably	56.0%	63.2%	38.5%	31
Liberals – somewhat	8.0%	5.3%	7.7%	4
Number of responses	25	19	13	57

Czechoslovak communist party's internal purge in the aftermath of the 1968 Prague Spring. Party members who had participated in developing Aleksander Dubcek's project of "socialism with a human face" were screened out.

4.5.2. Operationizing t_O: the Opposition's Tolerance for a Transition with Amnesty

Table 4.2 summarizes the responses to the question that operationalizes the tolerance of the opposition for a transition with the promises of amnesty kept, t_O: "How supportive of transitional justice was the opposition's electorate?" Although this question does not ask directly how attractive keeping the promise of amnesty was, it gauges more directly the opposition's actual payoff from a transition without transitional justice. When asked directly about their attitudes to breaking promises, politicians tended to overemphasize the costs of reneging on agreements. Indirect inquiry about how their voters felt about refraining from transitional justice seemed to be a more fruitful way of assessing the opposition's preferences.

The elite interviews suggest that the Polish elites believed that lustration was an important issue for the liberal electorate. Hungarian elites were more skeptical, and the Czechs were even less convinced. Hungarian elites, however, were not particularly eager to respond to questions about the liberal electorate. Fortunately, existing data allow directly gauging Hungarian attitudes toward dealing with their past. Figure 4.1 presents opinions of the liberal electorate regarding the issues more eagerly adopted by leftist, centrist, and rightist parties, respectively.

Table 4.2. *Operationalizing "how attractive is refusing negotiations with the autocrats for the opposition?" (parameter t_O) in Poland, Hungary, and the Czech Republic.*

How important was lustration for the liberal electorate? (t_O)	Poland	Hungary	Czech Republic	Number of responses
Considerably	57.1%	28.6%	20.0%	7
Somewhat	14.3%	28.6%	20.0%	4
Not at all	28.6%	42.9%	60.0%	8
Number of responses	7	7	5	19

Note: To avoid inflated polarization of elite responses, this parameter is operationalized with a question about how important lustration was for the liberal electorate.

% MDF electorate thinking that issue belongs to parties

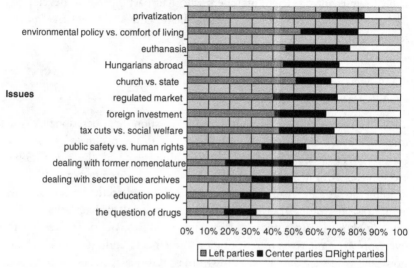

Figure 4.1. Issues taken up by Hungarian parties according to the liberal electorate.
Source: Median Opinion & Market Research, Budapest Hungary (Peter Olajos).

We see from the data that 32 percent of the liberal electorate indicates that centrist parties (who I refer to as "liberals," that is, groups originating in dissident movements that negotiated the transition) should deal with the former *nomenklatura (volt káderek eltávolítása)* and only 19 percent believe that centrist parties ought to occupy themselves with former secret police files *(mult feltarasa)*. By comparison, 26 percent of the liberal electorate considers "tax cuts vs. social welfare" an important issue for centrist parties. Furthermore, the percentage of liberal voters supporting transitional justice is considerably smaller than the percentage of all Hungarians supporting transitional justice. A poll of all the voters regarding their preferences for dealing with the past and removing communist cadres from office found that 47 percent of the electorate were against cadres' participation in public life and 26 percent support it, whereas 40 percent support opening the archives and 44 percent oppose such action (interviews 2004: CL4). The support among liberal voters is considerably smaller, suggesting that the Hungarian liberals' costs of transition with amnesty were relatively low. These survey data are consistent with findings from elite

Table 4.3. *Operationalizing "how attractive was holding out without initiating negotiations for the autocrats?" (parameter N_A) in Poland, Hungary, and the Czech Republic.*

Could the communists have held out longer? (N_A)	Poland	Hungary	Czech Republic	Number of responses
No	10.0%	0%	83.3%	6
Maybe	30.0%	37.5%	0%	6
Yes	60.0%	62.5%	16.7%	12
Number of responses	10	8	6	24

interviews: Transitions with amnesty were a far more tolerable option for the Hungarian electorate. Thus, one can conclude that whereas in Poland transition with amnesty was not a very attractive prospect for the opposition, in Hungary it was more tolerable, as it was in the Czech Republic.

4.5.3. Operationalizing N_A: Could the Communists Hold Out Longer?

Table 4.3 summarizes answers to the question operationalizing the parameter $N_{A:}$ "To what extent were communists forced to initiate negotiations and to what extent were they able to hold out longer?"

According to interviewed elites, in Poland and Hungary, the communists' survival prospects prior to roundtable (RT) negotiations looked much better than in Czechoslovakia. More than 60 percent of the interviewed Poles and Hungarians believed that the communists had an alternative to negotiating the terms of transition. Responses from the Czech Republic confirm that at the time that the communist leadership attempted to convene negotiations, the regime was perceived to be on the verge of collapse.

4.5.4. Evidence of Exchange of Amnesty for Free Elections at Roundtable Negotiations

One final claim that I back with evidence from elite interviews is that participation in roundtable negotiations was equivalent to an exchange of amnesty in return for free elections. The interview protocol included the question: "Were promises about refraining from transitional justice made at the RT? How explicit was the exchange of amnesty for

Table 4.4. *Perceptions of amnesty promises at roundtable negotiations in Poland, Hungary, and the Czech Republic.*

Were promises made at RT about refraining from TJ?	Poland	Hungary	Czech Republic	Number of responses
Explicit	33.3%	16.7%	30.0%	14
Tacit	37.0%	25.0%	0%	11
Made under communist pressure	7.4%	16.7%	0%	5
Explicit, but limited to elections	7.4%	16.7%	0%	4
No promises in any form	14.8%	25.0%	70.0%	13
Number of responses	27	11	10	47

democratization?" This question is not associated with any parameters of the model, but is important for presenting the argument that the transitions in East Central Europe can serve as an interpretation of the TSI model. The elite interview data provide enough information to present it in an aggregated format. Table 4.4 provides the distributions of interviewees in Poland, Hungary, and the Czech Republic according to their recognition of deals about refraining from transitional justice struck at the RTs.

In Poland, a plurality of respondents believed that promises made at roundtable negotiations were explicit. Less than 15 percent of the respondents did not believe that any promises were made. In Hungary, more than three quarters of the respondents believed that some form of promises had been made, although there was considerable variation with respect to how explicit these promises were.

In the Czech Republic, 70 percent of the respondents denied that any promises had been made at the roundtable negotiations. One can attribute this to the fact that in Czechoslovakia, the communist regime collapsed quickly and there was little room for negotiation. As a result, most of the opposition did not participate in whatever negotiations the outgoing regime tried to put together in the last minute. This is an important difference between Czechoslovakia and the countries with long roundtable negotiations – Poland and Hungary. The evidence from analytic narratives receives strong support from aggregate data presented systematically in Tables 4.1 through 4.4.

The combination of archival and historical data as well as evidence from interviews helps to estimate the critical parameters of the model in the

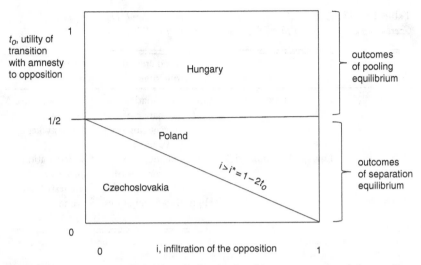

Figure 4.2. Hungary, Poland, and Czechoslovakia as outcomes of the pooling and separating equilibria in the TSI game.
Note: Assume that $1-2t_O \geq N_A$.

cases of Poland, Hungary, and Czechoslovakia. It is now possible to associate these three countries with the specific equilibria that I characterized in Propositions 1 and 2 and which I illustrated in Figure 3.2. The assignment and summary classification of the three countries is presented in Figure 4.2 and Table 4.5.

Starting with Poland, evidence from elite interviews suggested high levels of infiltration, a strong immunity of the communists to pressures to negotiate the transition, and a rather low tolerance for amnesty among oppositionists. This is consistent with the widespread experience with martial law that was ended as recently as in 1983. Under these circumstances, the model predicts an equilibrium in which the communists negotiate under high infiltration and the opposition responds with a mixed strategy, implementing transitional justice with some probability q and keeping promises of amnesty with probability $1-q$.[31] In this equilibrium, the opposition is able to learn about its level of infiltration from the fact that the communists initiated negotiations. The opposition interprets this action as a signal of strong infiltration. This is what in fact happened in Poland. Note that the strong resistance to lustration developed by the main negotiators in the roundtable, such as Adam Michnik, Bronisław Geremek,

---

[31] $q = (t_A - N_A)/(2t_O + t_A + 1)$.

Table 4.5. *The location of outcomes that took place in Poland, Hungary, and Czechoslovakia relative to the equilibria outcomes in the TSI game.*

Country	i	N_A	t_O	n_O	Predicted outcome	Observed outcome
Poland	High	High	Low	Low	Negotiations, q chance of reneging on promise	RT negotiations; promises of amnesty kept
Hungary	High	Medium	High	Low	Negotiations, promises of amnesty kept	RT negotiations; promises of amnesty kept
Czechoslovakia	Low	Low	Low	High	No negotiations	Regime implosion

Note: Hungary is also compatible with the outcome of the separating equilibrium that is associated with negotiations followed by q chance of reneging on the promise.

or Lech Wałęsa, quoted in the Preface, Introduction, and section 4.4.2.1 of this book is consistent with this interpretation.

In Hungary, the liberal opposition was equally heavily infiltrated but considerably more tolerant of amnesty than in Poland. I attribute this attitude to Hungary's less recent experience with attacks on dissident movements (the Soviet crackdown on the Budapest Uprising that also initiated internal purges took place in 1956). The communists' prospects for staying in office without negotiating the transition were perceived as almost as strong as in Poland. One should keep in mind that the Hungarian talks started about two months later than the Polish roundtable, and the prospects of communist regimes in 1989 were worsening quickly. However, even with considerably worse prospects, the TSI model's prediction is an equilibrium in which, depending on the level of infiltration, the communists decide to negotiate and the opposition applies a mixed strategy, refraining from promises of amnesty with probability q and keeping the promise with a probability $1-q$. The opposition's tolerance for a transition with amnesty can offset the effect of communists not being able to hold out as long as in Poland. In the equilibria matching the Polish and Hungarian cases, the opposition could update its beliefs about its infiltration levels.[32]

---

[32] There is another equilibrium in which the opposition cannot update its beliefs about infiltration levels and the autocrats step down no matter what. None of the East Central European countries analyzed here matches this equilibrium.

Note also the pooling equilibrium of the TSI model, where, irrespective of the level of infiltration, the communists initiate negotiations while the opposition honors the promise of amnesty. This outcome is also compatible with the Hungarian scenario, particularly if one emphasizes that lustration was not very important for the Hungarian liberal electorate. Czechoslovakia illustrates the second outcome of the separating equilibrium, where the communists do not initiate negotiations, because they cannot persuade the opposition that it is infiltrated. In Czechoslovakia, transition with amnesty was not an attractive option for the opposition since it was hardly infiltrated with secret police informers to the extent that Hungarian and Polish oppositions were. This was exactly the scenario that played out in Czecholslovakia, where even though, technically, RT negotiations were held, hardly any bargaining took place, so weak was the communists' position. As a result, the regime imploded.[33]

In this section, I have used data from elite interviews to reconstruct the critical parameters of the TSI game for Poland, Hungary, and Czechoslovakia. I then used the parameter assignments to predict equilibrium outcomes and compared them with the events that in fact took place. I found that the equilibrium outcomes do in fact match the trajectories of regime change and transitional justice in East Central Europe.

4.6. Summary of the Skeletons Argument

This concludes Part 1 of the book, in which I analyzed the puzzle of credible commitments applied to pacted regime transitions. These transitions resemble settlements in the aftermath of civil wars or peace agreements between warring countries in the sense that the parties to the conflict had the option *not* to negotiate. In the setting of transitions to democracy, autocrats negotiate deals about leaving power seemingly without credible assurance that after they are left powerless they will not be prosecuted. Almost all transitions to democracy from communism in East Central Europe have been peaceful. The only violent ones were

---

[33] There are more equilibria in the TSI game than just the pooling and separating equilibria outlined in this chapter. The ones that I discuss here involved pure strategies for the outgoing autocrats. Such equilibria were sufficient to cover the three cases for which data allowing the estimation of parameter values are at hand. There is, however, an important class of hybrid equilibria, where not only the opposition but also the autocrats would be playing a mixed strategy. The empirical interpretation of such hybrid equilibria is difficult and was not necessary given the small set of cases.

those in Romania and Yugoslavia – the two communist countries that remained outside of the Soviet sphere of influence. The causes for this pattern of events have remained underresearched by political scientists, perhaps because they still lack a firm grasp of the mechanism by which a monopoly of power can be credibly traded for amnesty. First, it is puzzling that promises about refraining from amnesty are routinely made. Second, it is unclear why there is such variation across countries in East Central Europe as to whether these promises are kept. Whereas the literature on credible commitments would predict that pacted transitions should never take place, not only do autocrats enter such agreements, but the promises that are made to them are sometimes kept and at other times broken. The solution to the credible commitments problem presented here exploits the power of secret information. The most popular transitional justice law in East Central Europe – lustration – relies on files of the secret political police containing information on persons who had collaborated with the ancien régime. This information is then used to verify who among candidates for public office had been a secret police collaborator. The content of secret files is unknown to opposition actors, although they do hold beliefs about who is implicated by the files. If the opposition believes itself to be seriously infiltrated, it will refrain from lustration, even when the opposition is in a position to implement it. Although this book focuses on cases from East Central Europe, the scope of findings goes beyond these cases.[34] The model presented here shows how agreements may be kept in the face of shifts in the underlying distributions of power. The second part of this book describes the circumstances of delayed lustration in East Central Europe. The reader will see how, sooner or later, lustration was eventually implemented in almost all countries. I use the remainder of the book to reconcile these observations with the theoretical insights from the Transitions with Secret Information game.

4.7 Alternative Explanations

Before outlining my own theory identifying causes for delayed transitional justice, I consider several possible alternative explanations for why in some countries the opposition was cautiously weary about punishing former autocrats. Since not all countries delayed the implementation of lustration,

---

[34] A select set of cases is discussed in the conclusion (Chapter 8).

we may try to identify other factors responsible for the cross-country variation.

Take, for instance, Czechoslovakia, where dissidents were eager to punish outgoing communists and where the roundtable talks, speedily put together by outgoing communists losing power by the hour, had hardly any significance. This can be compared to Poland and Hungary, where, in contrast, transitional justice was delayed; but then again, the roundtable negotiations came very early in the process and carried much more significance. Thus one might want to propose an alternative explanation according to which the relative "nastiness" of the communist autocrats would explain the significance of roundtable negotiations and subsequent repercussions. For instance, the Czech communist party (KSČ) was considerably more oppressive than its Polish, Hungarian, or Slovak counterparts. Anna Grzymała-Busse cites data according to which the purge carried out in the aftermath of Prague Spring stripped 28 percent of the communist party of its membership. For many former members, the purge resulted not only in the loss of affiliation with the communist party, but also in the denial of employment and educational opportunities. Grzymała-Busse notes that the trend of harsh lustration policies continued well into the 1980s. She quotes KSČ leader Milos Jakes, who in 1989 "argued that any attempt to come to terms with the events of 1968 would cause the party to fall apart" (Grzymała-Busse 2002, 35). This view is supported by other scholars. Grzegorz Ekiert notes that the Prague Spring movement failed to engage broad organizational and social resources that would withstand the communist crackdown on the freedom movement. He does not hesitate to point out that the Prague Spring events took place in the least favorable international context, with "the most conservative Kremlin since Stalin" (Ekiert 1996, 311). The United States engaged in Vietnam and could offer little diplomatic assistance in the Czechoslovak cause. Any traces of civil society that were born out of the Prague movement were left to wither away, unnourished. Thus, one is tempted to conclude that the Czechs speedily embraced a transitional justice program because among all the countries considered here, their experience with communist oppression was the most brutal and inhumane. This alternative explanation would make legacies of authoritarianism accountable for transitional justice timing. The more inhumane and brutal the previous regime, the stronger the desire for retribution later. Note, however, that this explanation leaves unresolved the credible commitment problem: Why would the opposition not exploit the communists' weakness *after* they had yielded power? Even if the Polish and Hungarian communists were less "nasty," the opposition still had a stake in lustration. If we ignore the infiltration mechanism, whether or not the Polish or Hungarian communists were "less nasty" relative to autocrats from other countries cannot explain why the opposition nevertheless would not lustrate. If the opposition were not infiltrated, it would improve its electoral prospects by implementing lustration. Second, although there are alternative explanations for the opposition's behavior, the infiltration story provides a more general explanation not only for the opposition's behavior but also for the communists' behavior. Furthermore, the infiltration story also explains the timing of lustration and is consistent with the mode of transition to democracy.

A related alternative explanation for the events we have described is that the Czech communists knew there was little that could be done to avoid retribution, so initiating roundtable negotiations was less urgent for them. Hence, the early regime transitions in East Central Europe were negotiations and all the subsequent ones were collapses, and while lustration followed the collapses almost immediately, it lagged behind the genuine negotiations. In this alternative explanation, the critical difference explaining the presence or absence of lustration was not the presence or absence of skeletons, but whether the communists were already collapsing or still negotiating from a position of power. And since the position of the ancien régime is closely related to the opposition's relative own strength, the Czech's opposition, feeling more secure in its demands than, for instance, Solidarity, may have more to do with coming late to the transition game (that is after the Polish and Hungarian communists had stepped down), than with their perceptions of infiltration.

A case that undermines this otherwise plausible explanation is Slovakia. Its delayed lustration is not consistent with the pattern that late comers had early lustration, while early comers had late lustration. Slovakia's transition was concurrent with the Czech transition, as both countries were part of the same federal union. However, a working lustration law was not adopted in Slovakia until 2002. The process by way of which Slovakia embarked on a lustration law is described in detail in the final part of Chapter 7.

In short, the alternative explanation relying on temporal order, like the alternative explanation relying on authoritarian legacies, can account for only part of East Central Europe's transition and dealing with the past, but is not sufficiently general to explain the mode of transition, the resolution of the commitment problem, *and* the timing of lustration. The skeletons story does offer such a general explanation.

Consider next the explanation that the first opposition cabinets pulled their transitional justice punches because of promises made at roundtable negotiations to the outgoing communist governments. This explanation offers a most favorable interpretation of the motivations of politicians in East Central Europe, but it requires the former opposition to act contrary to their political incentives. According to conventional wisdom, this opposition has incentives to renege on its promise of providing amnesty once the communists have stepped down and become powerless. However, the opposition, wishing to downplay its fear of infiltration with secret police agents, is likely to misrepresent the reason for its restraint in adopting lustration. In other words, former dissidents are more eager to attribute their leniency toward former autocrats to the norm *pacta sunt servanda* (agreements must be kept) than to their fear of infiltration. This is consistent with the following opinions from interviewed dissidents: "If I make a deal with somebody at the roundtable, then I am honorably obligated to keep the terms of the deal. We needed to give the communists some feeling of continuity, hence the presidency awarded to Jaruzelski" (interviews 2004: PL8). Even dissidents who were most skeptical toward lustration would remark, however, that the promise alone was not sufficient: "The other reason to appoint the general [Jaruzelski] to the post of president was to avoid provoking the ancien régime to use force, possibly with aid of 'friends' [from the Soviet Union]" (interviews 2004: PL8).

Another explanation for the communists' confidence that they would not suffer transitional justice in the aftermath of the roundtable talks is offered by Jon Elster (2004). According to this explanation, the communists knew how corrupt the court system was and they knew how unlikely it was to change into an independent judiciary compliant with norms of the rule of law. They could have been virtually certain that it would be long before post-transition courts would be ready to put on trial perpetrators responsible for crimes committed during martial law and other crimes against dissidents.

In a limited sense, this explanation can be reconciled with the events in East Central Europe. On the one hand, it is true that trials, property restitutions, and judicial forms of transitional justice have been few and far between and, instead, extrajudicial procedures – such as lustration and declassification – have become most prevalent in East Central Europe. It is possible that the outgoing communists did not anticipate transitional justice outside of the courtroom. On the other hand, this explanation still fails to explain why the oppositions in Poland and Hungary did not seize the opportunity to embark on lustration when the opportunity presented itself and while the blueprint of lustration from Czechoslovakia and East Germany was readily available to implement.

Finally, one should note that if the activity of constitutional courts can be any indication of how courts would handle transitional justice cases if given a chance, it is doubtful the courts would have protected former communists. The constitutional courts upheld lustration laws on numerous occasions, sometimes resulting in harsher legislation, as was the case in Poland when the court struck down the senatorial amendment in 2001 (see Chapter 7 for details).

To summarize these points, although the argument that communists were counting on judicial corruption shielding them from transitional justice helps explain why the communists felt confident leaving power, it fails to explain the opposition's compliance with this expectation. The best insurance against suffering transitional justice in the form of lustration was the opposition's uncertainty about the extent of its infiltration.

Out of the Closet

L e t us go back to Table 1.1. It is clear from the data presented there that throughout East Central Europe, lustration laws eventually did get adopted. Although the communists were able to shield themselves from transitional justice long enough to establish successful social democratic parties, toward the end of the 1990s lustration became the norm rather than the exception. This is not incompatible with my theory from the first part of the book. All that the skeletons model explained was that lustration will not get adopted by dissidents who suspect they are infiltrated with secret police agents. I argued that such fear is particularly widespread among dissident groups who actively participated in the roundtable negotiations. Furthermore, I argued that the communists were more likely to negotiate with those whom they had more information about and whom they could hold hostage to the threat of skeletons in the closet. Clearly, however, the communists' insurance device in the form of dissident infiltration could only last for a limited time. In transitions to democracy, one cannot be certain to whom exactly power is being transferred. In one of the most concise definitions of democracy – Adam Przeworski's minimalist definition – democracy is characterized as a "system where rulers lose elections" (Przeworski 1999). To be more precise, it is a system where the rulers *can* lose elections.

Clearly, the outgoing communists had a different idea of the system into which they were transitioning. Consider the following quote describing the communists' "biggest mistake during the negotiations" coming from one of the leading negotiators at the roundtable on the communist government's side:

We lacked political imagination. We couldn't see that, at some point, the [anticommunist] right would come to power and hold us accountable for the past.

At the time, we thought we were talking with the representatives of the opposition, but really we had no way of knowing whether or not we were negotiating with the representatives of this 10 million–person trade union. Solidarity, in the meantime, was playing its own game (interviews 2004: PC1).

At the roundtable negotiations, the communists thought that they were dealing with a well-structured dissident organization. Even if it appeared somewhat disorganized due to its underground character, its leaders were known, and choosing the persons with whom to negotiate was straightforward. The communists thought that the same leaders they were transferring power to after the semi-free elections would be forming governments for years to come. They were mistaken.

Uncertainty characterizes competitive elections. Outgoing communists should have expected that the opposition with whom they were dealing – that is, the infiltration-fearing dissidents – would eventually be voted out of power. They should have anticipated not always being in the position to hold the ruling party hostage to its threats. The new questions that I address now are the following: (1) Why was lustration adopted in 1997 in Poland and in Hungary? And (2) why did this happen at a time when the post-communist parties – the SLD and the MSzP – were in power?

This is the task for the second part of this book. I will explain why lustration gets adopted at a specific point in the political process and who the actors are who are involved in this event. I start with considering an explanation based on conventional wisdom: that by adopting lustration laws, parties, who want to win and maintain office, are responding to the demands of voters. The next chapter uses survey data to investigate this explanation in detail. I find that evidence of transitional justice driven by voter demand is not conclusive: Voter preferences alone cannot explain the appearance of lustration on legislative agendas. Thus, I explore in the two following chapters an elite-driven hypothesis. Chapter 7 examines developments in the East Central European party system – specifically the rise to power of groups with no history of dissidence or with a very specific underground structure, which provided them with immunity to infiltration by secret police agents. The final theoretical chapter of this book explains why transitional justice was adopted by post-communists, who – one would think – should try to prevent transitional justice legislation. I present a theoretical model that advances the explanation that anticipating inevitable and harsh lustration laws in the aftermath of the elections, the post-communists preferred to pass a mild lustration bill themselves.

5

Voters

TRANSITIONAL JUSTICE DEMAND

In the first part of the book, I explained how the opposition party's uncertainty about the extent to which it was infiltrated delayed the passage of lustration laws – this infiltration, of course, being the skeletons in the opposition's closet. The outgoing communists successfully persuaded the opposition to resist effecting transitional justice because they convinced the opposition that lustration would reveal more collaborators among the oppositionists than among communists. In the first few years after transition, the liberal opposition that was in power refrained from harshly punishing the autocrats – at least in some countries, such as Poland, Hungary, and Slovakia.

By the mid-1990s, those countries' autocrats' honeymoon with democracy ended abruptly as lustration laws became more appealing. Figure 5.1 presents – in a different way than Table 1.1 – the timing of lustration bills in Bulgaria, the Czech Republic, Estonia, Hungary, Latvia, Lithuania, Poland, Romania, and Slovakia. The number of all bills in each country has been normalized to 100 percent and represents only the bills that passed in a given country and were not struck down by constitutional courts or vetoed by the president. Specific country columns represent the distribution of bills across three five-year periods: 1990 through 1994, 1995 through 2000, and 2001 through 2005. This enables us to distinguish early transitional justice cases from moderately delayed transitional justice as well as from severely delayed cases. The figure illustrates that only four of nine East Central European countries successfully passed lustration laws between 1989 and 1994. But between 1995 and 2000, the total number of countries with such laws increased to six, and between 2001 and 2005, the number reached an impressive fourteen.

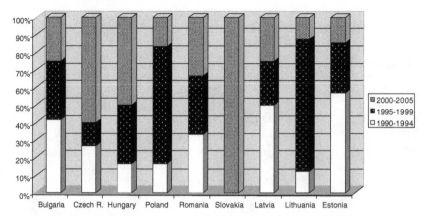

Figure 5.1. Timing of lustration and declassification in East Central Europe from 1990 to 2005.
Note: The longer the dark and light grey bars, the more bills were adopted recently. This represents delayed transitional justice. The laws passed in Czechoslovakia have been assigned to the Czech Republic rather than Slovakia, because it inherited the screening agency. Slovakia did not implement the federal bills (see section 7.4 for details).
Source: Author's database on transitional justice events.

What generated this revival of transitional justice? This chapter considers the hypothesis that that voters' demand for transitional justice policies determines their legislative timing. Common sense would suggest that it is plausible that transitional justice was implemented because the voters increasingly demanded it. After the economies of East Central European countries had picked up, those countries' electorates may have recognized the importance of truth and justice. They may have realized that the communists not only went unpunished for their past actions, but that those former autocrats were currently enjoying the riches of political office. Did it take time for dealing with the past to become a salient issue for East Central European voters?

This hypothesis is difficult to reconcile with the vast literature on emotions and transitional justice (Elster 1999; Petersen 2001, 2002). According to this literature, retributive emotions are most vivid in the immediate aftermath of transition. Nevertheless, the hypothesis can be reconciled under a theory of preference formation. Specifically, after the East Central European countries transitioned from state to market economies and they transitioned away from authoritarian rule, many other issues competed for the attention of voters. Joining NATO (ensuring sovereignty), reforming the economy, and integrating with Europe arguably became of primary importance. Next in priority was reform of the educational system, state administration, social security, and healthcare. Compared to these other, more salient issues, dealing with the past was not a priority. To be sure, although the need for transitional justice was not of utmost concern to the average voter in the immediate aftermath of democratization in East Central Europe, it was not a fleeting emotion either. Once the immediate demands of economic subsistence were settled, voters started calling for lustration and other forms of transitional justice.

Suppose, however, that this "voter demand → politics supply" explanation of lustration timing is incorrect, and that voters' preferences regarding transitional justice come from the parties for whom they vote. In other words, voters cast votes for politicians based on the more salient platforms; then, they identify with the transitional justice policies that their representatives pursue. Voters do not have strong preferences about lustration; nor do these preferences causally precede their voting behavior. In this model, the relationship between voters' transitional justice demand and the supply of transitional justice policies by politicians is reversed. It is consistent with the findings from the framing literature in American politics. This literature argues that voters' preferences regarding foreign policy, Supreme Court decisions, or even the economy are secondary to how politicians frame their decisions. At least on complicated issues, voters adopt the preferences of politicians for whom they voted (Iyengar et al. 1998; Iyengar and Simon 1993).

For transitional justice in East Central Europe, voters could be taking cues from politicians for two reasons. The first and obvious one is that transitional justice mechanisms are complicated. The second is that lustration only indirectly affects regular citizens. Directly, it targets elites and thus remains an entirely "elite affair." Elite interviews with Polish MPs support this theory:

The [lustration] declarations could not have worked, because public disapproval for lustration is secondary to punishing the informers. Whether or not the electorate approves of lustration is not independent of the political debate (interviews 2004: PN3).

People vote for those who declared [having been informers of the secret political police], because the informers were never held accountable for their past. People don't know that informing is wrong unless they see it punished. If those who informed had been punished they could never win elections again, but not because of the shame, but because the electorate learns what they did was wrong after seeing it sanctioned (interviews 2004: PA14).

If this model is correct, citizens voting for politicians against lustration should have a lower demand for transitional justice than those voting for politicians supporting lustration of the former opposition. Stated differently, despite the endogeneity problem involved with determining what comes first – voters' preferences or politicians' preferences – if voters' attitudes have anything to do with the timing of lustration, one should observe a correlation between voters' demand for lustration and the policy positions of politicians for whom they vote.

To test this general hypothesis, I use original survey data from Poland, Hungary, and the Czech Republic. However, because testing this hypothesis involves assigning policy positions regarding dealing with the past to political parties, I also draw on existing data from expert surveys for estimating spatial locations of parties.

The next section describes the conventional wisdom – namely, that politicians engage in transitional justice in response to demands from the electorate. I describe data from surveys that simultaneously asked voters and party members about attitudes toward dealing with the nomenklatura. I explain the limitations of measuring party positions on matters regarding lustration with manifesto data. To preview the argument of the chapter, I first present summary statistics from the surveys that undermine the conventional wisdom that politicians' transitional justice activity can be seen as a response to electoral demand. Following the presentation of these descriptive statistics, I specify what a model predicting voting behavior from voting demand would need to look like. This section requires a presentation of variables associated with demand for transitional justice that could predict voting for parties that have pro-lustration attitudes. The final section presents the results of regression and reaches the conclusion that a strategic as opposed to behavioral explanation is needed.

5.1. The East Europeans "Don't Need That"?

It is typical for local political and judicial elites, bureaucrats, and journalists to attribute lustration to voters' preferences. The chair of the Security Department in the Czech Ministry of Internal Affairs, for example, expressed such conventional wisdom:[1]

---

[1] The Security Department is the institution that has issued lustration certificates to hundreds of thousands of citizens applying for clearance to maintain their managerial positions.

The Slovaks don't need that [lustration]! It would tear their families apart, families made up of communists, fascists, Catholics, and protestants, all in one home. Clans rule in Slovakia and their members choose political and ideological affiliations according to the metaphor: when you're in a boat, you can't have everyone on the same side, or the boat will capsize and everyone will fall into the water! (interviews 2004: CN10).

The chair's remark expresses the conviction that the adoption of lustration is directly determined by what the voters want. This means that the more oriented the electorate is toward punishing collaborators of the former authoritarian regime, the more likely one is to observe transitional justice, because politicians respond to voters' preferences. Rather than conditioning their vote on economic performance or social policy issues, voters choose representatives according to their advocated transitional justice positions.

If politicians respond to voters' preferences and voters choose representatives according to politicians' advocated transitional justice positions, one should observe transitional justice only in those countries where voters consider transitional justice important. For instance, Slovakia would have delayed transitional justice because Slovaks did not consider it vital. However, polling information from Slovakia does not support the conventional wisdom of demand-driven transitional justice. In the immediate aftermath of the velvet divorce between the Czech Republic and Slovakia, more than half of the Slovaks polled by the polling company MVK agreed that the federal lustration law should be enforced in Slovakia. Yet politicians refusing to comply with this wish were reelected. In March 2005, the Slovak Institute for National Memory released the names of former secret police collaborators; at that time, a public opinion poll found that 82 percent of respondents believed that those listed as collaborators should give up their public posts (MVK Opinion Poll, 29 March 2005). Although respondents clearly preferred harsher lustration sanctions over merely revealing politicians' past collaboration, no legislative consequence followed.

Similarly, in Hungary, the anticommunist pressures for investigations into Prime Minister Peter Medgyessy's past and the appointment of the Mecs Committee to conduct such an investigation cannot be interpreted as responses to demands of the electorate. When a poll asked whether Medgyessy should resign due to his secret service past, only 28 percent of the respondents thought he should go, while 58 percent thought he should stay (Hungarian Gallup Institute

Poll 2002).[2] Most interviewees claimed that Hungarians are completely disinterested in coming to terms with their past. Given a moderate demand for transitional justice, it is surprising that the media are so keen on publishing lustration scandals. If nobody is concerned about lustration, why do the country's top dailies regularly publish articles exposing well-known public figures who had collaborated with the communist secret police? One of my interviewees thought that with so many media outlets, it is necessary to come up with a lustration scandal every once in a while. Prime Minister Medgyessy's popularity grew considerably after his work as undercover agent of the secret police was published by a right-wing daily associated with Fidesz (interviews: HO7 2004). Lacking the counterfactual, it is problematic to infer that the scandal itself had caused Medgyessy's surge in popularity (Fearon 1998). Had the scandal never surfaced, perhaps he would have been even more popular. Yet virtually all elite members I interviewed in Hungary described the scandal as an illustration of how disillusioned the Hungarian public had become with lustration. Revealing a famous politician as an ex-collaborator was a selling media story because Hungarians were so poorly aware of the secret police's presence in their lives under Janos Kadar's communism (interviews 2004: HA8, HA4, HL4, HL2, and HA9).

Finally, consider a series of surveys from Poland, conducted by the CBOS polling company five times between 1994 and 1999. The polls in June 1994, February 1996, December 1996, December 1997, and May 1999 asked respondents the following:

If it is revealed that a person holding positions of responsibility in a state institution collaborated with the secret police, do you believe that he or she:

-should be forced to give up the position or
-should be allowed to keep the position

The answers are summarized in Table 5.1.

The summary statistics only partially support hypotheses from the transitional literature on emotions. They support the prediction that, in the early aftermath of transition, public support for dealing with the past is greatest and

---

[2] The Hungarian Gallup Institute asked 754 randomly selected Hungarian citizens on June 19 and 20, 2002, whether they would like the prime minister to resign. Thirteen percent of those asked were unable or unwilling to give an answer. See www.gallup.hu for more details on how the poll was carried out.

Table 5.1. *Support for lustration among the general public in Poland, 1994 through 1999.*

	Responses according to timing of study (in percentages)				
"Persons holding public positions ..."	June '94	February '96	December '96	December '97	May '99
Should be forced to give up their positions	72	67	59	62	53
Should continue to hold their positions	15	17	23	21	28
Difficult to tell	13	16	18	17	18

Source: Komunikat 1999–24 CBOS, from "omnibus" surveys conducted on random-address samples of Polish adults.
Note: Full text of question is: "Do you believe that persons holding positions of responsibility in state institutions, if it is revealed that they had collaborated with the secret police . . . ."

then diminishes over time. The statistics are not consistent, though, with the part of the literature that assumes a direct link between emotions and political action. Nor do they support the hypothesis that public opinion drives the adoption of lustration laws. Agreement with "persons holding positions of public responsibility who collaborated with the secret police should resign" was highest in 1994 (at 72 percent) and dropped steadily over time (to 53 percent). Despite the steady decline in pro-lustration attitudes, between 1994 and 1999, the harshest lustration laws were implemented toward the end of that period. In addition, they were accompanied by the broad declassification program associated with creating the Institute of National Remembrance.

Although these illustrations are informative, they can be treated as little more than anecdotal evidence against the hypotheses that the driving force behind lustration is the desire to placate the voters. The goal of this chapter is to examine closely the relationship between voters' demand and actual adoption of lustration policies. The general hypothesis is the following: The timing of adopting lustration policies can be explained by the correlation between voters' demand for lustration and the policy positions of politicians for whom they vote. In the following section, I test this general hypothesis in a context broader than isolated polls from Slovakia, Hungary, and Poland. For that purpose, it is more useful to analyze data from cross-country surveys asking the same sets of specific questions.

5.2. Surveys with Questions on Transitional Justice

I consult data from a variety of sources, but the main source is the Transitional Justice Survey (TJS), which I designed and carried out in December 2004. It was based on 3,057 face-to-face interviews conducted in the respondents' homes by independent polling companies in Poland, Hungary, and the Czech Republic. All three parts of the survey used multistage clustered random samples of population (aged fifteen to seventy-five) based on the normal methods of sampling in these respective countries.[3]

In designing the Transitional Justice Survey, I relied on existing questionnaires – in particular, James Gibson's Legal Values Surveys (LVS). The LVS was carried out in six countries – including Poland and Hungary in 1995 to 1998 – to assess political tolerance, the legitimacy of existing institutions, and attitudes toward the rule of law. Gibson's survey covered six countries, including established as well as new democracies. The Polish and Hungarian versions of the questionnaire included a question about demand for transitional justice: "Do you believe communists should be allowed to run for political office?" I added to Gibson's question a number of specific measures of transitional justice demand, which I discuss later in this chapter.

Another survey I rely on in this chapter is Values and Political Change in Post-Communist Europe, conducted by William Miller. Miller and his team polled MPs alongside the general public in Hungary, Slovakia, the Czech Republic, Ukraine, and Russia. Apart from measuring voting behavior in great detail, one of the questions in his survey asked respondents to what extent they agreed with the following statement: "More should be done to punish people who were responsible for the injustices of the communist regime." Their answers can be used to assess preferences regarding transitional justice.

The next survey is the Party Policy in Modern Democracies (PPMD) project carried out by Ken Benoit and Michael Laver (Benoit and Laver 2007). The PPMD questionnaire asked experts about politicians' preferences among ways of dealing with members of the former authoritarian regime. Policy preferences were measured on a twenty-point

[3] There were 200 sampling points in Poland, 118 in the Czech Republic, and 100 in Hungary. The Polish survey was conducted by Pentor Company (n = 1006), the Hungarian survey was carried out by Hoffman Research International (n = 1049), and the Czech survey was administered by the Opinion Window Research International (n = 1002). The sampling methodology along with the question wording is presented in Appendix C.

thermometer scale, with 1 representing "Former communist party officials should have the same rights and opportunities as other citizens to
participate in public life," and 20 representing "Former communist party
officials should be kept out of public life as far as possible." A party's
position was measured as the average score across all experts.

There are other sources of data on parties' policy positions. One
prominent example is the Manifesto Data Project – an enterprise carried
out by Dieter Hans Klingemann and his colleagues originally for the
Organization for Economic Cooperation and Development (OECD)
countries. Recently the project has been extended to East and Central
Europe (Budge 2001; Klingemann 2006). Their teams coded election
programs on a scale from 0 to 100, on a variety of issues, among them
attitudes toward dealing with former communists and their collaborators.
Text containing the following "quasi-sentences" was coded as
"Communist: Positive":

1.1. "Cooperation with former authorities/communists in the transition period"
1.2. "Pro-communist involvement in the transition process"
1.3. "'Let sleeping dogs lie' in dealing with the nomenclature"
(Klingemann 2006, Appendix II, operationalization of variable 3052)
Text containing these "quasi-sentences" was coded as
"Communist Negative":
2.1. "Against communist involvement in democratic government"
2.2. "Weeding out the collaborators from governmental service"
2.3. "Need for political coalition except communist parties" (Klingemann 2006, Appendix II, Appendix II, operationalization of
variable 3053)

Statements 1.3 and 2.2 may initially appear to be good operationalizations
of expressed policy preferences regarding lustration. Using these data to test
the general hypothesis, however, poses a serious problem. It presupposes the
object of the test – namely, that voters elect politicians following transitional
justice policies they advertise. After all, manifesto data summarize electoral
programs in which politicians declare what they will do once in power.
Suppose we divide political parties into three groups: one group that contains "Communist: Positive" quasi-sentences in its manifestos, one that
contains "Communist: Negative" quasi-sentences, and one that contains
neither. Furthermore, if we found no correlation between voters' lustration
preferences and the type of party they voted for, it could just mean that the

politicians are "wrong" in deciding what to put in the manifestos. Stated differently, politicians mistakenly believe voters to be insensitive to transitional justice, while voters are sensitive to it but use different means of assessing which politicians they intend to vote for in order to get their preferred policy implemented. For this reason, when deciding where to place parties in the political issue space, I relied exclusively on the PPMD expert scores.

On a more practical level, the manifesto data would hardly code any of the parties as lustration supporters. Only 2 manifestos out of a total of 102 received non-zero in the "Communist: Negative" category. Although many more had positive scores on the "Communist: Positive" scale among the three countries that form my core cases, the highest scores were among the Czech parties, immediately after the transition. This is, ironically, exactly when Czechoslovakia adopted a harsh lustration policy. I present larger sections of these data in Chapter 7 of this book. One final argument in favor of using the PPMD is that the survey uses a 20-point scale. I decided not to divide parties into dichotomous categories of "lustration supporters" and "lustration resisters." Drawing the line between parties for and against lustration at 10 or the median score seemed arbitrary.

5.3. Summary and Descriptive Statistics

The argument that voting behavior induces politicians' compliance with the electorate's transitional justice preferences presupposes that transitional justice is a salient issue with the electorate. Consider, however, the combined evidence from the Legal Values Survey and from the Transitional Justice Survey, as shown in Figure 5.2. Here respondents from representative national samples in Poland, Hungary, and the Czech Republic were asked about characteristics they considered important for reelection. Four characteristics were proposed: (1) "talents and skills of politicians"; (2) "representing voters"; (3) "having the backing of influential groups"; and (4) "having a communist past."[4] Because the LVS was not carried out in the Czech Republic, the 1995 results reflect only Poland and Hungary. The timing in Poland and Hungary is particularly important,

---

[4] Even though "communist past" is not a very precise way of asking about lustration, retaining exactly the same set of questions from the LVS had the advantage of offering the possibility for making comparisons across time.

Mean Agreement That Characteristic is Important

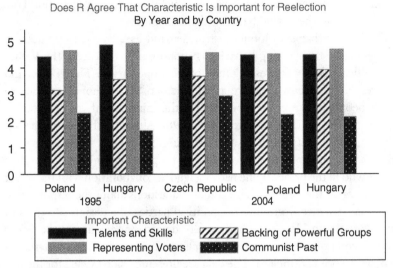

Figure 5.2. Saliency of lustration in Poland, Hungary, and the Czech Republic, 1995 and 2004.
Note: Attitudes on the question, "What helps politicians win elections?" were measured on a scale 1–5, where 5 = "Very Important," 4 = "Rather Important," 3 = "Uncertain," 2 = " Rather Unimportant," and 1 = Not Important at All."
Source: Legal Values Survey (1995) and Transitional Justice Survey (2004).

because the LVS was conducted before the adoption of lustration, while the TJS was conducted after the law was adopted.

Strikingly, the presence of a communist past is least relevant for winning (or losing) elections across the three countries and different time periods. Both in Hungary and Poland, respondents believe that representing voters is most important for winning elections, almost twice as important as not having a communist past. This is true even though in Poland and Hungary – in 1993 and 1994, respectively – post-communist parties did win elections. "Talents and skills" and "being backed by powerful groups" rated closely behind "representing voters" as reasons for winning elections. Pooling responses from all three countries in the TJS data shows that voters consider participation in the ancien régime less important for holding office than other factors. On a 1 to 5 scale of importance, respondents in Poland, Hungary, and the Czech Republic gave "communist past" the average score of 2.45, well behind "skills and talents" (4.45), "representing voters' interests" (3.67), and "being backed by powerful organizations" (4.56). It is intriguing that in Poland and Hungary over the course of ten years, respondents' answers have not changed much even though lustration laws were adopted in the period between the two surveys.

The theory that transitional justice demand as expressed by voters is endogenous to their voting behavior is supported by data from the Values and Political Change in Post-Communist Europe survey. There, MPs and their respective electorates were asked whether "More should be done to punish people who were responsible for the injustices of the communist regime" (Miller, White, and Heywood 1998). Although this is not specifically a measure of attitudes toward lustration, preferences regarding punishing former autocrats can serve as a proxy for positions on screening public officers who in the prior regime had engaged in collaboration with the secret police. Because the questionnaire contains questions about the respondents' ideological distance from different political parties, the design allows us to match voters with MPs from their preferred parties and compare the extent to which voter demand for transitional justice diverges from the preferences of voters' favorite politicians. The data are presented side by side for the five countries in Appendix B. One observes that in the Czech Republic, Hungary, and even Ukraine, political elites are systematically more extreme about adopting or avoiding lustration than their respective voters. Only in Russia is this trend reversed, with MPs preferring less transitional justice than their constituents.[5]

Figure 5.3 summarizes my main independent variable from the Transitional Justice Survey: demand for lustration measured with responses to "Do you agree with the claim that at this point in time lustration should be carried out?", broken down by targeted activity and targeted persons.

The most stunning observation is that fifteen years after the transition from communist rule in East Central Europe, demand for transitional justice is still extremely high. More than half of the polled citizens believe that lustration should continue to be effected. It is entirely possible, though, that for certain electorates, attitudes toward lustration are more important than for others. Indeed, this is what the histogram of my dependent variable, "pro-lustration voting," shows in Figure 5.4.

---

[5] Unfortunately, there is no data on MPs in Slovakia, but the public's preferences (on average at 3.64 on a scale from 1 [low] to 5 [high]) fall squarely in the middle of that scale in the Czech Republic (3.76) and Hungary (3.44). In Ukraine and Russia, the public's preferences are, on average, 3.22 and 3.13, respectively. This suggests that the Slovak public was not particularly different from other countries in the region – both those that adopted as well as those that refrained from transitional justice.

Voters: Transitional Justice Demand

Mean demand for lustration by targeted activity

By country

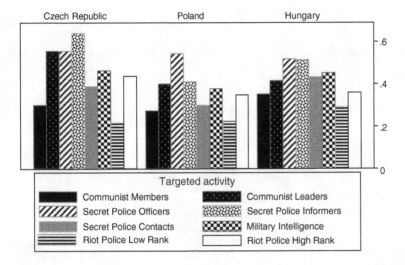

Mean demand for lustration by targeted persons

By country

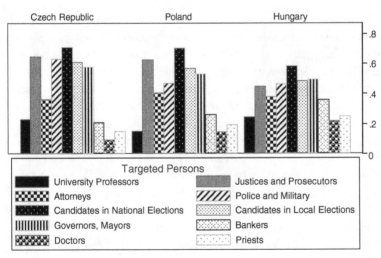

Figure 5.3. Demand for lustration according to TJS in December 2004.
Note: Bars show independent proportions of population who answered positively to the question, "In your opinion, should lustration cover the following persons?"

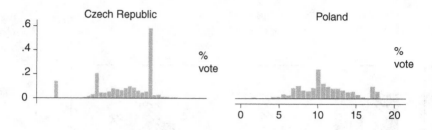

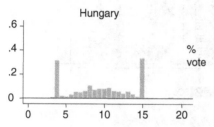

Figure 5.4. Histogram of pro-lustration voting by votes for parties ordered by parties' attitudes to lustration from ant-lustration (0) to pro-lustration (20). *Notes:* "Pro-lustration voting" is measured with questions about past voting behavior ("Which party did you vote for in the most recent parliamentary elections?").

"Pro-lustration voting" is measured with questions about past voting behavior ("Which party did you vote for in the most recent parliamentary elections?"). The responses were coded using measures from the Party Policy in Modern Democracies survey conducted by Benoit and Laver (2007) with experts in East Central European party politics. The PPMD questionnaire measured politicians' preferences over ways of dealing with the former nomenklatura on a 20-point thermometer scale. On that scale, 1 represented, "Former communist party officials should have the same rights and opportunities as other citizens to participate in public life," and 20 represented, "Former communist party officials should be kept out of public life as far as possible."[6] Thus, in Figure 5.4, the more skewed the histograms are to the right, the more voters are voting for supporters of lustration. The more skewed they are to the left, the more voters are voting for opponents of lustration.

[6] A party's position was measured as the average score over all expert opinions.

5.4. Factors Associated with Demand for Lustration

Let us here note an important fact related to the way our main independent variable is measured, however. Because pollsters in East Central Europe have been using the question for years and respondents are used to it, I used the question, "Do you agree with the claim that at this point in time lustration should be carried out?" In addition to asking respondents whether or not they support lustration, this question presupposes they know how the procedure is carried out. In this case, someone disagreeing strongly with the sentence may be a supporter of dealing with the past, but believe that it was not implemented adequately and therefore should not be performed. This is troublesome if one wants to measure attitudes toward screening politicians for their past. However, we are not interested in that exactly, but rather in how voters are willing to act politically as a result of their lustration attitudes. Nevertheless, to compensate for factors contributing to transitional justice demand that may be neglected by this question, I include in the model a selection of other variables related to transitional justice demand and their interactions with transitional justice demand. I describe them in the three subsections that follow.

5.4.1. Past Involvement in the Resistance Increases Demand for Transitional Justice

The legacy of authoritarianism is the first factor mentioned in the literature as generating demand for transitional justice. Scholars of normative transitional justice often interpret transitional justice as "victors' justice" and portray transitional justice procedures as motivated by revenge for past oppression (Rosenberg 1995; Schwartz 1995; Walicki 1997). James Gibson has tested a series of hypotheses relating "experiences of political repression" to reconciliation in South Africa (Gibson 2004). Even though his findings offer mixed support for the interpretation of transitional justice as "victors' justice," David Backer notes that this might be the result of a general tendency to overreport victimhood among citizens of postconflict societies in South Africa (Backer 2006). In reporting results from his own survey, Backer finds that victims' attitudes toward the truth and reconciliation process are systematically different from those of regular citizens. The general public is ambivalent about whether the Truth and Reconciliation Commission (TRC) played a significant role in the reconciliation process, but an overwhelming majority of victims see the TRC's role as vital. On the other hand, he finds little difference between victims' and the general public's attitudes toward "prohibiting former perpetrators from being employed by the state." Importantly, though, the transitional justice mechanism in South Africa was the TRC, not lustration. As transitional justice procedures, lustration and the TRC do share a similarity: Both are out-of-court procedures. Just as in South Africa, one could expect that in East Central Europe, victims of the ancien régime would have demands for transitional justice systematically different from the general public. Thus, persons with more ties to the former opposition would be more demanding of lustration and those with more ties to the ancien régime would be less demanding of it.

I operationalized this hypothesis by asking each respondent, first, how many people he or she knew who had worked in the former resistance, and second, how many persons he or she knew who had collaborated with the secret police. Directly asking, "Did you support or resist the former authoritarian regime?" was unlikely to generate sincere answers, because, in states where the autocrats were unpopular, such as Poland or Hungary, respondents were likely to misrepresent their pre-transition sympathies. This would yield responses biased toward participation in the opposition. This is a typical measurement error resulting from asking sensitive questions or questions about facts with respect to which respondents have strong feelings of obligation (Oppenheim 1992). For example, scholars of political behavior have noticed that American voters tend to overreport turnout, although they also have noted that this overreporting does not distort predictions of electoral outcomes on the basis of voting intentions (Cassel and Sigelman 2001). In the case of affiliations with the former autocrats, however, a bias toward overreporting ties to the opposition would decrease standard errors and could potentially exaggerate the significance of ties to the regime or ties to dissident movements. In Poland, Hungary, and the Czech Republic – as in South Africa – citizens tend to overreport victimhood, but we can separate actual victims from the rest by examining how they answer questions about their ties to a network of victims. In doing so, I draw on findings from the scholarship on informational networks (Huckfeldt and Sprague 1987). Assuming that persons with stronger ties to the former opposition or ancien régime know more persons from those respective camps, we can use the number of persons known as a proxy for the respective support or resistance to the regime.

5.4.2. *The More Citizens Feel Threatened by Communists, the Greater Their Demand for Transitional Justice Will Be*

One well-established relationship that scholars of political tolerance have identified is that "those who perceive their political enemies as threatening are more likely not to tolerate them" (Gibson 2004; Gibson and Gouws 2003, 227). James Gibson has measured political threat perceptions with twenty questions regarding the respondent's "least liked group." After conducting factor analysis, he distinguishes three main factors: "sociotropic threat," "group power," and "egocentric threat." The highest factor loading is associated with the following characteristic assigned to the least liked group: "they are dangerous to the normal lives of people" (Gibson 2004, 231). One of the ways Gibson measures political intolerance is by the degree of agreement with the claim, "Members of the disliked group should be prohibited from standing as candidates for elected positions," which is remarkably similar to my question regarding lustration. He finds that intolerance measured in this way is most closely related to sociotropic threat and that the "perceived power of the group has little, if anything, to do with the degree to which it is tolerated by South Africans" (Gibson 2004, 238). This finding challenges some widely held beliefs of scholars of democratic transition and consolidation, who have explained the lack of transitional justice in the immediate aftermath of transition to democracy by pointing to the popular fear of authoritarian backlash. They claim that uncertainty as to the possible reversal to an even harsher authoritarian system prevents leaders in new democracies from engaging in transitional justice (Diamond 1997; Huntington 1991; Linz and Stepan 1996). In this vein, Suzanne Choi and Roman David find in their study of political prisoners that individual empowerment – that is, reducing the inequalities between former perpetrators and victims – facilitates forgiveness. When victims feel constantly threatened by the power and prosperity of their perpetrators, they find it more difficult to forgive their wrongdoers (Choi and David 2006). Transitional justice in the form of lustration laws can effectively prevent former autocrats from reassuming positions of power.

Perceptions of authoritarian threat (in the case of my study, communist threat) were assessed with responses to the question, "How threatening to Poland's (Hungary's, or the Czech Republic's) way of life do you believe communists are?"[7] Respondents were offered options: "Extremely

---

[7] This question comes from James Gibson's Legal Values Survey (1998).

threatening" (5); "Somewhat threatening" (4); "Not particularly threatening" (2); and "Not at all threatening" (1). The reaction was only coded as "Hard to say" (3) only if the respondent refused to provide an answer. It is worth noting that this question had the strongest correlation with political tolerance in Gibson's South African surveys from 1996 and 2001.

But voters' demand for transitional justice may also be closely related to their conception of fairness. Suppose voters would prefer to see transitional justice done but doubt whether it is feasible to implement a reliable transitional justice procedure. This is another way in which my question about whether lustration should be carried out now may be seen as obscuring the true demand for transitional justice. An argument frequently raised in the literature on transitional justice is that unreliable evidence makes the use of lustration procedures unfair (Holmes 1994; Schwartz 1995). There are two sources of unreliability in the evidence. I will discuss them and their hypothesized effect on demand for transitional justice in the following subsection.

5.4.3. Sensitivity to Procedural Fairness Cuts Both Ways

The first problem of unreliability of the evidence arises because the files containing information about collaborators are incomplete. Over the course of transition, many files of the secret police were destroyed (Darton 1990; *Rzeczpospolita* 2001). Obviously, because secret police files contained evidence incriminating the secret police officers, these officers had incentives to destroy as many files as possible. Using incomplete files to carry out lustration raises the potential for both false acquittals as well as overlooking actual collaborators.

The second source of unreliability is that prior to the transition, false files – listing as informers persons who were innocent of collaboration with the secret police – had been created (Kavan 2002). There were two reasons why secret police officers had incentives to purposefully falsify evidence of collaboration.

First, the police officers were typically rewarded in proportion to the number of informers they recruited. Officers of the Polish secret police, for example, had to submit a report analyzing why a potential informer refused to collaborate if the officer was unable to recruit the candidate. This process was cumbersome and an officer who submitted too many such reports risked his chances for promotion. A long-time employee of the secret police archives admitted in a hearing with a special parliamentary committee that, prior to performance audits, the number of persons registered as new collaborators would rise (Committee 1992). Second, tricking a member of the anti-authoritarian opposition into signing a document of consent to collaboration was an excellent way to exercise blackmail. At some later point, the leading officer would threaten the oppositionist with releasing the signature to key people in the opposition movement unless he or she performed according to the officer's wishes.

Some of the political police units even maintained a special "department of misinformation," which was tasked with fabricating evidence of collaboration for popular members of the opposition. This evidence would be leaked to other opposition activists, who would infer that the person for whom evidence was falsified was a snitch. The idea was to disintegrate the trust-based social network of the underground opposition. If this fabricated evidence within the secret police archives is used in the transitional justice process, innocent people may be falsely convicted.

There is a trade-off between avoiding errors of false acquittal and false conviction. Harsh lustration laws, which require little evidence against a suspected collaborator before sanctions are issued, are likely to lead to fewer errors of false acquittal. But such laws are also more likely to result in false convictions because victims of fabricated evidence are more likely to be targeted (Nalepa 2008b). Thus, a priori, one would expect that the more sensitive a respondent is to false conviction errors, the less likely he or she is to demand transitional justice. In other words, sensitivity to errors of false conviction decreases transitional justice demand. On the other hand, mild lustration reduces risks of false conviction errors by requiring considerable evidence of collaboration before issuing sanctions. Conversely, such laws increase the chances of false acquittal. For some former collaborators, so much evidence could have been destroyed that what is left is insufficient to make them face responsibility. Thus, sensitivity to errors of false acquittal increases demand for transitional justice. To measure how sensitive respondents were to false conviction errors, I asked them to what extent each respondent agreed with the following statement: "The problem with lustration is that files of the former secret police are not reliable and using them may result in accusing innocent people." To measure sensitivity to false acquittal errors, I asked the degree to which respondents agreed with the following statement: "The problem with lustration is that files of the secret police were destroyed, so that many collaborators will not be uncovered

Table 5.2. *Summary statistics of the main variables.*

Variable	Czech Republic		Poland		Hungary	
	Mean	SE	Mean	SE	Mean	SE
TJ demand	3.328	1.209	3.586	1.265	3.005	1.486
False acquittal (FA)	3.900	.993	3.973	.899	3.596	1.205
False conviction (FC)	3.774	.969	3.777	.944	3.535	1.172
Pro-lustration voting	10.922	3.785	10.960	3.394	9.538	4.221
Communist threat	3.189	1.406	2.79	.366	2.481	1.220
Ties to opposition	1.306	.661	1.160	.545	1.083	.395
Ties to regime	1.455	.831	1.242	.731	1.122	.524
Settlement	1.859	.348	1.643	.479	1.643	.479
Age	40.258	13.239	43.044	16.412	48.209	17.650
Education	2.528	.787	2.486	.909	2.094	1.008
Sex	1.520	.500	1.509	.500	1.614	.487
Fascist threat	4.076	1.085	3.017	1.326	2.975	1.351

Note: Although these variables measure similar attitudes, the correlations between them are low. Apart from ties to opposition correlated with ties to regime at .632 and sensitivity to false acquittal correlated with sensitivity to false conviction at .57, all remaining bivariate correlations yield at most a correlation of .18.

anyway." Respondents were offered the possibility to "Agree Strongly" (5), "Agree," (4), "Disagree" (2), and "Disagree Strongly"(1). Again, if the respondent did not volunteer an answer, his or her reaction was coded as "Uncertain" (3). Table 5.2 provides summary statistics for all of the main variables.

5.5. The Statistical Model

In this section, I present an ordinary least squares (OLS) model with future lustration voting as the dependent variable and transitional justice demand, perceptions of communist threat, past experiences, and conceptions of fairness, as well as interactive terms as the independent variables of interest.[8] This model will allow us to test how much variance in pro-lustration voting is explained by transitional justice demand and factors hypothesized to affect demand for lustration that are not captured

---

[8] Interaction terms are composed of transitional justice demand and perceptions of communist threat, past experiences, and sensitivity to the two types of errors in the lustration process.

by my question. If the coefficients on anticommunist voting are significant, one cannot reject the theory that politicians are influenced by voters in their lustration policy choices, but if voters' transitional justice attitudes explain little variance in pro-lustration voting, this is still compatible with the fact that politicians do not *lose* their electorates by adopting lustration.

Results from running OLS regressions – with pro-lustration voting as the dependent variable and with interaction terms created out of transitional justice demand on the one hand, and ties to the opposition, threat perceptions, and sensitivity to false acquittal and false conviction on the other – are presented in Table 5.3.

For each country, I ran a model with and without interactive terms. I used the dichotomized version of the transitional justice demand (demand present = 1; demand absent = 0) for easier interpretation. The effects and standard errors for interaction terms have been calculated according to Brambor, Clark, and Golder (2007). The top two figures in each cell show the coefficient and standard error when transitional justice demand is present and the bottom two figures in the cell show the coefficient and standard error when transitional justice demand is absent.

The results show very weak support for any "voter demand → politics supply" theory, as the models with and without interactive terms have very little predictive power. The highest adjusted R-square is .0465. However, the factors explaining transitional justice demand significantly predict future pro-lustration voting behavior in intuitive ways. For instance, in Poland and the Czech Republic, communist threat perceptions reduce the propensity for pro-lustration voting in the absence of transitional justice demand. In Poland, in the presence of transitional justice demand, an increase in sensitivity to false acquittal increases future pro-lustration voting; in the absence of transitional justice demand, sensitivity to false acquittal also increases anticommunist voting, but this effect drops by almost 50 percent. In the Czech Republic, on the other hand, in the presence of transitional justice demand, sensitivity to false conviction decreases pro-lustration voting but increases pro-lustration voting when transitional justice demand is absent. All these effects are consistent with the Downsian model of transitional justice, but weak. The presence or absence of transitional justice demand does alter voters' propensity to elect anticommunists.

What about the independent effect of transitional justice demand? Although in Poland and Hungary transitional justice demand has an

Table 5.3. *OLS regression of pro-lustration voting on variables of interest with interactions.*

Variable		Czech Republic		Poland		Hungary	
Threat perceptions		**-.335** (.149)	**-.338** (.149)	**-.325** (.141)	**-.317** (.141)	-.070 .159	-.068 (.159)
Ties to opposition		-.153 (.308)	-.160 (.308)	-.049 (.357)	-.060 (.357)	-.199 .492	-.432 (.712)
TJ demand		.649 (.456)	1.96 (1.68)	**1.44** (.428)	-.314 (1.77)	**1.88** (.396)	1.40 (1.13)
FA sensitivity		-.101 (.242)	.124 (.369)	**.984** (.262)	**.693** (.387)	.151 .196	.155 (.196)
FC sensitivity		**.523** (.246)	**.526** (.245)	-.050 (.245)	-.050 (.245)	.177 .202	.176 (.202)
Sex		.003 (.396)	-.002 (.396)	.118 (.382)	.112 (.382)	.384 .396	.379 (.396)
Age		.032 (.015)	.032 (.015)	.006 (.012)	.006 (.012)	.019 (.011)	.019 (.011)
Education		.442 (.252)	.435 (.253)	**.884** (.219)	**.879** (.219)	.315 (.205)	.314 (.205)
Settlement		.456 (.560)	.437 (.561)	.182 (.406)	.201 (.407)	1.51 (.409)	1.51 (.410)
TJ demand interacted w/ threat	**Present**		-.269 (.175)		-.242 (.164)		-.030 (.197)
	absent		**-.502** (.276)		**-.561** (.278)		-.144 (.268)
TJ demand interacted w/ ties	**Present**		-.193 (.334)		.019 (.386)		.005 (.669)
	absent		.051 (.746)		-.446 (.922)		-.432 (.712)

TJ demand interacted w/ FA sens.	Present		-.214 (.279)		**1.15** .308		.323 (.227)
	absent		.124 (.369)		**.693** (.387)		-.169 (.292)
TJ demand interacted w/ FC sens.	Present		**-.495** (.278)		-.051 (.276)		.188 (.235)
	absent		**.754** (.399)		-.048 (.395)		.1556 (.301)
Constant	8.33 (1.72)		7.52 (2.04)	5.67 (1.51)	6.751921 (1.84)	6.46 (1.45)	6.54 (1.64)
Adj R-squared	.011		.011	.045	0.045	0.037	0.0363

Notes: A dichotomous version of the TJ demand variable has been used for easier interpretation of TJ demand as a modifying variable. This allows us to compare the coefficient on the independent variables of interest (IV) when TJ demand is present to when it is not present.

Standard errors for the interaction models and coefficients have been calculated (in stata) according to the following formula:

$$se(VI) = 221var(B_{VI}) + (TJ\ demand)^2 + 2(TJ\ demand)B_{INT}$$

$(\delta\ anticom/\ \delta\ VI) = B_{IV} + (TJ\ demand)B_{INT}$,

where B_{IV} is the coefficient on the independent variable of interest (threat perceptions, ties to the opposition, FA, or FC sensitivity), and B_{INT} is the coefficient on the interaction term between TJ demand and the independent variable of interest. Note that the second part of the expression drops out when TJ demand is not present.

For each country, the left column presents results from a model where the interaction is not included and the column on the right shows the model with the interaction term.

independent effect on anticommunist voting in the models without interaction terms, one cannot interpret the effect of transitional justice demand in the models with interactions just by looking at the OLS regressions output (Brambor, Clark, and Golder 2007). Since none of the independent variables of interest (ties to the opposition, threat perceptions, or sensitivity to fairness) are dichotomous, one cannot tell what happens to the effect of transitional justice demand once interaction terms are included without mapping out the marginal effect for different values of the independent variables of interest. I chose to focus on the modifying effect of sensitivity to false acquittal and false conviction, which in a maximum likelihood model showed considerable predictive power in the explaining transitional justice demand (Nalepa 2008a).

Transitional justice demand also has little effect on pro-transitional justice voting in the interactive models. In the Czech Republic, one observes a positive and significant effect of transitional justice demand on pro-lustration voting, but this effect decreases with sensitivity to false acquittal and with threat perception. In Hungary, while one still observes a positive effect of transitional justice demand on pro-lustration voting, this effect increases with higher threat perceptions of communists. Figure 5.5 presents the graphs leading to this interpretation.

The histograms in the background show the distribution of sensitivity to false acquittal (the top panel) and threat perceptions (the bottom and middle panel). Although transitional justice demand is a discrete variable, I imputed missing data, not constraining the values to fall into discrete categories 1, 2, 3, 4, and 5. This is justified because transitional justice demand functions here as an independent variable. The circled, inside line represents the change in the linear effect, while the diamond, outside lines represent the confidence intervals. The three panels capture all instances where the confidence intervals do not contain zero.

It is surprising that the slopes of the marginal effects against threat perceptions have opposite signs in Hungary and the Czech Republic. The intriguing influence of threat perceptions and transitional justice demand directly and indirectly on pro-lustration voting is puzzling in light of the history of communism in the region. Since the end of World War II, the communist party has been stronger in Czechoslovakia than in Poland or Hungary. It won a plurality in the first free and fair elections in the aftermath of World War II. Anna Grzymała-Busse (2002) notes that the Czech communist party is one of the few such parties in Eastern Europe

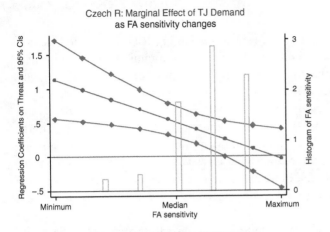

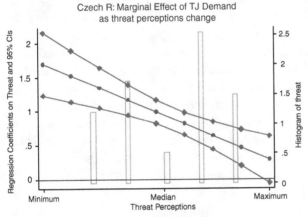

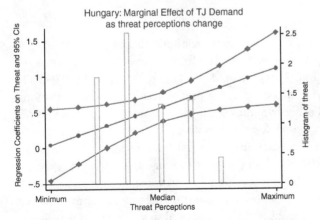

Figure 5.5. Changes in effects of transitional justice demand on pro-lustration voting, by fairness sensitivity.
Note: These graphs have been created by adapting the Stata code from Braumoeller (2004).

that still has not undergone reform readapting itself to the new democratic conditions. In contrast, Hungarian communists swiftly reformed their party organizations to a point where they could successfully compete in democratic elections. In the process, they completely disengaged themselves from communist ideology. It is thus surprising that Hungarians who feel threatened by communists would have transitional justice demand lead them to elect anticommunists, while Czechs who feel threatened would be less likely to elect anticommunists. Another puzzling result is that the more sensitive to false acquittals Czechs are, the smaller effect transitional justice demand has on casting pro-lustration votes.

These effects, although puzzling, are hardly significant. The most important conclusion from the preceding analysis is that demand for transitional justice is a poor predictor of voting behavior.

These results have important consequences for designing transitional justice regimes. Clearly, transitional justice involves more than settling accounts with the past. Voting behavior is the result of much richer processes than just voters' preferences regarding transitional justice. Although the passage of lustration laws does not cost parties with a pro-lustration agenda votes, transitional justice is not an issue over which electoral battles are fought. It would be unwise to attribute the timing or type of a country's transitional justice policies to the preferences of its general public.

5.6. Conclusions

This chapter investigated whether transitional justice policy making is driven by voters' preferences. I use data from a survey that I designed and conducted in Poland, Hungary, and the Czech Republic in 2004. The survey questionnaire measures voter preferences regarding transitional justice, along with other hypothesized determinants of transitional justice. very weak support I find for the hypothesis that voter demand was an important factor in shaping transitional justice. This forces us to look for other ways to explain the timing of lustration laws. In the next chapter, I proceed to explore the supply side of transitional justice – that is, the incentives and behavior of elites. I look at the emergence of anticommunist elites who had no skeletons in their closets and show how their appearance on the political scene can explain the "shock of transitional justice." If transitional justice is used strategically and is of a greater concern for political elites than it is for the general public, one would expect voters to take cues from politicians in deciding upon their preferred transitional justice policies. Thus, a "strategic elites" supply theory of transitional justice is consistent with the weak results presented here.

6

Strategic Elites

TRANSITIONAL JUSTICE SUPPLY

Chapter 5 showed that, empirically, a demand-based explanation for the variation in lustration regimes is not sustainable. Therefore, in this chapter, I turn to the "supply side" of transitional justice policies. This involves analyzing the preferences of relevant political decision makers and the institutional constraints that they faced in adopting lustration policies. Incidentally, this research strategy is similar to the approach taken in the literature on religious markets cited in Chapter 3. R. Finke and L. R. Iannaccone (1993) and others provide empirical evidence that religious awakenings are rarely a manifestation of bottom-up demand for spiritual guidance; instead, these religious awakenings are supply side–driven, as they are created by strategic spiritual leaders. Shifts in the supply side of religious production can be the effect of, for instance, deregulating religious markets. Similarly, lustration laws are not, I argue, a response to popular demand for holding former members of the ancien régime accountable for human rights violations. They are instead supplied by political elites who stood to gain from having lustration laws in place.

Consider once again Table 1.1 and Figure 1.1, showing the timing of lustration in East Central European countries. In the previous four chapters, I focused on explaining the long delay in passing lustration laws. In the chapters to follow, I explain what was responsible for the initially mild but increasingly harsh forms of lustration that came to be adopted.

Contrary to predictions from the normative literature on transitional justice (Huntington 1991; Nino 1996), lustration laws were not implemented shortly after the transition, when public support for them was greatest, but much later, in the late 1990s, when support for them was already dwindling.

I argued earlier that lustration laws can have far-reaching political consequences – which depend on who makes them, when they are implemented, and to whom they extend. Lustration can terminate the careers of certain politicians while enabling other politicians to pursue their careers without obstacles. I also showed that lustration laws have distributive effects: Depending on the distribution of infiltration across political parties, lustration affects parties unequally. Heavily infiltrated parties suffer losses while mildly infiltrated parties gain from transitional justice. When the specific level of infiltration is unknown to parties that would potentially gain from lustration, though, the process of revealing collaborators can be significantly delayed. It is possible, for example, that in the first years following the transition to democracy, parties that could potentially benefit from lustration were too concerned about "skeletons in their closets" to go about implementing lustration. I showed how reformed communist parties can use the opposition's uncertainty about how many skeletons it has hiding in its closet as insurance against transitional justice, at least in the first few years following the transition to democracy.

But the communists could not hold the former opposition hostage to the threat of skeletons in the closet indefinitely. Eventually, new parties untainted by secret police collaboration became competitive in democratic elections. They threatened to replace the former communist as well as the former dissident parties. Such newcomers to the political scene knew they were not infiltrated and had much to gain from implementing transitional justice that would reveal collaborators among former opposition parties as well as among former communists. This, of course, would clear the way for the newcomers' electoral victory. Such new parties would not be bound by roundtable promises. Additionally, if their party organizations did not originate in dissident organizations prior to the transition, they would not be afraid of having skeletons uncovered in their closets. They hardly had any skeletons. There are a number of ways in which a party can be counted as "new." One way is for the party to have young members. Another is for the party to have emerged from a dissident group that had been so firm in its anticommunist conviction prior to the transition that it carefully screened members, taking into account the likelihood that the secret police would attempt to recruit such candidates as informers. Dissidents groups that kept a low profile under communism made it difficult for the secret police to subject them to recruitment interrogations and pressures. As a result, in the transition aftermath, such groups were less infiltrated with the secret police agents. Finally, a party can be as good as new even if it uses an old label or is led by seasoned politicians but has departed from its original membership and policies by constantly reshuffling its membership to get rid of potential collaborators. In summary, parties have relatively few skeletons if their members are young, if their leaders were careful prior to the transition to avoid associations with those who may have been recruited as collaborators, or if they have been diligently eliminating such members from their ranks after the transition.

This chapter is organized as follows. First, I present two parties – Law and Justice (PiS) in Poland and FiDeSZ in Hungary – as model examples of pro-lustration parties. Following that, using manifesto data, Party Policy in Modern Democracies (PPMD) data, as well as data on individual legislators, I argue that parties advocating lustration were younger (in membership) and more recently established or reorganized than parties originating in the former liberal opposition and communist parties. Such parties, unburdened with links to the former secret police, were able to pursue lustration without risking having their own members exposed. I use manifesto data to show that older parties, over time, removed the anti-lustration rhetoric from their programs. Although as I mentioned in the previous chapter very few parties were willing to include pro-lustration rhetoric in their manifestos, demonstrating the trend of removing reconciliatory statements from manifestos still supports the thesis presented here.

The chapter concludes with a consideration of alternative explanations for delayed lustrations. Specifically, I discuss the possible influence of European Union (EU) accession and of binding promises made at round-table negotiations. It is in particular the evidence rendering this last alternative explanation implausible – the fact that lustration laws are adopted by former communists – that motivates the next chapter of the book, where the Transitional Justice Bill game is discussed.

6.1. The Origins of Pro-lustration Parties

I begin this section by explaining how political parties develop a pro-lustration agenda. Two parties are used to illustrate this phenomenon: PiS and FiDeSz. First, PiS exemplifies a party originating in closed and diffi-cult-to-penetrate dissident groups that are less infiltrated. This kind of party would benefit from lustration more than parties originating from open dissident groups. PiS is also an example of a party whose leaders came from other party organizations but which sheds members with skeletons in their closet when they switch parties. Thus, PiS presents an opportunity to present a model of a pro-lustration party that is made up of conspiring dissidents in a closed setting and contrast this model with an openly organized opposition that was easier to infiltrate.

I also discuss the Hungarian party of Young Democrats, FiDeSz. FiDeSz was established in 1988. But the party underwent a major metamorphosis in the twenty years following the preparatory talks for the roundtable. FiDeSz, which had originated as the SzDSz youth organization, completely changed its ideology, despite its pre-transition roots, from liberal and cosmopolitan to populist and nationalistic. By inducing those who disagreed with its leader, Viktor Orban, to leave the party, it managed to move across the ideological spectrum without resorting to splits and mergers, as the Kaczyński brothers (described in the introduction and the following section) had done. While undergoing these transformations, FiDeSz was shedding members who could be implicated by lustration without resorting to changing its party label entirely.[1] FiDeSz illustrates how parties that undergo extensive ideological changes are also able to purge their ranks of members vulnerable to lustration.

6.1.1. PiS

In Chapter 1, I presented a vignette about the Kaczyński brothers. I described how over the years following transition in Poland, they systematically collected information about the groups that had been infiltrated with secret police agents. The Kaczyński brothers distanced themselves from dissidents who had become stigmatized as former collaborators. They participated in a total of four political parties created as a result of split-offs from existing parties and mergers with other parties on the right side of the political scene. Although these splits and mergers cannot be viewed as direct responses to lustration (such activity was more likely to have been motivated by changes in the electoral laws), the Kaczyńskis could use them as opportunities to purge their party's ranks of suspected collaborators. This is consistent with the pattern of developing pro-lustration parties described in this section. Leaders who had not been

---

[1] As I describe in section 7.1.2, FiDeSz did change its name to Fidesz-MPP, but this change of label was merely a pretext to remove from its statute the age limitation of thirty-five that it had as SzDSz's youth organization.

collaborators themselves created new parties that were really just re-labeled old parties. They used this as an opportunity for getting rid of older members who had been or could be implicated by lustration. Those suspected of collaboration were replaced with younger members, who because of their young age were beyond suspicion of hiding skeletons in their closets. These young new members were eager to see former collaborators banned from office. Wiktor Osiatynski, for instance, notes the recruitment strategy of the Kaczyńskis in a *New York Times* editorial: "When the twins [Jarosław and Lech Kaczyńscy, Polish President and Prime Minister] decided to create the Law and Justice party, they turned to young people on the far right" (Osiatynski 2007). He, like many other western journalists, attributes this eagerness for lustration to a vindictive emotion to settle scores with the past. "Now, driven by resentment against an entire generation of older politicians, the Kaczyńskis are happy to see them purged from offices and replaced by their own [PiS] loyalists" (Osiatynski 2007). But it is unclear why young members of such parties as PiS would seek revenge for persecutions that never directly affected the young members. On the other hand, such young party members could safely engage in lustration, knowing that because of their age, they had no skeletons to fear. They could be certain that lustration would hurt only their electoral competition, helping to pave their own way to electoral victory.

6.1.2. FiDeSz

Scholars of post-communist party systems describe Hungary's as one of the most stable and most institutionalized party systems in East Central Europe. At the same time, they have noted the tendency of established political actors to change their policy positions frequently, even on the most important issues (Kitschelt 1999). A case in point is FiDeSz, the Alliance of Young Democrats. What preceded its rise to a prominent position in the Hungarian party system was a gradual but pronounced shift toward the political right. This shift was accompanied by arguing for lustration and dealing with the past.

FiDeSz originated as the youth organization of SzDSz, the Alliance of Free Democrats. The acronym for Young Democrats, FiDeSz, was adopted to match SzDSz's party label. Both parties jointly attended the roundtable negotiations, refused to sign the final version of the accords, and, in November 1989, organized the referendum over the presidency.

This was a brilliant strategic move that effectively saved Hungary from a communist president. In 1994, the split between SzDSz and FiDeSz seemed to be the result of a rather inconsequential coordination failure. However, after the elections, FiDeSz moved ideologically to the right, changing its language and its image. By 1998, it changed the spelling of its party name from the capitalized FiDeSz to Fidesz-MPP, derived from Latin *fidelity*, with MPP denoting civic movement instead of a party. This presented an opportunity to rewrite its mission statement and remove the age cap of thirty-five for members of a youth organization. At the same time, nationalistic and conservative values replaced the earlier liberal and democratic ones. One of my elite respondents remarked on how premeditated this change was:

FiDeSz had been a fringe youth organization kept in the shadow of SzDSz. It was marginalized because it had a radically liberal program. In the mid-1990s, after a few of the most liberal members left, it became more popular. That is when it discovered the potential for vote gain among the more conservatively oriented electorate. But to make full use of it, they had to make the ideological leap (interviews 2004: HN8).

Surveying lustration in Hungary, Elizabeth Barrett, Peter Hack, and Agnes Munkácsy write that FiDeSz had moved to the right in the years before the 1998 election and continued to do so during its term in office. They acknowledge that the deepening rift between FiDeSz and SzDSz – the two parties that had emerged from the same dissident group – was a surprising turn of events with very significant consequences for the ultimate lustration policy that Hungary adopted (Barrett, Hack, and Munkàcsy 2007).

The resulting policy difference between SzDSz and FiDeSz is documented by data on party policy positions. According to the Party Policy in Modern Democracies survey, the gap in attitudes toward the former communists between FiDeSz and SzDSz reached nearly seven points (Benoit and Laver 2007).[2] Yet, even more divisive than attitudes toward former communists were three other issues: foreign land ownership (11.74), nationalism (11.36), and social welfare (12.82). In Figure 6.1, the bars represent the scores of SzDSz subtracted from the scores of FiDeSz

---

[2] As described in the previous chapter, these attitudes were measured on a twenty-point scale, with, "Former communist party officials should have the same rights and opportunities as other citizens to participate in public life," as 1 to, "Former communist party officials should be kept out of public life as far as possible," as 20.

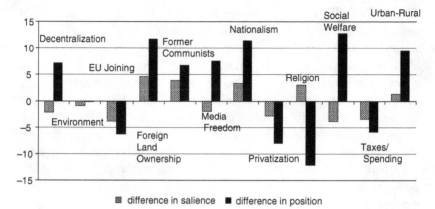

difference in salience ■ difference in position

Figure 6.1. Difference between FiDeSz and SzDSz in policy positions on twelve political issues (in percentages).
Note: Columns indicate differences between the positions and importance of twelve issues according to experts polled in the Party Policy in Modern Democracies (Benoit and Laver 2007). The questions operationalizing issues spanning from "Decentralization" to "Urban–Rural" are listed at http://www.tcd.ie/Political_Science/ppmd/ and were measured on a twenty-point scale.

on twelve issues. Light bars represent the differences in salience, while dark bars represent the difference in the parties' positions.

The narrative that follows uses quotes from current and former members of FiDeSz and SzDSz as well as independent observers to describe the transformation of FiDeSz.

HA2 was, along with Viktor Orban, one of the founders of FiDeSz. In 1993, he and two other FiDeSz members resigned their parliamentary seats. At that point, political analysts expected FiDeSz to win the 1994 elections but, according to HA2, its popularity suffered dramatically after his resignation. He attributed FiDeSz's decision to abandon its liberal position to "Orban's discovery of the winning potential in conservative values. By 1994, the conservative side of the political scene had been abandoned by MDF, which, compromised by its participation in the government coalition, did not have a chance of winning the elections. So FiDeSz tried to be the new conservative party. Contrary to MDF, it had not collaborated in any way with the ancien régime prior to the transition (its members were too young), so it could safely include demands for exposing links of politicians to the former secret political police in its political program (interviews 2004: HA2).

HA3, also a former member, described FiDeSz as one of the most popular parties in 1994 polls, showing 50 percent of popular support:

When, despite this popularity, they lost, they decided to embrace Christian and traditional values because they noticed that on the right side of the political scene, there were no credible political parties. But the decision was entirely motivated by discovering an electorate that they could capture. As dissidents, they would have never behaved like that (interviews 2004: HA3).

HA5 left FiDeSz in 1994, shortly after the elections, but believed that FiDeSz's ideological metamorphosis began in 1992. He claimed that FiDeSz, even in 2000, still used liberalism in its rhetoric but in the 1998 electoral campaign still could ensure right-wing voters that they were far from becoming a populist movement. However, the most radical part of FiDeSz – the "civic circles" – were spontaneous movements of right-wing extremists. As they started to gain popularity, the charismatic FiDeSz leader, Victor Orban, stopped using the word "party" to describe FiDeSz and began using the term "civic movement" more and more frequently. Also, the internal organization of the party changed, from being fairly democratic to being almost completely dominated by Orban. HA5 claimed that Orban had complete control over the candidate nomination process for elections and that he had been choosing people from right-wing movements to lead the lists. The rhetoric gradually changed from liberal and cosmopolitan to conservative – and, at times, even anti-Semitic. HA5 claimed that Orban deeply hated western style liberalism and came to power using an anti–EU agenda of national interests (interviews 2004: HA5).

HL2 was one of the leaders of the youth organization of the MDF, the conservative party of the early 1990s, which got pushed aside as a result of FiDeSz's rise to power. Similarly to HA5, he marks the beginning of FiDeSz's shift as 1992, when it saw a vast constituent to be captured by a more "sovereign-oriented" program, combined with deregulatory policies and swift economic reforms at the same time. According to HL2, prior to FiDeSz's shift to anticommunism, Hungarians didn't care about the past, but FiDeSz was responsible for polarizing the society in this way by arguing that you have to decide "whether you want to be for the agents or against them." This view is consistent with the supply-side hypothesis of voters' transitional justice demand presented in the previous chapter.

HL2 also divided FiDeSz's move away from SzDSz into two stages. The first was in 1992, when it moved in the religious authoritarian direction, after which SzDSz accepted MSzP's offer to become its coalition partner in 1994. The second took place in 1998, after FiDeSz won the elections and became the senior party in the cabinet coalition. It then replaced earlier free-market and deregulation positions with populist demands of social welfare and security. HL2's comment on FiDeSz's pro-lustration position was, "It could do so fairly safely: As a youth organization of a former dissident movement, its members were too young to be recruited as secret police collaborators" (interviews 2004: HL2).

6.2. Lustration Policies and Parties' Origins in Dissident Movements

The Kaczyński vignette in Chapter 1 illustrates another reason why parties may be supportive of lustration. The secret police found certain dissident groups that preceded party organizations created after democratic transition to be easier to infiltrate than others. Consider the following comment, from a post-communist elite respondent, about the uncertainty of communist representatives as to the type of opposition they were facing:

During the roundtable negotiations, we were constantly uncertain about street demonstrations and about strike activity. We had the impression that Solidarity could not control the situation. Why did we deliberate with them anyway? Because, at least, we had access to information about them. Since we were relying on secret police reports, the only opposition that existed for us were those people who were featured in secret police reports. And that was the KOR [Laborers' Defense Committee] and people like Geremek, Michnik, and Kuroń. We also believed that this was the extreme part of the opposition. Why was the secret police providing such information on people from the KOR? Probably because to them they seemed tough and resistant to their interrogation techniques. Secret police officers would put a lot of effort into breaking them, but with very meager results. So the secret police considered them to be the true enemy and gave them a reputation of the devil himself. The PZPR leadership was convinced that it was talking with representatives of the most radical opposition. Accusations that the roundtable amounted to negotiations in which the secret police spoke with their own agents make no sense. The table had to be legitimate (interviews 2004: PC1).

In his last comment, the respondent distanced himself from a popular, albeit radical, interpretation of the roundtable negotiations – namely, that the secret police negotiated the transition with its own agents. Although I argue in this book that the opposition negotiating the transition with the communists was more infiltrated with secret police agents than the opposition that did not participate in negotiations, this is far from saying that the secret police acted as negotiator. The claim of PC1 that the talks had to be legitimate is consistent with the theory that the negotiations were meaningful. A deal struck between agents of the secret police and their leading officers would not be binding; nor could it be respected by the society at large. PC1 continued to say that "they [the communists] lacked the imagination that later the opposition that comes to power would want to hold them [former communists accountable]." He believed he was talking to *the* anticommunist opposition – in other words, to the only politicians who in the foreseeable future could become significant representatives. That is why he regarded their promises as made on behalf of a 10 million member–strong trade union.

But the huge organization that Solidarity had grown to was far from unified. Especially after it went underground, following its de-legalization on December 13, 1981, there were many competing ideas for organizing anticommunist resistance. Roughly, the different strategies fall into two main categories: that of an open opposition and of a clandestine conspiracy.

6.2.1. Open Opposition

This idea first originated in the group of oppositionists who in 1976 formed the Laborers' Defense Committee (KOR). The goal of the KOR was to provide aid to laborers who were being repressed for participating in strikes in response to drastic price increases that took effect in June of that year. It was the first non-underground opposition group in communist Poland. The founding declaration was signed by fourteen members. Although KOR had members with very different political outlooks (from Christian Democrats and conservatives to social democrats and even socialists), it began its activity by issuing an open letter to the communist authorities signed by its founding members, who disclosed not only their true names but also their addresses and telephone numbers. Only four lawyers who had been successful in defending oppositionists in political trials preserved their anonymity as founding members; otherwise, the communist authorities would have attempted to withdraw the lawyers' licenses, a move that eventually would have hurt the opposition. Within a few weeks, KOR began to publish its samizdat bulletin. It was one of the first underground publications in the Soviet bloc. Over time, the number of KOR activists grew.

In 1977, the communists started cracking down on the movement. The counteroffensive culminated in the murder of a Krakow student, Stanislaw Pyjas. His death shook the entire opposition movement, which organized Catholic masses and black processions and distributed fliers describing the circumstances of Pyjas's death. One of the protests led to the organization of a Student Committee of Solidarity (SKS), with the aim of creating an authentic and independent representation of students. SKS demanded that the communists provide a complete account of the circumstances of Pyjas's death. As a result of the events in Krakow, KOR members Jacek Kuron, Adam Michnik, and Antoni Macierewicz were arrested along with forty-seven people. On May 20, 1977, most of those arrested were released, save for nine of the most prominent activists. To accelerate their release, the remaining KOR members staged hunger strikes, which again boosted participation in the movement.

The main aim of the KOR, SKS, and oppositionists grouped around them was to expand the anticommunist resistance. The ease with which Solidarity acquired nearly 10 million members, after signing the agreements with representatives of the communist government in August 1980, can be attributed to the openness of KOR and the network of associations around it. Since these civic groups had been semi-open to begin with, when Solidarity became legalized, it needed very little time to acquire a large membership. However, being easy to join, it was also very easy to infiltrate.

One of the respondents in my series of elite interviews in Poland was a professor at a university department involved in the anticommunist resistance. He claimed that the Polish secret police aimed to have ten thousand collaborators infiltrate the resistance groups each year. The civil society that grew around Solidarity was an easy target.

According to my interviewee cited in Chapter 4, in 1981 the communist government's press secretary, Jerzy Urban, proposed the following idea: Since Solidarity by 1981 had become a force increasingly difficult to control, he suggested the implementation of martial law as a coverup leading to a series of arrests of thousands of Solidarity leaders. According to this scenario, the goal of the arrests would be to screen midlevel leadership in Solidarity for persons constituting "weak links" who could be cowed into collaboration. All of the interned leaders would be offered the possibility to collaborate. The offer would be backed with some mild threats, but mostly convincing arguments. Those who declined would be released and no further repercussions would follow. After all, if a person was unwilling to cooperate, to punish him would be just a waste of resources. The goal of the secret police officer would be to present the oppositionist with a different decision problem than the one that he was in fact facing. The dissident was supposed to think that *refusal* would bring upon him undesirable harassment, whereas *agreement* would end all harassment for the mild price of disclosing some seemingly irrelevant information about the underground opposition. In reality – and this is the information that was available to the secret police officer, but not the dissident – refusal ended the game with a payoff of unconditional release. However, agreement was just the beginning of an everlasting process of harassment for more information, as the dissident would be constantly threatened that refusing to cooperate would lead to the disclosure of his or her identity to fellow dissidents.[3]

Urban's scenario was implemented with martial law coming into force on the night of December 12, 1981. The special secret police operations that outlined the strategy for recruiting collaborators were described earlier in section 4.4.2.1 and are backed by archival evidence cited in the bibliography of archival sources. For instance, the plan outlined by Z. Bielecki (1981) included conversations with "persons whose anti-socialist activity had started to subside" or "had not been elected to the leadership circle of Solidarity even though they had exhibited dissident activity in the past," that is, when Solidarity was legal. The plan anticipated that some of those interviewed would sign a "declaration of loyalty [to the communist authorities]" (lojalka). After eighteen months of functioning as a legal trade union, Solidarity was banned. Fifteen thousand of its members were arrested while others went underground.[4] Nevertheless, thanks to two secret police operations – Jodla (internment) and Klon (media takeover) – 1,597 persons were recruited as collaborators (MSN 1982).[5]

Solidarity was easy to infiltrate because its members wanted to create an underground civil society, the larger the better. It was to be a loose, semi-open network of organizations presented as an alternative to the communist party. Many of its leaders believed that increasing the circulation of underground publications was more important than intensely screening potential members for connections to the enforcement apparatus. The benefits of outreach outweighed the cost of increased infiltration. It seemed to be a more efficient way of bringing about the fall of communism. Most of the participants of the roundtable negotiations had KOR backgrounds. It was reasonable for them to negotiate with the communists

---

[3] This deception mechanism can be represented with a formal model equivalent to the "generic screening test with an uninformed rookie" analyzed in Kaminski (2004, 44–5).

[4] The extent of repercussion was presented in Table 1.3.

[5] See also Milewski (1980), MON (1982), Taka Sluzba (1993), Okraj (1981), and Bielecki 1981.

because even partial liberalization was better than prolonging the authoritarian regime – again, even if that meant a small degree of infiltration by the secret police (Dudek 2004).

As a consequence, in the aftermath of transition, politicians associated with dissident groups surrounding the KOR were more likely to be former collaborators of the secret police and thus targets of lustration than were politicians from dissident groups that conspired more intensively and advocated the second idea of organizing resistance, the clandestine conspiracy.

6.2.2. Clandestine Conspiracy

An underground civil society was compatible to some extent with an oppressive communist state. But a full-blown, open challenge to the communist regime was not. This meant that the open existence of other opposition groups – such as Solidarity '80 (S'80), Fighting Solidarity (SW), and most importantly, the Confederacy for Independent Poland (KPN) – posed risks that were to sever the communists' unchecked retention of power. The names of these organizations succinctly describe their strategies of noncooperation.

First, KPN ignored the communist regime's ban on registering political parties, and in September 1979 established itself as a political party essentially by sheer declaration. Its leaders likely spent as much time in prison as outside of it. In 1989, KPN distanced itself from the roundtable negotiations. Following the announcement of the June 1989 elections with 35 percent seats open to noncommunist candidates, KPN leaders tried to field candidates, creating a joint list with Solidarity. Lech Wałęsa's cell for managing Solidarity candidate lists, the Civic Parliamentary Committee (OKP), offered KPN too few seats. In the end, KPN ran its own candidates, none of whom was elected (Dudek 2004).

Among the factors explaining KPN's low electoral support was its complete lack of recognition among voters. This was partly because KPN's leaders spent most of their pre-transition lives in prison. KPN's obscurity, however, was magnified by its complete absence from the communist media, even as a negative point of reference. While communist media frequently bashed the KOR, routinely referring to it as a counterrevolutionary terrorist organization, the KPN was hardly ever mentioned. At the height of the communist regime's unpopularity, being criticized by the communist media was actually a good thing. Hence, at the beginning of the transition, the KPN immediately found itself at a disadvantage.

After the elections, KPN started a campaign to make the sixty thousand Soviet troops stationed in Poland leave the country. To a certain extent, this was a strategy to gain more popularity. KPN maintained its popularity long enough to win a 10 percent representation in the 1991 parliament. But in 1991, after the Macierewicz list identified KPN leader Leszek Moczulski as an agent, KPN's popularity dipped again and remained too low for it to get into parliament again in 1993.[6] Moczulski spent the next couple of years clearing his name in the courts. In 1997, KPN became a member of Electoral Action Solidarity (AWS), and after its victory in the September 1997 elections, KPN joined the ruling coalition. It then also became one of lustration's most vocal supporters.

Solidarity '80 (S'80), a group of Solidarity members who wanted to stay loyal to the original idea that brought Solidarity to life in the Gdansk Shipyard in 1980, and Fighting Solidarity (SW) were created after martial law was implemented. SW's leader, Kornel Morawiecki, was not nearly as wed to the idea of nonviolence as was Lech Wałęsa. Morawiecki believed that programmatic nonviolence signaled weak bargaining power. Both split-off organizations were skeptical about roundtable talks, did not even run in the semi-free elections, and severely criticized the joint government of Solidarity, PZPR, and communists' satellite parties led by Tadeusz Mazowiecki (Dudek 2004).[7]

It was difficult to become a member of groups like KPN, S'80, or SW. The screening process for potential secret police agents was extensive and did not presume that potential candidates were innocent. The smallest doubt about the candidate's background was regarded as a reason to terminate his or her candidacy. This manner of ending all ties with a dissident under even the slight suspicion is illustrated well in Krzysztof Kieslowski's 1981 movie *Blind Chance*. As a result, clandestine conspiracies had little reason to fear infiltration.

My respondent, PA12, did not associate himself either with the KOR or with its competitors. On the one hand, he opposed the idea of clandestine

---

[6] The lustration resolution that led to the circulation of the Macierewicz list was described in the introduction to this book.

[7] The strategy of "letting bygones be bygones" adopted by the Mazowiecki government was described in Chapter 4.

conspiracies because he feared they would lead to the disintegration of the opposition by disconnecting particular dissident cells from one another. On the other hand, he worried that the establishment of any centralized structure would expose its members to easier infiltration. If the secret police was expected to recruit ten thousand collaborators each year, it would obviously focus on the cells that were easier to penetrate.

An important caveat that should be noted here is that the two modes of organizing opposition activity described in this chapter should be treated as "ideal types." Every dissident organization had both an "above-the-ground" and an "underground" part. However, in the case of organizations exhibiting the "open opposition" approach, most of the operations were above the ground. A majority of its members did not conspire, and some were even publicly known – artists, writers, and figures of authority. At the same time, there was a small leadership group that remained below the surface. This was, for instance, the case with Solidarity's Temporary Coordination Committee (Tymczasowa Komisja Koordynacyjna, or TKK). On the opposite end of the spectrum were, for instance, underground publishing houses that kept complete secrecy to maintain efficient production and avoid harassment from the secret police. Publishing houses were so secretive that workers of the same firm did not know each other's names. Of course, there were exceptions. The publishing house Nova, for instance, received financial support from western governments and pro-democratic NGOs and consequently needed to maintain a public image.[8]

The way in which the two modes of organizing dissident movements correspond to the distributive effects of lustration is rather intuitive. Groups that practiced strict screening procedures and were very careful about associating with potential agents had fewer collaborators among their ranks. This meant having fewer participants to help distribute dissident ideology widely. But they also had less to fear from lustration and more to gain from it. To extend the distributive effects of lustration to post-transition parties' attitudes to lustration does require an inferential leap, albeit a small one. But if parties are seat maximizers and politicians are office seekers, one should expect parties originating in clandestine conspiracies to favor lustration more than parties founded on open opposition. Most parties that originated in dissident movements compete for roughly the same electorate. When lustration procedures expose dissident collaborators among parties

---

[8] Marek Kaminski, personal communication.

originating in the open opposition, postdissident electorates may transfer their support to parties originating in the dissident movements based on clandestine conspiracies. Dissident groups that were either actually or seemingly small (as no conspirator knew more than a few co-conspirators by their last names) were notorious for placing unwieldy demands on their members. This is documented in samizdat manuals for dissidents, such *The Little Conspirator*, which instructed dissidents on how to resist the secret police and how to refuse to collaborate even under the threat of imprisonment or physical pain (Anonymous; after 1981). Only those dissidents most committed to overthrowing communism would opt into these small cells of the opposition movement. Thus, in the aftermath of the transition, parties originating from these small dissident groups could be confident that they had fewer collaborators than parties that grew out of large opposition organizations where the barriers to entry were low and the demands placed on participants were considerably more manageable.

Evidence from elite interviews corroborates this analysis. Asked which groups are the biggest losers under lustration, Polish elite respondents characterized it this way: Post-communist voters knew about the collaboration of communists from the PZPR and were not discouraged by the revelation of collaborators among PZPR's ranks. But Solidarity's electorate was very sensitive to collaboration with the secret police. Candidates who showed up on the ballot as former collaborators would be ostracized (interviews 2004: PA2, PC2, PL2, PL3, PL4, PA4, PN3, PL7, PL11, PC4, PA14, PA15, PC6).[9]

Some elite respondents went so far as to say that SLD's electorate assigned positive values to former collaboration (interviews 2004: PA8). Others offered examples of post-communist politicians, such as Jerzy Szeliga, who collaborated with the intelligence department while working as an intern in East Germany. Szeliga claimed in his lustration declaration that he collaborated in order to prevent Poles from being recruited by the Stasi (the East German secret police). My respondent insisted that despite filing a positive declaration, Szeliga easily won the election as a candidate of SLD (interviews 2004: PC2, PA15).

---

[9] The Polish lustration law provides incentives for candidates running for public office to reveal whether or not they had collaborated in the past with the secret police. Statements revealing collaboration are disclosed on the ballots, although the candidate in question is still allowed to run. For details of how this procedure affects false acquittals and false convictions resulting from lustration, see Nalepa (2008).

Respondents were eager to add that electoral success following an admission to being an informer would not have been possible for former dissidents (interviews 2004: PA4). Party functionaries were obligated to collaborate with the secret police. There was nothing clandestine about the collaboration – it was practically voluntary (interviews 2004: PO8). Although meticulous records were kept of party informers, they were not recorded in registers of agents, but rather in special operational files. These files were, incidentally, also the first to be shredded once the secret police started its systematic operation of document destruction (Dudek 2004). Moreover, PZPR functionaries collaborating with the communist state could not be viewed as an act of betrayal. After all, by supplying the security apparatus with information helpful in fighting dissent, these party informers were just protecting the communist state. In 1970, a special instruction banned secret police officers from recruiting party members, although it was not always followed (interviews 2004: PC6). Respondent PC6 added, however, that although providing the secret police with information came naturally to party functionaries, it is not clear exactly how useful the information provided by party functionaries was compared to the information from dissidents themselves. Another respondent insisted that although lustration is less damaging at the individual level, at the group level lustration first and foremost affects post-communist parties. This is because lustration invited research into departments in which the party functionaries were permitted to collaborate, such as for military intelligence and counterintelligence:

Initially, the post-communist SLD believed that the lustration law would hurt it somewhat, but thought it would affect the former dissidents to a much greater extent. Only since 2000 has the situation started changing, with people like Jozef Oleksy and Jerzy Jaskiernia having lustration cases in court for collaborating with the intelligence. Yet, there will always be many post-communists eager to replace them (interviews 2004: PN10, PL7).

Respondents widely believed that most of the destroyed files implicated the communist party, but most of the preserved files implicated the opposition (interviews 2004: PL12). Party functionaries could, at most, work in the military counterintelligence, but lustration did not reach that far until 2001 (interviews 2004: PN8). This is far from saying that lustration served the interests of post-communist parties. For one, certain institutions, such as the military or the ministry of foreign affairs, recruited as collaborators exclusively party functionaries . It is difficult to craft a lustration law that would exclude those divisions of the secret police where party functionaries were employed. It is likewise difficult to avoid having lustration spill over into other forms of transitional justice, such as trials and expropriations of former communist party assets (taken over by their successors, the post-communists). Lustration can open a can of worms by sparking transitional justice debates that could escalate quickly. In light of this, only parties that originated in clandestine collaborating groups such as the Independent Student Union (NZS), KPN, Ruch Wolnosc i Pokoj, S'80, and S'90 could feel relatively safe from lustration. Members of most of these groups united in the Electoral Action Solidarity, created in 1996. Parties emerging from dissident groups that had been less selective and careful about their recruiting practices suffered from lustration in the aftermath of the transition. Such parties were Freedom Union (UW), Labor Union (UP), the Liberal Democratic Congress (KLD), the Civic Parliamentary Committee (OKP), the Polish People's Party (PSL), and, to some extent, the Civic Platform (PO). These are ostensibly the same parties that fall on the lower range of the PPMD anti-lustration (or post-communist) to pro-lustration (or anticommunist) scale.

The thesis that dissidents who were part of the open opposition had greater reservations about lustration than dissidents coming from clandestine conspiracies is supported by data collected in 1988 (during the Magdalenka talks) by the Center for Public Opinion Polling (CBOS). CBOS was a survey initiative of the communist authorities created in 1983. It conducted surveys to monitor the general public's attitudes so that another martial law scenario could be avoided. Because the objective of the polling institute was to provide the authorities with reliable data, the survey institute worked hard at instilling confidence in people it interviewed that their responses were fully confidential.[10] Therefore, the usual criticisms directed at surveys conducted in authoritarian states – that respondents are too intimidated to provide reliable responses – are not as applicable to CBOS data, especially in the late 1980s.[11] Their survey analysts were not rewarded for delivering results that presented the

[10] The idea of providing incentives for supplying the communist authorities with a true rather than favorable outlook of social attitudes dawned upon the martial law authorities in the early 1980s when it became apparent that in estimating the popularity of Solidarity, they were relying on misleading survey data, produced by pollsters who felt discouraged from reporting figures disappointing to the authorities.

[11] In fact, even in the early 1980s, CBOS succeeded in separating itself from the communist enforcement apparatus. In data reported by Grabowska and Sułek (1993), respondents were asked about their affiliation with Solidarity in 1980–1. Although at the time the polls were taken (between 1982 and 1987) Solidarity was an illegal organization, 38 percent of the respondents declared they had been members of the trade union, even though at its peak membership in the trade union was only 30.4 percent strong.

communist authorities in favorable light, but instead for information that reflected actual attitudes harbored in society. In Figure 6.2, I present part of the data from a survey gauging attitudes toward dissidents, communists, and Catholic Church representatives who were being considered as candidates to serve as negotiators in the roundtable talks. The questionnaire first asked respondents whether they recognized the candidate's name. Next, they were asked whether they trusted or mistrusted the candidate. In presenting the results, though, one of the variables is redundant because trust and mistrust are expressed as conditional on name recognition. Figure 6.2 graphs attitudes toward twelve Solidarity leaders. I ordered the ex-dissidents according to their attitudes toward lustration (measured by the party they ended up joining by the time the PPMD expert survey was carried out). It is worth noting that the first and last post-communist presidents of Poland – Lech Wałęsa and Lech Kaczyński – are located on opposite ends of both scales: the PPMD measuring attitudes to lustration and the trust/mistrust CBOS scale. This is also consistent with the thesis of this chapter: Lustration skeptics tend to be those politicians whose past is associated with an open opposition movement. Open oppositionists were more popular in the transition aftermath than the clandestine conspirators. Politicians' attitudes toward lustration are consistent with the expected payoffs that lustration laws deliver to parties that are not infiltrated.

Two other findings are striking in this survey, although they confirm the lack of authoritarian bias in the way the questions were answered. First, the dissidents from Solidarity had, on average, considerably greater name recognition than leaders from the party apparatus or the Catholic Church.[12] This is counterintuitive, because following its de-legalization in 1981, Solidarity operated underground. Meanwhile, leaders of the communist party had exclusive access to the media, and Catholic clerics who fairly openly performed religious functions had considerable visibility, (Dudek and Gryz 2003). Curiously, the average mistrust of Solidarity members exceeded the average level of trust. On average, close to 10 percent of the communist candidates were mistrusted, but close to 15 percent had earned the trust of respondents.[13] Note that, although

---

[12] The variable of "name recognition" is not presented in Figure 6.2, but can be directly derived from adding "trust" and "mistrust" columns.

[13] It should be noted that this 10 percent reflects not mistrust to the communists in general, but toward those whom the regime was thinking of seating to negotiate at the roundtable. It is reasonable to assume that, according to the communist regime, these were the *most* trustworthy elites on hand.

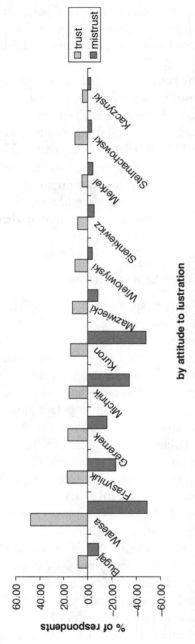

Figure 6.2. Trust and mistrust toward members of the opposition considered as candidates for Solidarity representatives at the roundtable talks.
Source: CBOS.
Note: Dissidents are organized according to the revealed preferences for lustration (measured by the lustration position of the dissident's party in 2002, according to PPMD).

counterintuitive, this result strengthens our confidence in the survey results. If CBOS respondents suspected that recognizing opposition members could be detrimental to them, surely they would not admit to recognizing their names.

In the next section, I look at the "birth" and "death" of parties as well as MPs' pro-lustration positions according to experts and the parties themselves. I use PPMD and manifesto data. The following section takes the analysis to an even more micro level, using multivariate analysis on data about the age of individual legislators, their party affiliation, their tenure in parliament, and their position on lustration. These empirical sections help us evaluate theories about the origin of pro-lustration parties outlined previously by testing hypotheses about whether newer parties were more likely to support lustration than were old parties.

6.3. Do Parties Exhibit More Support for Lustration over Time?

Both manifesto data and expert surveys can answer whether parties exhibit greater support for lustration over time. Recall the "quasi-statements" from the manifesto data that were used by Dieter Hans Klingemann and his colleagues that I described in section 5.2. The "Communist: Positive" set of quasi-statements included "'let sleeping dogs lie' in dealing with the nomenclature" (Klingemann 2006, Appendix II, 3052). This is clearly a statement opposing lustration. Among the "Communist: Negative" statements was "weeding out the collaborators from governmental service" (Klingemann 2006, Appendix II, 3053), which is a statement of pro-lustration preferences. However, since the beginning of the transition, in Poland, Hungary, and the Czech Republic, only two parties included any "Communist: Negative" statements in their manifestos (less than 2 percent of all electoral programs). There is not enough variation in the data to analyze "Communist: Negative" (or pro-lustration) quasi-statements. Thus the analysis that follows looks only at "Communist: Positive" (or anti-lustration) quasi-statements. The three panels of Figure 6.3 present the number of "Communist: Positive" quasi-statements for all parties and all electoral terms, by country. The manifestos are ordered by the time of their publication. Note that parties that ran in successive electoral terms changed their manifestos, thus they appear in the series more than once.

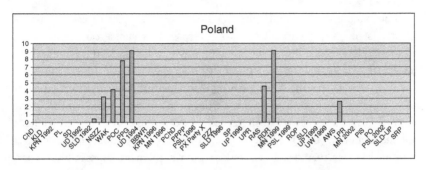

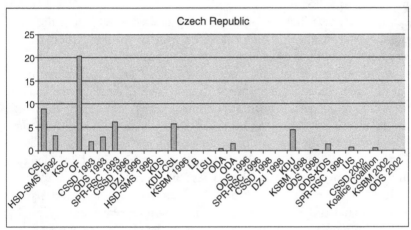

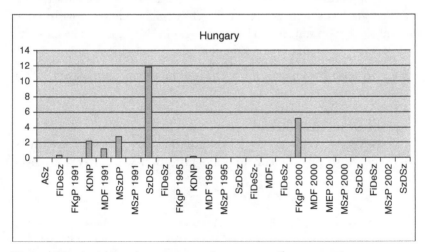

Figure 6.3. Anti-lustration statements in party manifestos over time.

The manifesto data in Figure 6.3 first show that parties are not particularly keen on using manifestos to advertise their stance on dealing with former collaborators; if they did so at all, it was more likely in the immediate aftermath of the transition to democracy rather than recently. Over time, in all three countries, statements supporting reconciliation have disappeared from manifestos. This is consistent with parties preparing for implementing transitional justice laws. Two Polish parties are exceptions: AWS and Movement for the Republic (RdR). These two, after defending members of the ancien régime in their manifestos, rushed to punish them as soon as they were positioned to do so.

Manifesto data illustrate what parties promised to do before the elections. Next, consider the empirical evidence on the entry and exit of parties as a function of their pro and anti-lustration positions.

A line starting at each parliamentary party's "birth" and ending in its "death" represents its life span in Figure 6.4. The lines are stacked according to the parties' positions on lustration as estimated by experts in the PPMD. Those opposing lustration are at the bottom and those supporting it are at the top portion of each panel. Where a party's legislative seat share changed considerably between its life and death, I included this information in a box next to the parties' "life line."[14]

It is striking that in Poland and Hungary, pro-lustration parties emerged later (note the shorter lines in the upper right) and achieved a significant representation in parliament in the late 1990s. In contrast, these patterns are less prominent in the Czech Republic, although parties that are anti-lustration still tend to be older (signified by the long lines closer to the bottom). Overall, I observe the following regularities:

- Parties with preferences for harsh lustration laws appear later rather than sooner.
- Parties with preferences for mild lustration appear sooner in parliaments rather than later.
- Parties with preferences for harsh lustration win more seats over time.
- Parties with preferences for mild lustration win fewer seats over time.

---

[14] Appendix D provides the full dataset that was used to construct these figures. It lists parties' positions on dealing with former communists (on a normalized scale of 0 to 1), provided that they held at least 5 percent of the seats in the legislature. The columns provide data on the date of the party's first appearance in parliament, the date of its last appearance in parliament, and the percentage of its respective seat share.

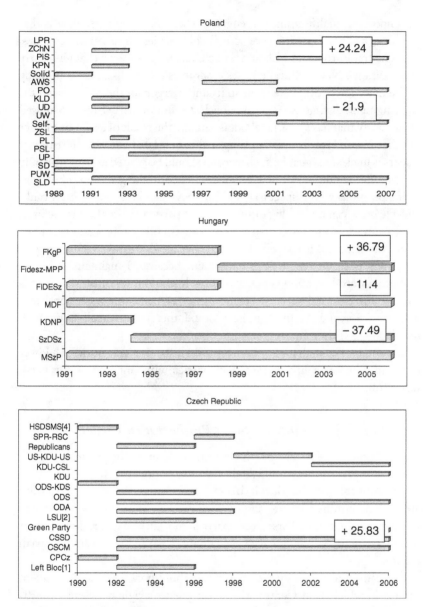

Figure 6.4. Survival of parties in East Central European legislatures by attitudes to lustration.

An important qualification to recognize when analyzing these data is that many of the "new" parties were actually old parties disguised as new ones. East Central European legislatures are characterized by ever-changing party compositions. New political entities emerge as others disappear, but many of the newcomers originate from splits and mergers of the older ones. It is challenging to distinguish unambiguously a *truly* new party from a disguised "new" party that has a new label but is actually the result of a split or merger (Tucker 2006). How to treat a group with a new label but with the original leaders is unclear. Arguably, such a group should be treated as truly new only if a significant number of new members joined it along the way. For analyzing positions with respect to lustration, new members, even merely rank-and-file ones, can make a big difference. The party may use the change in its label as an excuse to purge its ranks of former collaborators and reemerge under the same old leadership. On the other hand, treating such a party as truly new is consistent with my argument because, I maintain, a party's attitude toward lustration depends on how lustration will affect that party's chances for electoral success. Having fewer ex-collaborators is consistent with a more favorable attitude to lustration. I, therefore, treat all parties with new labels as if they are truly new.

In sum, parties with preferences for mild lustration are "born" at a lower rate and "die" at a higher rate than parties with preferences for harsh lustration.

6.4. Do Younger Legislators Select Pro-lustration Parties?

I have argued so far that pro-lustration preferences originate in beliefs that one's party is less infiltrated with secret police collaborators than other political parties. But if beliefs concerning levels of infiltration are also determined by the age of parties, they must also be related to the age of their members. New parties can survive lustration if their members are too young to have been collaborators under the authoritarian regime.

We cannot test directly the hypotheses about how the type of dissident groups in which East Central European parties originated explains attitudes to lustration. This would require data on the pre-transition activities of politicians. We can, however, quite easily test whether young parties and young legislators prefer more stringent transitional justice policies than older parties and more seasoned legislators. In this section, I use data collected on individual members of the Polish legislature over all electoral terms between 1991 and 2005. This is to see whether the age of its members has an independent effect on the pro-lustration policy of the caucus they chose to join once elected to parliament.

The two principal hypotheses tested in this section are that (1) a legislator's age determines the type of party that he or she selects (defined by its lustration policy) and (2) the longer a legislator's tenure in parliament, the less likely he or she is to support stringent lustration policies. I evaluate these hypotheses while controlling for the parliamentarian's education, the term in which his or her caucus was formed, and the current parliamentary term.

In addition, I included two regional dummy variables to control for the type of district from which the legislator was elected. There is a rich literature on Polish elections that illustrates how historical determinants explain variations in voting behavior across electoral districts. For example, between 1772 and 1918, Poland was under the "partitions." Its territory had been divided among three empires: Russia, Austria, and Prussia. Scholars have shown how today voters living in the territories of the former partitions exhibit markedly different voting patterns. (Jasiewicz 1993, 2000; McManus-Czubinska et al. 2004; Markowski and Tucker 2005, 2008). There is no research yet on how partitions influence legislative behavior, but I nevertheless used two dummy variables to control for the possibility that the three regions affect legislators differently.

The Polish parliament (Sejm) is composed of 460 MPs and, at the time of writing, it is in its sixth term. The fifth term was extraordinarily suspended,[15] and I was unable to incorporate data on the fifth term into my dataset. Thus, my universe of cases contains 1,839 MP terms, only 1,442 of which were not independents. A small minority of the MPs appear more than once in the dataset. In virtually all such cases, the MP reappears as a member of a new or different party. Thus, because the dependent variable is the pro-lustration ideology of the party to which the MP belongs, it makes sense to treat each such MP term as a new observation. The dependent variable is pro-lustration ideology (of the legislator's caucus) measured on the normalized PPMD expert scale described in section 5.2 (Benoit and Laver 2007). The independent variable of interest is the individual legislator's age (in years) and the number of terms served in

---

[15] The suspension of the parliamentary term resulted from a non-confidence vote that brought down the ruling coalition led by Jarosław Kaczyński. Given the distribution of seats in the current parliament, a new cabinet could not be formed. It was dissolved by President Lech Kaczyński, who called for new elections in October 2007.

Table 6.1. *OLS regression of individual legislators' attitude toward lustration.*

Independent variables	Dependent variable: Lustration	Position (PPMD)
Legislator's age	−0.00151**	(0.000639)
Current term	−0.000765	(0.00554)
Legislator's tenure in parliament	−0.0268***	(0.00544)
Legislator's education	−0.0149	(0.0147)
Age of legislator's caucus	−0.0566***	(0.00200)
Birth of legislator's caucus (in years since transition)	0.00649**	(0.00271)
Austrian partition	0.0212	(0.0167)
Prussian partition	−0.0275**	(0.0118)
Constant	1.028***	(0.0575)
Observations	1,442	
R-squared	0.711	

Note: Robust standard errors in parentheses, *** $p < .01$, ** $p < .05$.

parliament, ranging from zero to five. (On this scale, I allowed for tenure from one legislative term prior to the transition to count as well.) The other variables for which I controlled are the parliamentary term (ranging from 1 to 4), the legislator's education (four levels – vocational, high school diploma, college diploma, or graduate degree), and the historical partition of his district (dummies for Prussia and Austria, with Russia as the base category). Table 6.1 presents the OLS regression results.

OLS analysis shows that, of the variables previously considered in the party-level analysis in section 6.3, a party's age measured since its first appearance in parliament is significant. Younger parties are more eager to embrace stringent lustration policies.[16] Also, legislators elected from districts that were under the Prussian partition are less likely to be members of pro-lustration parties. We see also, however, that individual characteristics of MPs are highly significant. Young and less educated MPs gravitate to parties with pro-lustration agendas, while those who are older and have more degrees join parties that do not pursue lustration. The effect of age is highly significant, albeit small. This is true

[16] Since the unit of analysis is an individual legislator, while the result is about parties' age and policy position, this result can be interpreted as weighed by the number of legislators in the party.

even though age is measured in years, whereas the scale of transitional justice ideology ranges only from 0 to 1. Holding all else constant, a legislator who is twenty years older is a member of a party that is 3 percent less supportive of lustration. Note that these data are also consistent with an analysis in which the causality of the observed phenomena is reversed – that is, pro-lustration parties intentionally select younger candidates for MPs. This is plausible in light of Poland's closed-list PR system (in most of the electoral cycles analyzed here), in which party bosses determine the composition and ordering of party lists. These data support the theory linking age of individuals to pro-lustration attitudes.

6.5. Alternative Explanations

Is the difference in infiltration the only explanation for the emergence of pro-lustration parties? Before I move to the next chapter explaining the specific strategic interaction among post-communists, the liberal opposition, and anticommunist dissidents that led to the passage of lustration laws in Poland, Hungary, and Slovakia, I consider some alternative explanations for delayed lustration that are consistent with the emergence of pro-lustration parties described in this chapter.

6.5.1. Substitute Topic

One alternative explanation is suggested by David Ost (2005) in his analysis of the Solidarity trade union. Ost describes the transformation of the independent trade union from a representative of labor interests, across regions and industrial sectors, to a political party, actively participating in a series of economic reforms in the spirit of neoclassical liberalism. Ost argues that the political extension of Solidarity, created to capture the union vote, included among its programmatic pursuits appeals to populist policies, such as banning abortion and minority rights. Lustration is not the focus of Ost's book, but in passing, the author places the adoption of lustration in the context of "exclusionary illiberal policies." Ost claims that lustration limited access to office for vast groups of the population: "When parliaments pass radical lustration or privilege one religion or nationality over another, they are being illiberal by creating whole groups of citizens subject to persecution by the state" (2006, 10).

There are at least a few reasons that associating lustration with illiberal policies on a par with restrictions on gay and ethnic minority rights is problematic. First, lustration directly does not affect the general public, but elites. It affects labor, the primary subject of Ost's research, least of all. Unless a blue-collar worker is planning a political career, he or she is unlikely to have any direct interest in lustration. Such individuals are not subjected to screening to keep their jobs. To the contrary, lustration affects whether professional elites can hold public office. Second, implicitly, Ost's treatment of lustration evinces a skepticism toward one of the normative arguments supporting lustration – namely, the backward-looking argument of *fair representation*, according to which a new democratic regime can be entrusted with representing voters only if its leaders and civil servants are not tied to the former regime. Broadly speaking, according to this argument, victims of the totalitarian regime should be able to trust politicians in office; citizens who were politically prosecuted under authoritarian rule should not be rehabilitated in the new regime by the same judge who ruled against them previously. Similarly, the police officers responsible for law and order in the new democratic state should not be the same as the ones who participated in suppressing anti-authoritarian demonstrations and spied on political dissidents.

This argument, however, provides much weaker support for lustration than the forward-looking *corruptibility* argument. Under this view, if collaboration with the previous regime is kept secret, public officials become corruptible because they are vulnerable to blackmail by those who have access to secret police files.[17] In other words, there is an implicit electoral cost, or loss of popularity, associated with the official's collaboration being exposed. In such a case, elected officials may be tempted to avoid such cost by corrupt means (Kunicova and Nalepa 2006).

Third, Ost confuses at least three different political parties: the Solidarity Election Action (Akcja Wyborcza Solidarność, or AWS), Self-Defense (Samoobrona, or S), and the League of Polish Families (Liga Polskich Rodzin, or LPR). All three parties at various times advocated Christian values and employed antigay rhetoric to some extent. But only

---

[17] The possession of files of secret collaborators was documented in the confiscation of 2,612 pages of documents from the apartment of former military intelligence chief Jerzy Fraczkowski in March 1993. The documents contained files that the secret police had created regarding dissidents: Bogdan Borusewicz, Lech Kaczyński, Bogdan Lis, Jacek Merkel, and also Lech Wałęsa (see Cenckiewicz and Gontarczyk 2008, 529, for a report documenting the takeover of the files).

AWS supported neoclassical liberal reforms. It also supported EU expansion, whereas Self-Defense and LPR did not. Finally, while LPR and AWS advocated harsh lustration laws, Self-Defense did not (as I show in the following section). There are, therefore, significant differences among the parties that Ost has decided to lump together.

6.5.2. NATO Expansion and EU Accession

Another explanation I consider is that the prospect of EU accession spawned the emergence of new parties with a populist agenda (Markowski and Tucker 2008). Populist parties, this argument runs, felt secure – just like new parties, parties with young membership, or parties originating in clandestine conspiracies – that lustration would spare them yet undermine their competing parties. For the first ten years after transition, nearly all political parties in East Central Europe shared two common goals: joining NATO and joining the EU (O'Dwyer 2006, 610).

For Hungary, the Czech Republic, and Slovakia, joining NATO meant closing a historical chapter that began with the Soviet military's crackdowns on anticommunist protests in 1956 and 1968. For Poland, joining NATO represented permanently removing the threat that almost materialized in December 1981.[18] For others, it meant removing the Soviet troops stationed on their territory. Indeed, for the entire Soviet bloc, NATO and EU expansion represented the end of Yalta commitments.

Just as joining NATO ensured military security, joining the EU carried a promise of economic security and a symbolic return to western civilization. It is not surprising that virtually all political parties in East Central Europe in the early 1990s equally supported their country's EU accession. Although there was broad consensus among political parties on joining the EU, the electorate's appetite for joining the EU gradually dispersed. This occurred especially as negotiations progressed and the European community mounted greater demands on the candidate states. As Euroskepticism in the electorate grew, existing political parties with

---

[18] Just before martial law was introduced in Poland, many Solidarity members feared Soviet intervention would ultimately end the "eighteen months of Solidarity." General Jaruzelski later used this fear to his advantage as an excuse for implementing martial law, by saying that it was the "lesser evil" (Jaruzelski 1993, 2008). This book has a better account of the martial law and subsequent excuses for his actions produced by Jaruzelski.

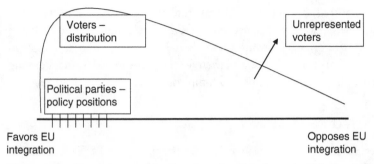

Figure 6.5. Downsian model of voter and political parties' ideal points on the "joining EU" dimension.
Note: Voters' preferences are presented as a continuous distribution; parties' ideal points are presented as discrete points over the pro-EU to anti-EU joining cleavage.

stakes in the ongoing negotiations could not easily shift their support to catch up with their constituents. In the summer of 2003, referenda for ratifying the accession treaties for the new member states provided the ultimate incentive for new parties to emerge. The referenda asked voters a single question: whether or not they supported joining the EU.

It is useful to represent this situation with a Downsian model of politics, according to which parties chose their positions in response to voters' preferences. The Downsian representation of this situation is a one-dimensional model with most of the old political parties on the pro-EU side of the spectrum. The distribution of voters, on the other hand, although still skewed in the pro-EU direction, was more symmetrical. Figure 6.5 represents this hypothetical situation.

Clearly, the significant cleavage of EU expansion created incentives for the emergence of new parties capable of credibly committing to a Euro-skeptic agenda. The crude model outlined in Figure 6.5 leads us to expect new parties to emerge. This is consistent with Radoslaw Markowski and Joshua Tucker's finding. In an article based on surveys with elites and electorates in Poland following the EU referendum, they conclude that political representation on the issue of EU membership did matter to Polish citizens by helping inform their political choices and attitudes, and that political parties clearly seemed to have been aware of this fact and reacted to it. Markowski and Tucker also notice the irony in the fact that although this is a positive result for the development of political representation in Poland, it may ultimately threaten the quality of democracy by providing mass support for radical and anti-systemic parties (Markowski and Tucker 2008).

This trend is further reflected in the PPMD data, described in section 5.2. That survey asked expert respondents to evaluate party positions on a 1 to 20 scale, with 1 representing "Opposes joining the European Union" and 20 representing "Favors joining the European Union." Apart from the authentic, unreformed communist parties that survived the transition, such as the Bulgarian Communist Party, the Communist Party of Slovakia, and the Communist Party of Bohemia and Moravia, almost all the EU skeptics emerged in this century as referenda for deciding EU membership were being conducted. In this section, I describe the emergence of parties of noncommunist origin whose normalized scores on joining the EU were less than .5 on the normalized PPMD scale.

In Bulgaria, the most anti-EU party, the Bulgarian National Movement (VMRO), which was created in 2001, did not even cross the threshold necessary for winning parliamentary seats in that year. But in 2005, two years before Bulgaria joined, VMRO entered parliament with a 5.7 percent representation. In the Czech Republic, the Republicans of Miroslaw Sladek, the rightist anti-EU party, was created in 1998 but never managed to clear the threshold for entering parliament. In Slovakia, in addition to the communists, the Slovak National Party was classified in 2002 as Euroskeptic. The Slovak National Party was very popular in the years just before the breakup of Czechoslovakia. In 1990, it obtained 14 percent of the vote share, but in 1994, after the elections, the Slovak National Party garnered only 5.4 percent of the votes. Its popularity began to increase again, though, as Slovakia's prospects for joining the EU improved. Despite its Euroskepticism, however, this party never adopted a pro-lustration agenda, which is reflected in its score on attitudes toward former communists (in the PPMD, it has a score slightly below the median in Slovakia).[19]

In Estonia, the only Euroskeptic party – aside from the Social Democrats (the communist successor party) – has been the Estonian Christian People's Union. This party has never entered parliament. In Lithuania and Romania, there are no parties with a lower EU joining score than .5. In Latvia, the only two such parties are the ethnic Russian advocacy parties, the People's

[19] This is consistent with the history of Slovak nationalism. In communist Czechoslovakia, in the aftermath of the Prague Spring, most of the dissident elites who escaped degradation to blue-collar jobs were sent to work in government and academic institutions in Slovakia, where they would often take jobs of less skilled Slovaks who had been working. This sparked nationalism and eagerness among some degraded Slovaks to collaborate with the secret police in providing information on Czech dissidents who had deprived them of prestigious jobs.

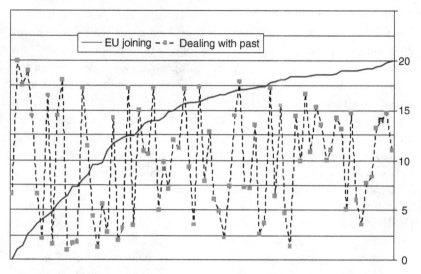

Figure 6.6. PPMD scores on lustration policy and joining the EU sorted by attitudes toward EU joining.

Harmony Party and For Human Rights in United Latvia. As most KGB officers and collaborators were Russians, these parties are not very keen on lustration. In Poland, the three parties that are shy of .5 on joining the EU are the League of Polish Families (LPR), Samoobrona (S), and the Polish People's Party (PSL). The PSL was technically a successor communist party and has been on the political scene since the early 1990s. Its attitude toward lustration is quite close to the post-communist SLD's. Self-Defense and LPR, on the other hand, were brand new parties that appeared on the political scene right before the accession referenda. Samoobrona was never especially supportive of lustration (with a score of .32), but LPR was more anticommunist (with a score of 1). Since 2006, however, when information about infiltration in the higher echelons of the Catholic Church appeared in the news, LPR has become more reserved regarding lustration.

This discussion leads to the conclusion that although many new illiberal parties emerged in the period of the EU referenda, there is little overlap between these parties and groups insisting on harsh lustration. There is, in fact, no correlation whatsoever between PPMD scores of members of parliamentary parties in their attitudes toward joining the EU and their attitudes toward former communists (–.002). These points are summarized in Figure 6.6, which plots by party expert-assigned scores on dealing with communists against scores on joining the EU. To make the figure easier to read, the party averages have been sorted according to PPMD scores on EU joining, from Euroskeptic to Euroenthusiatic.

6.5.3. Roundtable Negotiations

A final alternative explanation for delayed lustration that is consistent with the empirical evidence concerns parties originating in dissident groups of the clandestine conspiracy type. These groups, which distanced themselves from the roundtable negotiations, were not bound by the promises made at those negotiations, while the open opposition groups were. Many of the contacts established between the communists' negotiators and the opposition's outlived the negotiations themselves. After months of bargaining in a secluded Warsaw suburb, social connections between representatives of the two sides were bound to emerge.[20] Thus, although promises to refrain from transitional justice were not credible (as I argue in Chapter 3 of this book), members of the liberal opposition may have felt constrained by personal ties created by the roundtable proceedings. Daniel Pawlowiec, one of the youngest MPs in the Polish parliament from LPR, expressed just this view:

My parliamentary caucus, the League of Polish Families, did not make any promises in Magdalenka [a Warsaw suburb] at the roundtable negotiations and therefore is not bound by any agreements or deals. I believe that the problem of lustration and decommunization should have been solved long ago. And now I fully support the proposal of Law and Justice (PiS) because we need to finish what was started long ago (Program Trzeci Polskiego Radia, "Debata o Deubekizacji").[21]

This explanation accords with the conventional wisdom for parties' eagerness to lustrate, particularly in Poland. In Chapter 3, I used game theory to demonstrate that no such promises could bind the opposition after the communists relinquished power. The model is further supported by interviewed elites who said that any promises about refraining from transitional justice at the roundtable (RT) negotiations were meaningless (if they were made at all). One respondent, PL12, even explained his "transformation from a personal Decalogue to a political Decalogue":

---

[20] Antoni Dudek mentions that among these communication channels was one between Janusz Reykowski and Bronislaw Geremek and between Jacek Kuron and Aleksander Kwasniewski. These contacts were so well known that one of the Political Bureau members suggested their coordination (Dudek 2004a, 430).

[21] See http://www.polskieradio.pl/_repository/_folders/f_99_890/7795.mp3.

Some of them [participants of the RT negotiations] felt that they could not break a word given to the communists and they felt that since they had struck a deal with the communists, the terms of that deal should be kept. That's why Jaruzelski was still elected to presidential office, even after the communists had lost so dramatically. But with time, many of us began thinking that those promises need not be kept any more, although we ought to be discrete as we break them (interviews: PL12).

I asked if the reputation of being a "promise breaker that cannot be trusted" could damage a politician's reputation when he or she tried to establish cabinet and voting coalitions. PL12 replied "absolutely not, the conditions of any such agreement are always dictated by the winner; that is where its credibility resides." Ironically, PL12's "collaboration" was one of the first "skeletons" that the Macierewicz list exposed. After spending years clearing his name in the courts, he became an adamant supporter of lustration procedures that allow politicians to volunteer themselves for screening if the media start spreading rumors about their past involvement with the secret police. But PL12 did not consider himself a victim of lustration and declined to attribute the delay in lustration to any roundtable promise.

Finally, the history of actual lustration legislation in Poland, Hungary, Bulgaria, and Romania refutes the plausibility of this explanation. The first time that working lustration laws were actually adopted in these two countries, it happened at the hands of the post-communists themselves. The next chapter of this book addresses this final puzzle.

6.6. Conclusions

I have shown in this chapter that strategic concerns delay the adoption of lustration, as illustrated in Table 1.1. Younger parties have more to gain from lustration than older parties because, on average, they have fewer links to the former communist police. Although adopting lustration does not cause parties to lose their electorates, the supply-side explanations for engaging in transitional justice policies reinforce demand-side theories. The demand for transitional justice among voters has been constant or declining throughout East Central Europe, but lustration laws have become ever so popular with politicians.

The findings of the last two chapters demonstrate that, compared to other legislative dimensions, politicians' stated positions on lustration can plausibly be considered their authentic policy preferences. For positive political theory, this is critical. Neo-institutionalism takes preferences of political actors as given. Yet the literature on politicians' behavior has shown that they are guided by at least three objectives: policy, winning office, and rents (Bawn 1999; Persson and Tabellini 2000). This presents a critical problem for the political scientist who has to decide on which type of preferences to focus. Legislation on lustration, however, deals with this problem remarkably well, because it allows us to separate preferences over policy from rent-seeking and office-seeking behavior. I consider rents first. With a few exceptions, lustration cannot be a substantial source of rents. Among the exceptions are rents from privatization of state-owned companies that are controlled by highly placed secret police collaborators. Thus, extending lustration to include directors of state-owned enterprises would deprive former collaborators of rents. Although it is clear that former collaborators in control of privatized companies would lose rents if lustration were thus extended, it is not immediately obvious how parties not infiltrated would stand to capture those rents.[22]

Second, policy preferences of political elites are not conflated with behavior directed at catering to voters' preferences. Since voters are not terribly concerned about lustration, politicians are not adopting lustration to capture their constituents' approval. In short, if politicians care about lustration (because they want to retain office) but appeal to voters on other dimensions (that are substantially more important to voters), positive political theory can be used to explain strategic behavior with regard to lustration. Lustration may be a mediocre tool for winning votes, but it can certainly be a powerful strategic weapon in political competition. An effective lustration bill can deprive a former secret police collaborator of political office and can make that office more accessible to non-collaborators by precluding or hindering former agents of the ancien régime from running.

The current chapter linked the adoption of lustration laws across East Central Europe to the emergence of anticommunist parties. But a significant puzzle remains: In two of the countries with delayed transitional justice, Poland and Hungary, lustration laws were passed by *post-communists*, that is, by successor communist parties. The next chapter confronts this puzzle.

---

[22] Note, however, that including rents as a motivation for lustration is not entirely inconsistent with the infiltration story: Uncovering who was and who was not a secret police collaborator at state-owned companies may have hurt the oppositionist collaborators hiding among the labor force and low-ranking *nomenklatura*.

7

The Transitional Justice Bill Game

Throughout this book, I have been trying to resolve the puzzle of delayed transitional justice in East Central Europe.[1] Why did some countries embark on purging public officials so late? In my explanations, I have been making a case for a positive approach to transitional justice. I have been arguing that rather than becoming a matter of retribution or "coming to terms with the past and moving on," transitional justice legislation became a dimension of strategic interactions among actors eager to maintain their offices and advance careers. Thus, in Chapters 2 and 3, I explained why outgoing communists were not anxious that after leaving power, they would be punished with transitional justice and why the former opposition indeed refrained from exerting this type of punishment.

Unsurprisingly, the communists could not hold the opposition hostage to its threat of skeletons in the closet indefinitely. As one sees in Table 1.1, lustration was eventually adopted in virtually all East Central European countries. In the previous chapter, I explained this as the result of the emergence of new political parties with a pro-lustration agenda. I showed that lustration laws helped these parties weaken electoral competition and establish themselves as just and incorruptible. Their party manifestos no longer contained vows to reconcile and "let sleeping dogs lie." It was virtually certain that after coming to power they would declassify secret police files and lustrate. Indeed, their threat of retribution was so imminent that it induced successors of the former communist parties to adopt

---

[1] A generalization of the model of the Transitional Justice Bill game into a model of strategic preemption is provided in an article coauthored with Marek Kaminski, available at http://repositories.cdlib.org/csd/. The version presented here is based on Nalepa (2005) and is sufficient to explain the cases of delayed transitional justice in Poland and Hungary.

transitional justice preemptively themselves – another paradox of democratization that has not yet been explained. Figure 1.1 shows that the delayed lustration laws in Poland and Hungary were implemented when post-communist parties held parliamentary majorities. In this chapter, I will present a model that explains how legislative institutions enabled post-communist parties to adopt lustration preemptively in a milder form than that preferred by anticommunist parties, as described in the previous chapter. I will argue that by appeasing the legislative median with this milder form of lustration, the post-communists shielded themselves from the harsh forms of transitional justice that the anticommunists would have introduced.

This chapter is organized as follows. After providing more details about the puzzling behavior of post-communists in East Central Europe, I show that the literature on transitional justice fails to provide us with any clues as to why Polish and Hungarian post-communists engage in such puzzling behavior. Next, I introduce the recent literature on legislative institutions and explain why it makes sense to employ existing models of agenda setting to explain our puzzle. The argument of strategic preemption is presented in the following section. In this section, I formalize the argument in a Transitional Justice Bill game and define conditions under which it is rational for post-communists to lustrate. Next, I derive predictions from the main results and analyze the cases of legislative action or inaction in Hungary and Poland. Another case of delayed transitional justice is that of Slovakia. As it turns out, however, the Slovak case can also be explained within the agenda-setting framework, albeit one which incorporates the atypical transitional status quo – the lustration bill that the Slovaks inherited from the federal state of Czechoslovakia.

7.1. The Wave of Post-Communist Lustrations

In April 1997, the Polish post-communists[2] proposed and adopted a bill requiring MPs, judges, prosecutors, and persons holding top positions in

---

[2] As a reminder, throughout this chapter I refer to members of successor communist parties – that is, parties that have reformed the authoritarian communist party organizations to the point where they can compete in democratic elections – by the term "post-communists." I use the term "anticommunists" to refer to parties that have been created anew after the transition to democracy and insist on dealing with members of the prior authoritarian regime in a harsh way.

the state and the public media, as well as candidates for these positions, to declare whether or not they had worked for or consciously collaborated with the communist secret services between 1944 and 1990. The statements were published and, on that basis, voters or the appropriate authorities would decide whether a given person may be elected or appointed to a particular post. A Lustration Court was established to verify statements of the politicians. If the judges found a statement to be untrue, the relevant ruling of the Court would be published, while the person concerned would be banned from holding a particular position for a period of ten years (Ustawa Lustracyjna 2004).

The post-communist camp also initiated a law on opening the communists' secret police archive to the public (*Rzeczpospolita* 1999). This motion was put forward by the post-communist president Aleksander Kwaśniewski (Kwaśniewski 1997). He proposed the establishment of a Citizens' Archive – an institution for collecting, organizing, and distributing copies of the ancien régime's documentation, similar to the famous Gauck Agency in Germany.

A similar scenario unfolded in Hungary, where both the screening and secret files acts were passed in 1996 by the votes of post-communists, who had been holding a bare majority in the Hungarian parliament since 1994. The Historical Office in charge of the secret files opened to applicants on September 1, 1997 – less than a year before the post-communists lost the elections.

A considerable body of literature in comparative politics finds the comeback of post-communist parties in Eastern Europe surprising and makes attempts to explain the phenomenon (Bozóki 2002; Druckman and Roberts 2005; Grzymała-Busse 2002; Ishiyama 1999). It is indeed surprising that successors of parties responsible for decades of authoritarian rule, who were so extremely unpopular in 1989, would be winning elections only a couple of years later. But even more surprising than their unexpected revivals is that they adopt policies that scholars of comparative transitions and democratization have rendered harmful to such parties – so harmful that many of these scholars predicted that fear of transitional justice might even prevent transitions from occurring. In the literature on negotiated transitions, scholars predict that leaders of authoritarian regimes will concede to democratization only after they are guaranteed that the new democratic institutions will not prosecute members of the ancien régime (Colomer 1991; Colomer 2000; O'Donnell and Schmitter 1986; Omar 1996; Przeworski 1992). Ratifying constitutions that render retroactive legislation illegal (as in Hungary in 1990 and South Africa in 1995) or designing electoral laws that give the outgoing regime an upper hand (as in Chile) are examples of such institutional guarantees.[3] The reasoning that leaders of authoritarian regimes step down from power only after they are convinced that they will not be prosecuted is difficult to reconcile with the empirical observation that once they find themselves in positions to do so, they punish themselves with lustration laws. A first place to look for explanations of the post-communists' puzzling behavior is the literature on transitional justice. In Chapter 2 of this book, I described transitional justice as an interdisciplinary field concerned with how new democracies deal with collaborators of the past regime. Transitional justice has a normative component, originating in the literature on legal and constitutional theory, and a positive component. The normative literature examines the possible justifications of retroactivity (Holmes 1994; Sa'adah 1998) and problems created by retroactivity, such as, "To what extent should the ideals of rule of law and peaceful reconciliation be jeopardized for the sake of punishing the wrongdoers?" and, "Can acts that were legal according to the authoritarian constitutions be prosecuted?" (Nino 1996; Welsh 1994, 1996). Another component of transitional justice research seeks explanations for empirically occurring phenomena. Scholars of democratic transition and consolidation have inquired why new democracies attempt to rectify wrongs committed by the ancien régime (McAdams 1997, 2001; O'Donnell and Schmitter 1986), who are the actors responsible for implementing transitional justice measures (Elster 1998, 2004), and whether these institutions have led to reconciliation (Gibson 2004). Neither the literature on negotiated transitions nor that on the normative and empirical components of transitional justice offers explanations of the post-communists' strange behavior. In this chapter, I use the tools of positive political theory to answer the question of why post-communists lustrate. The explanation I pursue is that the post-communists act under constraints of a combination of approaching

---

[3] These institutional constraints may have adverse effects. Post-communists' attempts to manipulate electoral institutions to grant them more representatives in the future legislature were unsuccessful both in Hungary and Poland (Benoit and Hayden 2004; Benoit and Schieman 2001). In South Africa, although members of the apartheid regime tried to write a blanket amnesty for human rights violations into the constitution, what they ended up with was individual amnesty granted only after testifying to the character of one's crime (Boraine 2000).

elections and legislative institutions. According to spatial models formulated by Thomas Romer and Howard Rosenthal (1978, 1979), the final outcome of this process results from an interaction between the proposer and median in the legislature. The most interesting scenario unfolds under closed rules of parliamentary decision making: If the post-communists do not adopt any bill but, as a result of the elections, lose proposal power to anticommunist-oriented forces, they will have to put up with a very stringent transitional justice bill. This is the case because the median of the legislature is ready to accept even a very stringent lustration bill instead of putting up with no lustration. Post-communists can prevent this punishment by implementing a mild bill themselves. If this bill is sufficient to appease the new parliamentary median, it prevails when they lose power. I formalize this argument in an "agenda-setter" model that I present in the next section. The main results form the basis of my argument and allow for the formulation of the following testable hypotheses:

1) Under closed rules of procedure for parliamentary decision making:
   a) toward the end of an electoral cycle after which post-communists expect to lose proposal power to anticommunists, they will propose a bill at the ideal point of the anticipated median of the new electoral cycle and
   b) if the post-communists' expectation is fulfilled or if the post-communists overestimate the median's position, there is no transitional justice of that type in the new electoral cycle.
   c) If they underestimate the median's position, the new electoral cycle witnesses hard-line transitional justice amendments.
2) Under open rules of procedure for parliamentary decision making:
   a) post-communists will not propose transitional justice bills toward the end of the electoral cycle even if they expect to lose the upcoming elections.
   b) If they indeed lose the upcoming elections, the new electoral cycle witnesses moderate transitional justice legislation.

The organization of the chapter is as follows. The next section formalizes the argument and defines conditions under which it is rational for post-communists to implement lustration. Next, I explain how adopting lustration in the late 1990s in Poland and Hungary satisfies the equilibrium conditions. I also summarize how cases from other countries, such as Slovakia and the Baltic states, fit into the hypothesized patterns.

7.2. The Model

I open this section with an intuitive example illustrating the mechanism at work in my argument. This example, which assumes complete information, is followed by a model that relaxes this informational assumption.

7.2.1. Example

The following simple model illustrates the main idea of this chapter, that is, the strategic introduction of a transitional justice bill by members of the ancien régime. Let PC represent the post-communists' party, M represent the legislative median, and A the anticommunists, whose emergence was described in Chapter 6. The issue space is [0,1]. Preferences are Euclidean, that is, the payoff of each party associated with a given outcome is the negative distance from this outcome to the party's ideal point. The parties' ideal points are 0, m, and 1 as represented in Figure 7.1. Without loss of generality, assume $m \geq \frac{1}{2}$. One may think of these points the following way: 0 represents a situation of no transitional justice, which is the plausible ideal outcome from the post-communists' point of view. 1 represents a situation of the most stringent lustration law, the anticommunists' ideal point. For instance, the Czech 1991 lustration-decommunization act, which required over 420,000 persons to obtain lustration certificates from the Ministry of Interior, would be a bill close to 1 in the transitional justice issue space, whereas the Hungarian 1996 bill (Act 57/1996), covering only 600 persons running for highest public office, would be closer to 0. The transitional justice issue space is portrayed in Figure 7.1.

The game begins with a status quo at 0. In period 1, party PC can unilaterally introduce an alternative status quo $y \in [0,1]$. In period 2, A can propose an alternative legislation x. Finally, in period 3, party M decides between the status quo (0 or y, depending on the choice of PC) and x. This is a game with complete information. Thus, the subgame perfect equilibrium can be found by reasoning resembling that of backward induction. If PC proposes $y \in [0, m)$, M will accept any $x \in [0,m)$, and A will have an incentive to propose $min\{2m-y, 1\}$. If PC proposes $y \in [m,1]$, no proposal $x \neq y$ will be accepted by M, but any policy in $(m,1]$ will make PC worse off than m. Hence, PC's optimal strategy is to change the status quo to $y = m$, that is, to propose a bill exactly at the median's ideal point.

Figure 7.2 presents the game tree for this simple model. What this model explains is that under certain circumstances, incumbent post-

Figure 7.1. The transitional justice issue space.

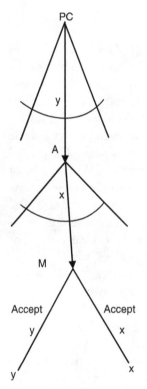

Figure 7.2. Game tree to the agenda-setting game with switching proposal power.

communists will propose and enact transitional justice legislation quite different from their ideal point. In particular, they will abandon their ideal policy, 0, and propose m.[4]

---

[4] The assumption of Euclidean preferences is not necessary to demonstrate this result. To see this, let X be the set of outcomes and let each of the players $\{PC, M, \text{and } A\}$ have rational preferences defined over X. Define the status quo as $sq \in X$. For any subset Y of X, let $C(Y)$ denote PC's most preferred outcomes in Y and assume that $C(X)$ is a singleton = $\{sq\}$. Let $H(Y)$ denote A's most preferred outcomes in Y and $P(z)$ denote the set of alternatives that M weakly prefers to z. The order of play is as follows. Player PC moves first

Notice that the description of this game represents adopting bills under *closed rule* procedures (Baron 2000; Baron and Ferejohn 1989; Gilligan and Krehbiel 1986; Weingast 1989). Under this institutional design, the proposer is different from the median in the legislature. The proposal, which is drafted in the appropriate committee or ministerial department, cannot be modified once it is on the floor of the legislature. The median has to "take it or leave it."

Now consider a modified version of this game, in which party M proposes the alternative status quo in period 2. In this version, in period 2, M will propose and adopt its ideal point m, irrespective of what the action of party PC was. Thus, foreseeing this event, PC has no incentive to leave its ideal point at 0.

This modified description represents adopting bills under *open rule* procedures. Under this institutional design, the role of the proposer of bills is insignificant, since whatever he or she proposes can be freely amended once it reaches the floor. The bill favored by the median voter in parliament is ultimately the proposal that gets passed. Thus this situation can be represented by identifying the party M as the proposer. Note that in this modified game, as in the original version, m is the final outcome of the interaction. However, under the closed rule, to secure this outcome, the incumbent post-communists had to change the status quo from their ideal point to a policy that hurts them. They need to "scratch themselves a little bit to avoid a blow."[5]

This simple model assumes, however, that the incumbent knows with certainty the position of the future legislative median. A more realistic representation should account for his or her behavior in the face of uncertainty, that is, what is the post-communists' optimal strategy when they are uncertain as to *where* exactly the party M may be. This inquiry is the subject of the remainder of this section.

7.2.2. The Model with Uncertainty

The Transitional Justice Bill game is a sequential game with imperfect information. The players are the post-communists *(PC)*, the anticommunist hard-liners *(A)*, and two small, moderate parties: left-leaning *(L)* and

---

and may retain sq as the status quo or choose $y \in X$. Next, A moves proposing $x \in X$. In the last stage, M chooses between x and y. It is easy to verify that generically PC's rational choice is $C(HcP(sq))) \neq sq$.

[5] I am grateful to John Huber for coining this metaphor to describe the actions of post-communists.

Figure 7.3. Transitional justice issue space in a model with uncertainty.

right-leaning *(R)*. Their favorite transitional justice policies from the unidimensional transitional justice issue space $T\mathcal{J} = [0,1]$ are depicted in Figure 7.3.

In period t_1 a transitional justice bill is to be adopted. The post-communists hold full control over the legislative process in this period and they may adopt any bill $y \in T\mathcal{J}$ – ranging from 0 (no transitional justice) to 1 (stringent transitional justice). They have proposal power and because the current state of transitional justice is at 0, the median will approve any post-communist proposal to the left of his or her ideal point. But it is common knowledge that the hard-line anticommunists will win the upcoming elections and form a government with one of the moderate parties. The new cabinet will be a connected coalition consisting of anticommunists up to the moderate party, which has the median position in parliament. The post-communists hold ex-ante beliefs about the new median's location.

Parliamentary elections occur in period t_2 and they are won by the challenger – the hard-line anticommunists. This outcome is known from the beginning of the game. What is uncertain is the position of the median. I have assumed, for simplicity, that there are only two possible medians, L and R, who are chosen with probability p and $1-p$, respectively.

In period t_3, the proposer is specified. Under closed rules of procedure, the proposal power goes to the larger party in the coalition – the anticommunists. Thus, $q = 0$ represents a situation where the anticommunists have agenda-setting power. If the parliamentary decision-making procedure is restricted – that is, a closed rule is used – proposal power is critical. The proposer (a cabinet minister or committee chair) can make "take it or leave it" proposals to the median; $q = 1$ represents open or "unrestricted" rules of procedure, meaning that proposals originating in the committee or respective ministry can be freely amended on the floor. This is equivalent to the situation where the median is the proposer. Thus, the parameter $q \in \{0,1\}$, describing the rules of procedure, can be interpreted as the probability with which the median rather than the anticommunists becomes the proposer. That q is dichotomous reflects the fact that there is certainty among players as to the type of rules of procedure – open or closed – that is used.[6]

Due to strict party discipline, all members of the same party will vote as if they had identical preferences. All players have Euclidean preferences – that is, each has a unique ideal policy point in TJ, they prefer policies closer to their ideal points, and their utility decreases with distance from their ideal point at the same rate. The leftist party L prefers no transitional justice to the tough bill and has an ideal point at l. The rightist party R prefers the stringent bill to no bill and has an ideal point at r. Hence, $l < r$.

In period t_4, depending on the nature of the political system, a new proposal is put forward. The new proposal is a bill x from TJ. Under the closed rule system, either the minister of justice or a transitional justice parliamentary committee, both institutions controlled by the anti-communists, drafts the transitional justice bill, and this proposal is final. Under the open rule system, it can be amended on the floor by $M \in \{L,R\}$, reflecting that the median is the actual proposer under open rules.

In period t_5, the proposal is voted in the legislature. If it is accepted by the median, the bill x becomes law; if it is rejected, bill y prevails as the reversion bill. This model allows for bills to originate and be modified at three levels of the legislative process: on the floor of the legislature, in the cabinet, and in standing committees. The first case exemplifies unrestricted rules of procedure; $q = 1$ describes the open rule system in the model. The parliamentary procedure employed in the Hungarian parliament from 1990 to 1994 falls into this category. The next two cases exemplify restricted decision making represented in the model by $q = 0$. In Poland, proposals of a "take it or leave it" character are made in standing committees, whose chair has ultimate control over the agenda. It is also typical for a standing committee to be chaired by a member of the party who won the elections. Beginning with the second parliamentary term in Hungary, a majority of proposals have originated in cabinet ministries and have not been amended on the floor. Both these procedures fall into the closed rule category. The type of decision-making procedure is, of course, common knowledge to all parties of the game.

---

[6] A possible generalization of this model would be to let q vary from 0 to 1, which would represent that incumbents are uncertain about the future rules of procedure. I owe this suggestion to Jeff K. Staton.

It is also assumed here, as it was in the case of both Poland and Hungary, that when the post-communists adopted transitional justice legislation, they were expecting to lose their dominant position in the legislature to the hard-line anticommunists as a result of the upcoming elections. Excluding pathological cases, using opinion polls and information about preelectoral collations (Golder 2006), it is often quite easy to predict which of the major parties will form a cabinet. What is difficult to foresee, especially when there is more than one moderate party, is the exact position of the legislative median. However, the optimal location of the lustration bill issued by post-communists depends critically on where they expect the new median to be. Under the closed rule system, the post-communist bill establishes a reversion point for the median after the elections, when anticommunists have proposal power. If the post-communists correctly anticipate who the new median will be after the elections, and they adopt a bill exactly at the median's ideal point, the anticommunists are powerless in attracting the new median to any new proposal. For example, if the post-communists anticipate that a moderate party with an ideal point at r will be the median, they will adopt r as the transitional justice bill, and if in fact R is chosen, it is impossible for A to win the median's approval of any other bill. If PC succeeds in appeasing the median, the new anticommunist proposer is powerless. But if PC fails to predict the position of the new median correctly, the hard-line proposer may still get the median's support for his or her new amendment.

The crucial variable determining what sort of transitional justice bill is adopted by the post-communists is thus the anticipated position of the median after the new elections. Figure 7.4 presents the game tree of the Transitional Justice Bill game.

The Transitional Justice Bill game is a sequential game, where the players are post-communists (PC) with an ideal point at 0; a left-leaning moderate party (L) with an ideal point at l; a right-leaning moderate party (R) with an ideal point at r; and anticommunists (A) with an ideal point at 1. $0 < l < r < 1$; $p \in [0, 1]$ is the probability that L becomes median, and $1-p$ is the probability that R becomes median (M) in stage t_2; $q \in \{0,1\}$ is the probability that the median will be the proposer (P) in stage t_3; $TJ = [0,1]$ is the Transitional Justice space; $A_{PC} = [0,1]$ is PC's action space in stage t_1; $A_P = [0,1]$ is A's and L or R's action space in stage t_4; and $A_M = \{x, y\}$ is L and R's action space in stage t_5. The solution concept is Subgame Perfect Nash Equilibrium.

I have assumed here Euclidean preferences over final outcomes of the legislative process. In the case of this model, these assumptions are fairly

Players:
PC, M_R, M_L, A
TJ issue space = $[0,1]$
x,y bills in TJ
$q=0$ represents closed
rules of procedure;
$q=1$ represents open
rules of procedure

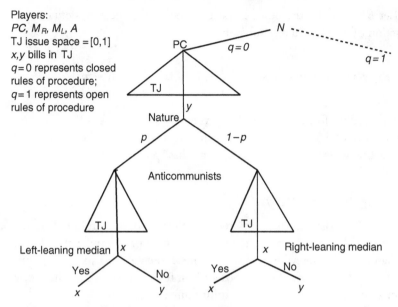

Figure 7.4. The Transitional Justice Bill game.

innocuous, as I demonstrate in the robustness analysis provided in Appendix E. However, they simplify greatly the demonstration of the model. Let M and P denote the party chosen to be the median and proposer in stages t_2 and t_3, respectively, and b_M and $b_P = 1$ denote their respective bliss points. The payoff functions are given by

$$u_M(a_M) = \begin{cases} -|x - b_M| & \text{if } a_M = x \\ -|y - b_M| & \text{if } a_M = y \end{cases}$$

$$u_{PC}(a_M) = \begin{cases} -x & \text{if } a_M = x \\ -y & \text{if } a_M = y \end{cases}$$

$$u_P(a_M) = \begin{cases} -|x - 1| & \text{if } a_M = x \\ -|y - 1| & \text{if } a_M = y \end{cases}$$

7.2.2.1. Solving for the Median and Proposer's Best Responses in the Four Subgames Given any post-communist strategy y, there are four possible subgames, each characterized by who the median is. Only the median and proposer can take actions in the proper subgames.

Let $BR_M(y,x)$ be the best response action of the median, defined as a function of y and x. In any subgame

$$BR_M(y,x) = \arg\max_{v \in \{x,y\}} u_M(v) = \begin{cases} x & \text{if } |x - b_M| < |y - b_M| \\ x,y & \text{if } |x - b_M| = |y - b_M| \\ y & \text{if } |x - b_M| > |y - b_M| \end{cases}$$

The preceding formula states that given two alternatives – the anticommunist proposal and the post-communist reversion bill – the median will choose that which is closer to his or her "bliss" point. Define now the set Z as follows:

$$Z = \{x | u_M(x) \geq u_M(y)\}$$

The set Z consists of all points representing proposals preferred by the median to the post-communist reversion bill. For example, if L is the median and y is somewhere between 0 and l, then Z consists of all points within $l-y$ distance of l. The proposer's best response to y is thus that point from Z that maximizes his or her utility function:

Let BR_P $(y, BR_M(x,y))$ be the best response action of the proposer, defined as a function of y.

$$BR_P(y) = \arg\max_z u_P(z)$$

For the closed rule system (with the anticommunists as proposer), the two cases representing L and R, respectively, chosen as medians are illustrated in Figure 7.5.

If L is the median and y is to the left of the median, the proposer will maximize his utility function by choosing the point in Z that is closest to his "bliss" point. This is given by $2y-l$. If y is to the right of the median, the proposer cannot offer anything the median would accept without making himself worse off than with the post-communist reversion bill, so his best response is just $x=y$. Similarly, if R is the median, the anticommunist proposer maximizes her payoff by offering $2y-r$. The following lemma summarizes the equilibrium results of the subgame played between the hard-line proposer and median for a reversion point given by the post-communist bill.
Lemma 1: The best responses of the proposer and median to each other are given by:

$$BR_P(y), BR_M(y,x) = \begin{cases} \min\{1, 2m - y\}, x \text{ if } y \in [0, m) \\ y, y \text{ if } y \in [m, 1] \end{cases}$$

The Transitional Justice Bill Game

a) optimistic estimates

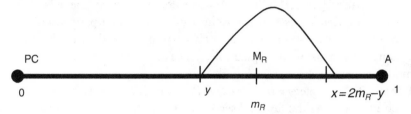

b) pessimistic estimates

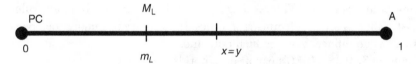

Figure 7.5. Hypotheses about post-electoral behavior.
Note: M_i *(i= L,R)* represents the median that actually gets chosen as a result of the elections; in (a), the *PC* are too optimistic and propose lustration at y; *A* exploits *PC*'s mistake by proposing $x = 2m_R - y$, which M_R accepts, since it is equally distant from its ideal point as y; in (b), *PC* also makes a mistake, but in this case, *A* cannot further exploit the mistake to its advantage. M_L will decline any proposal farther to the right from its ideal point than y.

Table 7.1. *Equilibrium outcomes of the subgames played between the proposer and median defined for four different medians and four types of reversion bills.*

Median/Proposer	$y \in [0,2r-1)$	$y \in [2r-1;l)$	$y \in [l,r)$	$y \in [r,1]$
L/ L (open rule)	l	l	l	l
L/A (closed rule)	$2l-y$	$2l-y$	y	y
R/R (open rule)	r	r	r	r
R/A (closed rule)	*1 (one)*	$2r-y$	$2r-y$	y

Notes: Any strategy y in $[0,2r-1)$ of *PC* is weakly dominated by $y = 2r-1$.

Proof: By equations (1) and (2).

Under open rules of procedure, the median simply proposes and accepts his or her ideal point. Table 7.1 summarizes the outcomes if the median and proposer are playing their best response strategies.

7.2.2.2. The Post-Communists' Optimal Strategy

The next two lemmas use the best response solutions from the previous subsection to narrow the optimal choices of post-communists to a subinterval of the transitional justice space: $[2r-1,1] \subset [0,1]$. Assume for simplicity that $2r-l \leq 1$. This assumption states that the right-leaning moderate party's position is closer to the left-leaning moderate's party position than to the anti-communists. This is very plausible, since both possible medians are moderate parties.

Lemma 2: Any strategy y in $[0, 2r-1)$ of PC is weakly dominated by $y = 2r-1$.

Proof: Comparing the first and second columns in Table 7.1, notice that for any $y, y' \in TJ$ if $y < 2r-1 \leq y'$, then $2l-y > 2l-y'$. Also, if $y' < l$ & $2r-l < 1$, then $2r-y' < 1$.

Lemma 2 says that whatever the post-communists' ex-ante beliefs about the median, they never have an incentive to propose a bill closer to their bliss point than $2r-1$. This result is especially important for the closed rule system, for as the next lemma establishes, PC's choice of y under the open rule has no influence on the final outcome.

Lemma 3: If $q = 1$, PC's payoff does not depend on y.

Proof: By comparing in Table 7.1 the columns of the second and fourth rows that are relevant for the case of the open rules of procedure.

Lemma 3 together with lemmas 1 and 2 implies that under the open rule, the post-communists need not propose any transitional justice bill. Finally, a proposition establishes the post-communist's optimal strategy as a function of the rules of procedure and their beliefs about the future median's position. These variables are represented by the two parameters q and p, respectively.

After deleting the weakly dominated strategies, the expected utility function of the post-communists can be derived from Table 7.1, as follows:

$$EU_{PC}(y)$$
$$= - \begin{cases} pql + p(1-q)(2l-y) + (1-p)qr + (1-p)(1-q)(2r-y) & \text{for } y \in [2r-1, l) \\ pql + (1-p)qr + p(1-q)y + (1-p)(1-q)(2r-y) & \text{for } y \in [l, r) \\ pql + (1-p)qr + p(1-q)y + (1-p)(1-q)y & \text{for } y \in [r, 1) \end{cases}$$

and further simplified to

$$EU_{PC}(y) = - \begin{cases} y(1-q) - (1-q)(2lp + 2r(1-p)) - \Delta & \text{for } y \in [2r-1, l) \\ y(1-q)(1-2p) - 2r(1-p) - \Delta & \text{for } y \in [l, r) \\ y(q-1) - \Delta & \text{for } y \in [r, 1) \end{cases}$$

where $\Delta = pql + (1-p)qr$.

The Transitional Justice Bill Game

Table 7.2. *Equilibrium outcomes in the Transitional Justice Bill game defined for three types of post-communist beliefs.*

	Rules of procedure		Open rule: q = 1
	Closed rule: $q = 0$		Open rule: q = 1
PC's beliefs	$p \geq 1/2$	$p < 1/2$	$0 \geq p \geq 1$
Outcome if L is median	l	r	l
Outcome if R is median	$2r{-}l$	r	r

Note: Shaded cells illustrate what happens when the post-communist's ex-ante beliefs are realized. Transparent cells illustrate what happens in the case of post-communists' underestimation. An unsuccessful attempt to appease the median results in the anticommunists' persuading the actual median to adopt a bill to the right of its ideal point.

Proposition: If $p < \frac{1}{2}$ and $q=0$, *PC*'s optimal strategy is $y^* = r$; If $p > \frac{1}{2}$ and $q = 0$, PC's optimal strategy is $y^* = l$; if $p = \frac{1}{2}$ ($q = 1$), PC's optimal strategy is any $y \in [l, r] \subset ([0,1])$. The proofs are provided in Appendix E.

Under closed rules of procedure, if the post-communists believe that the leftist party has more than a 50 percent chance of winning the median, their optimal strategy is to adopt the leftist party's favorite bill. If they believe the rightist party has at least a 50 percent chance of winning the median, their optimal strategy is to adopt the rightist party's ideal point. Under open rules of procedure for parliamentary decision making, as has already been shown in Lemma 3, the post-communists' payoff is the same regardless of which transitional justice bill they adopt.

Table 7.2 combines the results from Lemmas 1 through 3 and the proposition to describe the equilibrium outcomes of the post-communist transitional justice bill game.

The shaded cells (top-left to bottom-right diagonal of the left part of the table) illustrate what happens when the post-communists' ex-ante beliefs are realized. The closed rule of procedure case leads to more interesting results than the open rule case. Under the closed rule, if the post-communists correctly estimate the position of the legislative median, the new legislature does not amend their bill. Neither is it amended if the post-communists overestimate the median. The first situation is illustrated by one of the case studies from Hungary in the following section. However, if the post-communists underestimate the median's position, the anticommunists will reap the benefits of the post-communists' mistake. The transparent cells illustrate what happens in the case of the post-communists' underestimation. An unsuccessful attempt to appease the median results in A's persuading the actual median to adopt a bill to the right of its ideal point. This last situation will be illustrated by the Polish case study described in the next section.

Before I proceed, it is useful to note the implications following the fact that the Transitional Justice Bill model is symmetric. Symmetric results hold when the roles of anticommunists and post-communists are reversed. That is, if the anticommunists are enjoying control over legislation prior to the elections but expect to lose the upcoming elections and proposal power to a government led by post-communists, they will have incentives to legislate transitional justice. Under a closed rule system, they will propose mild transitional justice legislation different from their ideal point; under the open rule system, they have no incentive to abandon their harsh transitional justice ideal point. This symmetric result is presented in the corollary that follows. The game is redefined so that the A and PC exchange strategy sets, that is, in period t_1, A chooses a transitional justice bill $y \in [0,1]$, and in period t_3, if $q = 0$ (under the closed rule), PC proposes an alternative transitional justice bill, $x \in [0,1]$.

Corollary: If $p < \frac{1}{2}$ and $q = 0$, A's optimal strategy is $y^* = r$. If $p > \frac{1}{2}$ and $q = 0$, A's optimal strategy is $y^* = l$, and if $p = \frac{1}{2}$ $(q = 1)$, A's optimal strategy is any $y \in [l, r]$ $c[0,1]$.

The first case study from Hungary presented in the following section serves as an empirical illustration of the preceding corollary.

7.3. Case Studies Explained by the Model

The theory presented in the preceding section can be supported by many instances in which transitional justice legislation was adopted in Central and Eastern Europe after the fall of communism. In particular, one may relate the timing of adopting transitional justice legislation to approaching elections. Table 1.1 presented the passage of the screening laws in parliaments of a few selected countries over the last fifteen years. The diagonal striped cells mark the periods when the post-communists were the governing party, whereas transparent cells mark periods of noncommunist rule, whether moderate or hard-line. Although conclusive inferences cannot be drawn by projecting the results of elections onto expectations about losing power, the data otherwise show remarkable conformity to the model's predictions. Virtually all new lustration laws that were adopted were introduced in the close proximity of elections. However, the hypothesis that political actors adopt lustration laws to eliminate political competition and stay in power receives moderate support. In fact, one observes that in a majority of cases in which lustration is passed, the party that adopted it loses subsequent elections. Even in cases where post-communists never win office, such as Czechoslovakia (before 1993), the Czech Republic (after 1993), Estonia, and Latvia, turnovers in power do occur, but only within parties created from scratch, after the transition.[7] These last three cases are consistent with the theory that incumbents introduced lustration effectively enough to safeguard against the post-communists' winning a significant number of seats.

One can further combine the data from Table 1.1 with the framework from Table 7.2, associating different outcomes of the Transitional Justice Bill game with different incumbent beliefs about the median's position (columns) and the actual realization of the elections (rows). Table 7.3 matches cases of legislating lustration in East Central Europe with the model's predictions.

The cases where incumbents correctly predicted the median's position are the diagonal, shaded cells. These are Hungary '96, Lithuania '01, and Bulgaria '01. The diagonal, transparent cells mark the incorrect predictions: the underestimation of the Polish post-communists and the overestimation of the Slovak (2002) and Bulgarian (1993) incumbents. Notice that the equilibrium outcomes are preserved in all but the underestimating case, as in Poland 1997–8.

For this reason, the Polish case is of particular significance to the argument presented in the previous section. The case in which post-communists adopt a bill prior to elections only to see it amended after the elections cannot be explained in plain English as "policy prevention." If the Polish post-communists were trying to prevent a harsh lustration bill by adopting a mild one to appease the median, clearly they did not succeed. Instead of

---

[7] For instance, in Czechoslovakia, and later in the Czech Republic, the turnovers have been occurring between the neoliberal Civic Democratic Party (ODS) and the Czech Social Democratic Party (ČSSD); and in Estonia between the Pro Patria Union, the Coalition Party, and the Estonian Center Party. In East Central Europe, most of the recent democratic elections bring turnovers in power. This can be attributed to the fact that governments in countries undergoing transitions often are forced to sponsor unpopular economic reforms, which causes them to lose electoral support. To the student of, for instance, American politics, this "incumbent disadvantage" may seem very puzzling.

Table 7.3. *Fitting the passage of lustration laws in East Central Europe to the model's predictions for different combinations of beliefs, electoral outcomes, and rules of procedure.*

	Rules of procedure		
	Closed ($q = 0$)		Open ($q = 1$)
PC's beliefs' realization	Leftist median ($p > 1/2$)	Rightist median $p < 1/2$	$0 \geq p \geq 1$
Leftist Median	Hungary '96	Bulgaria '93 Slovakia '02	Hungary '94 Poland '92
Rightist Median	Poland '98	Bulgaria '01 Lithuania '01	Czechoslovakia '91 Czechoslovakia '96 Czechoslovakia '01

attributing Polish post-communists' failure to preempt a lustration bill to their irrational behavior, I use the Polish case to illustrate why it is so important to use a game theoretic model of incomplete information. Without this framework, one would not be capable of explaining lustration before and after the elections in Poland. The remainder of this chapter presents two trajectories of adopting transitional justice: (1) a correct prediction by post-communists in Hungary and (2) the underestimated case of Poland.

7.3.1. Hungary

The first Hungarian case concerns the adoption of lustration laws by Hungarian anticommunists under open rules procedure. This illustration pertains to the corollary model mentioned in section 7.2.2.2. The law was eventually struck down by the Constitutional Court. The second case, mentioned in the introduction to this chapter, describes the post-communists' adoption of a screening law and the opening of secret files. Both can serve as illustrations of the model's predictions in situations where the ex-ante expectations as to the position of the median are confirmed by the actual events. The identities of the political actors are as follows:

- MSzP (Hungarian Socialist Party): post-communists (PC)
- SzDSz (Alliance of Free Democrats), FKgP (Smallholders): moderate left-leaning party (L)
- KDNP (Christian Democrats), FiDeSZ (Federation of Young Democrats): moderate right-leaning party (R)

- MIEP (Justice and Life, after 1994), Fidesz-MPP (Fidesz-Hungarian Civic Party)[8]: anticommunists (A)

7.3.1.1. Before the 1994 Election After the first free elections, in 1990, a government ruling coalition was created of three parties originating in the former democratic opposition: MDF, KDNP, and the Smallholders. Despite the constitutionally strong position of the government, its influence on final versions of legislation was rather miniscule. The committee system was also underdeveloped. The rules of procedure for this first democratically elected parliament, although vague and unclear, seem to point toward the open rule. Atilla Ágh and Sandor Kurtan (1995) found that "the government dominated in drafting proposals, but shifted the whole job of bill preparation from the ministries to parliament, almost achieving the model of a governing parliament. A high percentage of amendments and interpolations came from ruling parties' MPs – a phenomenon totally unknown in West European parliaments." Thus, in terms of the TJB model, presented in the previous section, the Hungarian political system in the years 1990 to 1994 can be characterized by the parameter value $q = 1$. As early as 1990, deputies from the SzDSz submitted a draft screening law aimed at the informers of the III/3 section of the communist Ministry of Interior – the secret police. The parliament never got to vote on the draft. Subsequent amendments were proposed and debated, but no consensus was arrived at between members of the ruling coalition. In the meantime, rumors circulated that former III/3 agents were still present in several parties, including the governing party (Barrett, Hack, and Munkàcsy 2007). Between 1991 and 1993, on numerous occasions, some information from the secret files would leak to the press, discrediting some politician and creating an accompanying scandal. Finally, early in 1994, only a few months before the elections, lustration legislation returned to the parliamentary agenda.

In the spring of 1994, each of the three ruling parties had less than 10 percent of voter support. It was dubious that as a coalition they would win

---

[8] Recall from Chapter 6 that Fidesz was originally called FiDeSz (Fiatal Demokraták Szövetsége [Alliance of Young Democrats]), the youth organization of the Free Democratic Party. In 1998, the organization changed the capitalization of the name and used instead just the Latin meaning of *fides* (fidelity). Fidesz-MPP represented Magyar Polgári Párt (the Hungarian Civic Party). In the year 2002, the organization changed its name once more to Fidesz-MPSZ (Fidesz–Hungarian Civic Alliance). Fidesz abandoned the Young Democrats version to distinguish itself from the SzDSz, as they moved ideologically to the right, eventually purging liberal values from their program in favor of nationalistic and traditional ones.

enough seats to form a cabinet in the approaching elections. Nevertheless, they proposed and passed a law that arguably was very close to their ideal lustration policy. Act No. 23, "on the Control of Persons Filling Certain Important Posts," was designed to hurt the governing coalition. The minimal criterion for collaboration was providing signed declarations or receiving money for written reports to the secret police agency. The definition of collaboration extended also to the semimilitary armed corps established after 1956, something that the Socialist prime minister, Gyula Horn, who served in that corps, complained about considerably (Mora 1994). Another way of ensuring that lustration extended to former communist officials was to make receiving reports of the secret police prior to 1989 a lustrable offense.[9] Screening was entrusted to panels of three justices, who were to review the documents made available to them by the National Security Commission of the parliament. Their proceedings were closed to the public and no one besides the targeted person could be present. The panel's report qualified as state secrets. Any person found guilty would be asked in a private letter to resign within thirty days. Upon his or her refusal, the committee would publish its findings. The decision could be appealed in a court meeting in a closed session. If the targeted person resigned of his or her own will, the process would conclude without revealing the reason behind the resignation.

This harsh bill agrees with the model's predictions stated in the corollary. Under the open rule ($q = 1$), the payoff to the proposers is not dependent on their initial proposal y. Thus, the Hungarian ruling coalition had no reason to refrain from adopting their transitional justice bill, even if this was pretty stringent.

7.3.1.2. Before the 1998 Election

The parties constituting the ruling coalition – MDF, KDNP, and the Smallholders – lost the May 1994 elections to the post-communists. MSzP won in 149 out of 176 constituencies. The composition of the Hungarian parliament before and after the 1998 elections is presented in Figure 7.6.

In a mixed proportional representation (PR) and first past the post (FPP) electoral system, 33 percent of the vote secured them 54 percent of

---

[9] In terms of the scope, current positions covered not only MPs, the president, and cabinet ministers, but also judges and state attorneys, department heads in ministries, mayors, the president and vice presidents of the National Bank, state secretaries, ambassadors, army chiefs, police department captains, and even leading state media officials, deans of universities and colleges, editors of the largest newspapers, and managers of state-owned companies.

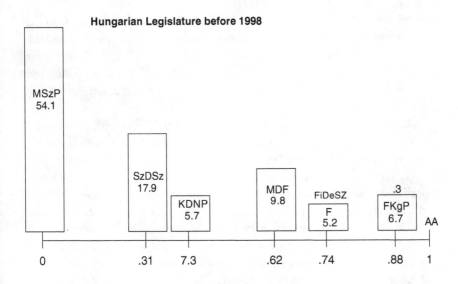

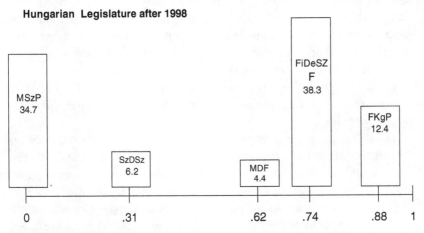

Figure 7.6. Hungary: composition of the legislature before and after the 1998 elections (in percentages of seatshare).

the seats.[10] Predictions drawn from Table 7.2 suggest that after the elections, the screening law should have been amended by the post-

---

[10] The disproportionality between voter support and seat share also favored the largest party at the expense of the runner-up. This pathological characteristic of the electoral law came to haunt the post-communists in 1998, when even though they gained votes, they lost over 20 percent of the seat share.

communists. Not only did they hold proposal power, but they also won the median in the legislature. It turned out, however, that before they had the opportunity to do so, the Constitutional Court struck the bill down for violating the principles of equality before the law (Halmai and Scheppele 1997). This reversed the status quo to 0 on the transitional justice bill space.

Meanwhile, with the increasing professionalization of parliament, legislators began to acquire political expertise. According to Ágh (1999), this was reflected in the "growing activity of legislative committees." According to his data, 68 percent of resolutions passed by the second parliament were initiated by the government and 24 percent by committees (1999). Bartlet (1996) describes the institutional design of the Hungarian government as a democratic polity distinguished by an unusually high concentration of power in the office of the prime minister, whose strong position is enforced by a constructive vote of confidence (Huber 1996). Among the consequences of this design are high stability, low government turnover, and strong party discipline, with low accountability to the legislative floor (Ágh 1999). The emergence of proposal power located outside of the floor of the legislature indicates that the rules of procedure in the new parliament evolved toward a closed rule system. Thus, in terms of the model presented in the previous section, the Hungarian legislative process evolved in the years 1994 to 1998 toward restricted decision-making procedures characterized by the parameter value $q = 0$.

By 1996, the popularity of MSzP had decreased to around 20 to 25 percent, which was significant compared to 1994, and occasionally the party would be overtaken by the MIEP, with FiDeSz coming in close behind. The more general trend is reflected in public opinion data collected on popular support for political parties in Hungary between 1995 and 1998 by Szonda Ipsos. FiDeSz's lead was solidified with the break out of a privatization scandal involving the post-communist government (the "Tocsik Affair") toward the end of 1996. The support of the Fidesz-MPP increased to 26 percent.[11] Under these circumstances, the model predicts

---

[11] The *Financial Times* reported in December that, "The Socialists...have lost ground since winning one third of votes and 54 per cent of parliament in the last general election.... Opposition parties, however, especially Fidesz, a former liberal youth movement that has now positioned itself on the centre-right, have been boosted this autumn by the 'Tocsik affair,' a highly-damaging scandal over illegal payments to a consultant by APV, the state privatization agency" (Marsh 1996).

that the post-communists would adopt a transitional justice bill different from their ideal point, equal to where they expect the new median to be. According to public opinion polls released in daily papers at that time, this position would go most likely to SzDSz or the Smallholders (Marsh 1996). The proposition from section 7.2.2.2 states that when the left-leaning moderate party is more likely to become median than the right-leaning moderate party, the post-communists' optimal strategy was $y = l$. Indeed, in July of that year, a new lustration law (Act 57/1996) was passed and approved, although not without controversy. Most former liberal respondents argued that it did not go far enough to make public administration free from those who had a tainted past. The proposal, however, did gain approval of the moderate parties in parliament (Halmai and Scheppele 1997). Relative to the 1994 proposal, the number of officials to be screened was reduced from ten to twelve thousand to only about six hundred. Only those public officials who had to take an oath before the parliament or the president would be screened. The scope of collaboration was also narrowed. Signing a declaration indicating willingness to spy was no longer sufficient. Having collected a salary from the III/3 agency for the performed work was a necessary form of evidence. Other secret service agencies were excluded. Little time was given for screening officials – the process was to conclude by July 1997. The law also established the Historical Office for housing the secret archives of the political police, which beginning in September 1997 was to make its archives accessible to the public. Victims had their access to files severely restricted, however. They could read only files about themselves and the names of informers were blacked out. Victims of the secret informer network complained that the files were incomplete and manipulated.[12]

Even though in 1997 the MSzP began regaining popularity while the MIEP started drastically losing public support (see Figure 7.7), Fidesz won the 1998 election and formed a cabinet led by Viktor Orban, a

---

[12] One journalist and former dissident wrote, "In 1990, when the single-party system was in its last throes before the country's first democratic elections in 40 years, state employees received whispered calls from friendly bosses to rewrite their curriculum vitae and omit the fact that they had been members of the state party. At the same time, a vast part of the secret service files mysteriously disappeared, with state party officials saying the files had been destroyed. But people who knew they were watched and followed by the communist secret police claimed that so much material could not have been burnt. Some went so far as to go to paper mills to try to trace the fate of the documents from the amount of recycled trash paper" (Szamado 1997).

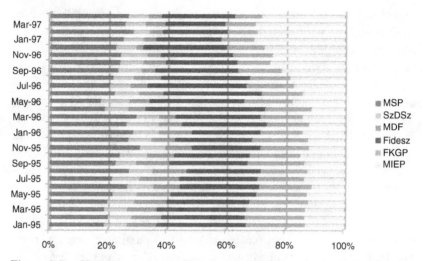

Figure 7.7. Hungary: anticipated median in legislative elections according to opinion polls taken from 1995 through 1997.
Source: Szonda 2006.
Note: The figure summarizes results of opinion poll surveys held between January 1995 and May 1997 (the elections took place in May 1998). It illustrates that the identity of the median varied from MDF to FiDeSZ. In April 1997, at the time that the screening law was adopted, the post-communists could expect FiDeSz to be the median, but were probably not aware of how far FiDeSz would move to the right in its preferences for stringent lustration.
Source: Rose and Munro 2006.

staunch anticommunist. SzDSz occupied the median position and the very weak screening law and secret files' law remained in force. This also matches the TJB's predictions from Lemma 1 and Table 7.2. The post-communists' beliefs about the median's position were realized. Their optimal strategy of adopting a screening law at the estimated median's position prevented them from suffering a harsher transitional justice bill, after the anticommunists took over power. Post-communists in other countries did not guess the median position so well, however. In the next section, a study from Poland illustrates a case where the post-communists were unsuccessful in predicting the median position.

7.3.2. Poland

Poland's is the more troubling case to explain, because both the post-communist screening law and the proposal for opening the secret police archives were amended later by the anticommunist hard-liners. The post-communist initiative, even though it seems irrational ex-post, was ex-ante rational, in light of the results from section 7.2.2. The identities of the players can be assigned as follows:

- SLD (Democratic Left Alliance): post-communists (PC)
- PSL (Polish People's Party), UP (Labor Union): moderate left-leaning party (L)
- UW (Freedom Union): moderate right-leaning party (R)
- AWS (Solidarity Election Action) and ROP (Movement for the Reconstruction of Poland): anticommunists (A)

7.3.2.1. Before the 1997 Election

The rules of procedure in the Polish parliament are closed. Proposals originate in standing committees. The most influential figure in the committees is its chair. As a rule, chairs are members of the senior party in the cabinet coalition (Olson and Crowther 2002; Olson and Norton 1996). Thus, although the composition of standing committees is proportional to the number of seats won in the elections, proposal power goes to the winners. This political system is represented in the model by the parameter value $q = 0$. Prior to September 1997, the post-communists had vast control over the legislative process: They were the major party in a cabinet coalition whose minor party was the median voter in parliament. The president was a post-communist and SLD alone had enough influence to uphold his veto. However, this power resulted to a large extent from the fragmentation of post-Solidarity parties rather than voter support (Kaminski, Lissowski, and Swistak 1998). By the end of 1996, the post-Solidarity right had finally united from a number of fragmented parties into a major coalition called AWS, thus adjusting to the 1993 electoral law favoring larger parties.[13] AWS instantly gained popular support and was expected to form a cabinet coalition with the nearest moderate party (or parties) sufficient to gain majoritarian support in the legislature. Being a major party in that coalition, AWS was expected to hold proposal power. Thus it became clear, many months before the elections, that SLD would lose power to AWS.

The fact that the AWS would form a cabinet could be predicted much earlier and easier than who the median voter in parliament would be.

---

[13] As a result of the 1993 electoral law reform, three important parameters were changed: Saint Lague divisors and Hare quotas as seat apportionment methods were substituted with a d'Hondt divisor method. Nationwide thresholds were introduced and the average district magnitude decreased from 10.6 seats to 7.3 (Kaminski, Lissowski, and Swistak 1998).

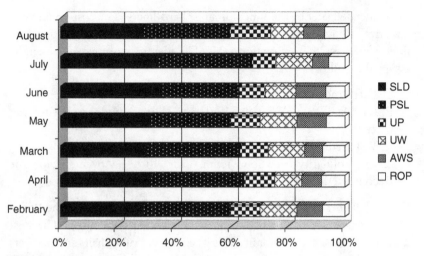

Figure 7.8. Poland: anticipated median in legislative elections according to 1997 opinion polls.
Source: OBOP 1997.
Note: The figure summarizes results of opinion poll surveys held between February 1997 to the elections that took place in September 1997. It illustrates that the identity of the median varied from PSL to UW. In April 1997, at the time that the screening law was adopted, the post-communists had March 1997 data at their disposal. They could expect the PSL to be median – its support was close to the 50 percent line and was increasing. In addition, surveys had a reputation of being biased to the disadvantage of post-communist parties.

Figure 7.8 summarizes the results of opinion poll surveys held between February 1997 and the time when the elections took place, in September 1997. It illustrates that the identity of the median varied from PSL to UW.

In April of 1997 – at the time the lustration law was adopted – the post-communists had March 1997 data at their disposal. They could expect the PSL to be median; its support was close to the 50 percent line and rising. Declaring support for the ancien régime's successor party was still embarrassing for many respondents, who would rather declare support for the post-Solidarity UP or UW. Given this bias, post-communist parties could count on even greater support on election day than indicated by the polls.

The proposition from section 7.2.2.2 indicates that if the left-leaning moderate party is more likely to become the median than the right-leaning party, the post-communists' optimal strategy is $y = l$. Indeed, it can plausibly be maintained that both the April 1997 lustration law and the presidential declassification proposal were close to PSL's ideal point. According to the

1997 presidential proposal, the Secret Files Archive was to be merely a storage place for secret files. Victims were not to be able to conduct further inquiries or to initiate investigations against those who had spied on them. The president would also nominate a third of the Archive's authorities. Bogdan Pek, a member of PSL who chaired the special committee for dealing with screening issues on a number of occasions, advocated the 1997 screening bill as a fair and safe way of dealing with the past (Pek 1998). The presidential secret files initiative aroused similar reactions in the PSL.

On the other hand, UW politicians publicly admitted dissatisfaction with the transitional justice legislation state of affairs as of 1997 (Litynski 1998). Poland had long been delaying the implementation of a lustration law act, and many of the post-Solidarity leaders felt threatened by the possibility of political blackmail with forged or incomplete files if a law regulating the use of secret files was not implemented (Bachman 1996).

7.3.2.2. After the 1997 Election

The parliamentary elections of September 1997 were in fact won by the AWS, which formed a cabinet with the moderate right-leaning UW. Although the post-communist expectations about maintaining the PSL median seemed reasonable in April of 1997, in July 1997 – only two months before the elections – an unexpected natural cataclysm hit: the largest flood of the century occurred in Poland. The SLD/PSL government's reputation was damaged as a result of various shortcomings of handling the emergency situation, supplying aid, and managing reconstruction. Figure 7.9 portrays the sudden drop in support for the governing coalition over the summer of 1997. SLD and PSL were not able to make up for that loss before September.

As a result of the elections, UP did not manage to cross the national threshold for entering the parliament and the median appeared to be UW. Figure 7.9 illustrates the exact distribution of seats across parties in the new parliament.

After the elections, the chair of the Secret Files Committee became, as expected, a member of the AWS. The model predicts (see Table 7.2) that his best response to the post-communists' $y = 1$ was $x = 2r - 1$. Indeed, although initially accepted by the parliamentary committee as a working project, the Presidential Secret Files proposal was dismissed immediately after the 1997 elections in favor of an AWS (governmental) project establishing a National Remembrance Institute. This institution, apart from taking care of the files, would also conduct research and assume the role of an investigative body. The proposal lifted statutes of limitation for

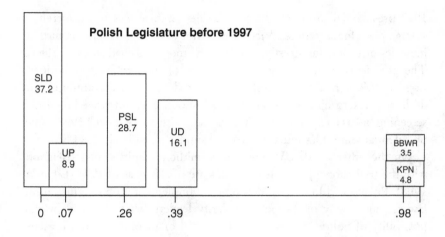

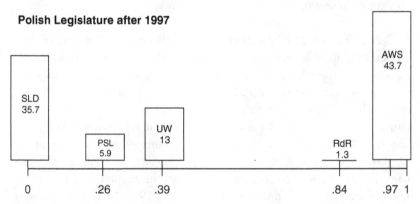

Figure 7.9. Poland: composition of the legislature before and after the 1997 elections.
Source: Rose and Munro 2006.

"communist crimes" committed between 1944 and 1990. The new limitation period established for those crimes would start running in 1990 and last for twenty years (Prezes 1998, art 4). Victims could supply further information to the archives and could also initiate additional investigations. They could also learn the names of their perpetrators. The Institute would have multiple locations throughout Poland and would operate electronic data, making access to the files much easier than the Citizens' Archive. Candidates for public office, before filing their screening declarations, were prevented from accessing the Archives to find out what information had been stored in their files: Anyone wishing to access her files would have to declare whether she was a victim, secret informer, or professional agent. Finally, the choice of authorities leading the institute would be entirely controlled by the legislature. The president could not nominate any persons in charge. In the end, the AWS bill was adopted by the Secret Files Parliamentary Committee as a working project. The parliament, after overturning a presidential veto, voted it into law.

UW's best response was to accept the new proposal (x), rejecting the post-communist reversion bill (y). As a result, the final outcome was a new lustration bill that was very close to the anticommunists' ideal point. The 1997 post-communist lustration bill was amended in a similar process. Immediately after the post-communists lost the elections, the president proposed a lustration amendment to the Sejm. His amendment was tougher on collaborators than the original bill. This motion could be interpreted as the president's attempt to appease the new, unexpected median. Since leaders of the AWS were deeply dissatisfied with the 1997 bill, the president's proposal invited a slew of amendments and proposals from both houses of parliament.[14] A new subcommittee in the Committee of Internal Affairs was appointed to handle them. It was headed by an AWS member and quickly submitted its own proposal incorporating most of the amendments making lustration more stringent. Instead of a lustration court, whose twenty-one volunteer judges were difficult to appoint, the law created an institution of a state prosecutor to be chosen by the Supreme Court to verify the statements on the basis of materials from the secret files. If the statements were inconsistent with the prosecutor's findings, the politician could be accused of a lustration lie and tried before the Appellate Court. Those accused were no longer granted two instances of appeal. Additionally, the files of agents working for the post-transitional secret service and military intelligence were admitted to the lustration procedures. One SLD MP said that the hard-line amendment had changed 70 percent of the statute (Dziewulski 1998). Another MP complained, "this is a record! Out of 43 articles in the lustration bill, the senate (hard-line) proposal recommends to change 31!" (Zemke 1998). Politicians from both sides of the aisle agreed that for all practical purposes this was like a new

---

[14] In an interview with the author, Antoni Macierewicz , a staunch supporter of harsh lustration, said: "That [1997] bill was rather an anti-lustration bill. Its aim was to mislead the public by calling it a lustration bill. It wasn't until the amendment that it finally got its teeth. Today's shape of the bill is completely different, which is why only formally one should refer to it as an amendment. For all practical purposes, it is an entirely new bill" (interviews 2004: PA8).

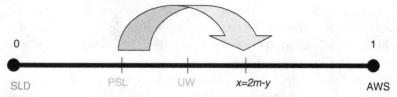

Figure 7.10. The Polish post-communists' mistake.
Note: SLD believed PSL would become the median and adopted a TJ bill at
PSL's ideal point, *y*. After the election, which gave the median to UW, AWS
could exploit the distance between UW's ideal point and the TJ policy adopted
by SLD, *y*, by proposing a bill *x = 2m−y*.

bill (interviews 2004: PA8). The bill adopted by the post-Solidarity coalition in 1998 was considerably more stringent than its predecessor,
adopted by the post-communists in the last year they were in power.

The Polish case fits the model's predictions: Although post-communists
were pursuing their optimal strategy, $y^* = l$, given their beliefs regarding
the anticipated position of the post-electoral median, the more stringent
bills, $x = 2r-l$, were adopted. The post-communist ex-ante mistake is
illustrated in Figure 7.10.

The post-communists believed that the median would be the PSL, with
an ideal point at l, and their best response to that belief was to propose l.
However, due to an exogenous shock (the flood), the median turned out to
be UW, with an ideal point at r. As a result, the anticommunists, who took
over proposal power, could exploit the distance between l and r to their
advantage and propose a bill at $2r-l$. Although the screening and secret files
laws were amended by the AWS-UW coalition, this does not mean that the
post-communists were playing a suboptimal strategy. They chose an optimal strategy given their beliefs. The anticommunist proposer had more
information available to him at the time he was making a decision. Given
their beliefs, the post-communists' strategy was ex-ante rational, that is,
the expected payoff was higher than the payoff corresponding to "doing
nothing." In light of what actually happened, it was a mistake ex-post.

Before concluding this chapter, I devote a few paragraphs to explaining
the remaining cases of delayed lustration – in Slovakia and the Baltic states.

7.4. Slovakia: Agenda Setting with an Atypical Status Quo

Looking at Table 1.1, it is striking to see that Slovakia was the very last
country to adopt TJ, but interpreted in a direct way, neither the skeletons

model presented in Part I nor the Transitional Justice Bill game outlined in this chapter explain why.[15] Slovakia's is not a typical East Central European transition. On top of democratization, Slovakia experienced the breakup of the federal Czechoslovak state and, consequentially, instead of the transitional justice status quo of 0, it inherited the Czechoslovak lustration law that was passed just two years prior to the "velvet divorce." Following the "divorce" that took place on January 1, 1993, all federal legislation was by default to be valid in each of the two successor states unless overruled by their respective parliaments. However, despite the partition statutes, the federal lustration was not implemented in Slovakia at all.[16] Given that formally the law remained on the books in both republics, one would expect the same form and extent of transitional justice to be implemented in both the Czech Republic and Slovakia, but just the opposite happened. The Czech Republic not only fully implemented lustration, but went above and beyond the federal lustration law, which was to be valid until 1996. The Czech parliament passed amendments that continued lustrations past this date and created a large and efficient implementing agency at the Czech Interior Ministry. Slovakia did not even start to implement the federal law.

Following the Czecho-Slovak breakup, the Slovak Republic inherited the lustration agency for implementing the law. It was up to the Slovak executive to propose legislation that would charter an office responsible for issuing lustration certificates. No such agency was appointed.

For almost six years following the velvet divorce, power was in the hands of Vladimír Mečiar, a former communist. His party, the HZDS (Movement for a Democratic Slovakia), was to a large extent made up of former communists. Scholars of democratic transition and consolidation have argued that the presence of former autocrats in positions of power following the transition presented an obstacle to the country's engagement in transitional justice (Elster 1998; Huyse 1995; O'Donnell and Schmitter 1986). However, the cases of Poland and Hungary, presented earlier in this chapter, show clearly that the fact that successor communist parties controlled the legislative process in Slovakia in 1992 to 1998 is alone insufficient to account for this country's lack of lustration. Indeed, prior to 1994, Mečiar's cabinet

---

[15] This subsection relies heavily on Kunicova and Nalepa 2006.

[16] The Federal Law No. 451/1991, dated October 4, 1991, commonly known as the "Lustration Law" designed to govern the lustration procedures in Czechoslovakia, was passed in the Federal Assembly in 1991 and is described in detail in Appendix F, along with similar legislation from Poland and Hungary.

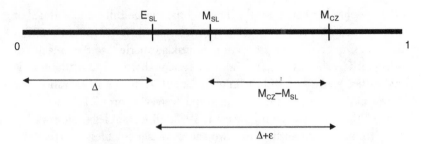

Figure 7.11. Slovakia's transitional justice issue space with relevant actors' ideal points.
Note: 0 represents "no transitional justice"; E_{SL} represents the transitional justice ideal point of the Slovak executive; M_{SL} represents the transitional justice ideal point of the Slovak median; M_{CZ} represents the transitional justice ideal point of the federal (Czechoslovak) median identical with the federal bill; 1 represents the "harshest possible" transitional justice bill; $\varepsilon > 0$ and preferences of all actors are Euclidean.

worked on empowering the Slovak Information Agency (SIS) to deal with the secret police files. These efforts came to a standstill when it turned out that the SIS would have to implement the federal law, which was too stringent for HZDS's liking. Mečiar also tried to remove the federal lustration law by petitioning the Constitutional Court about its inconsistency with the Charter of Rights and Freedoms, but the Slovak court refused even to consider the petition. The explanation the court gave for this decision was that the federal court had already deliberated the exact same question and reached the conclusion that the law was consistent with the charter (CTK). Thus, the Slovaks were not politically in a position to abolish the federal lustration law after the breakup. It was, however, up to them to create a lustration agency. If such an agency was created, it would implement the federal law adopted in Czechoslovakia. In the absence of such an agency, however, no law could be enforced.

In this section, I explain how Slovakia's delay in implementing lustration can be attributed to its inheritance of an atypical status quo from the federal Czecho-Slovak state. Instead of beginning the legislative process with a situation of "no transitional justice," as all other post-communist countries did, Slovakia started with the very harsh bill. This situation is illustrated in Figure 7.11.

We assume as before that all possible transitional justice bills are ordered on a single-dimensional issue space, from 0 (no transitional justice) to 1 (most stringent transitional justice). Let M_{SL} and M_{CZ} represent the ideal transitional justice policies of the median legislator in the Slovak parliament and the Czechoslovak Federal Assembly, respectively. Let E_{SL} represent the ideal policy of the Slovak executive. In the Slovak parliament, Mečiar and HZDS's positions on transitional justice were to the left of the executive and legislative median in the Federal Assembly. The institutional constraints were as follows. The bill passed by the Federal Assembly in 1991 would become operational if a law appointing a lustration agency had been proposed by the Slovak executive and voted in by the Slovak legislature. In the absence of a lustration agency, the situation of "no transitional justice" would prevail. There is an important difference between the *adoption status quo* and *implementation status quo*: While the status quo in terms of adopted legislation in Slovakia was close to 1, the implementation status quo remained at 0 until 2002. The model presented here explains why this was the case. Henceforth, when I refer to the "status quo," I mean the law on the books, not the actual implemented outcome.

Repealing the lustration law was an arduous task. Note the interesting asymmetry: It would have been much easier to make the lustration law harsher, if the actors so desired, but very difficult to amend it "down" or repeal it altogether. Softening lustration laws is difficult, because politicians arguing that a lustration law should be abolished come under suspicion of being collaborators themselves. The literature describes debates following lustration proposals in the early 1990s in post-communist countries where such proposals, unlike in Slovakia, were discussed in parliament. In Czechoslovakia, Poland, and Hungary, all amendments proposed to a lustration bill submitted for debate were in one direction only – toward making the law more stringent, either by adding new categories of collaboration to be targeted, by adding new positions to be screened, or by introducing harsher sanctions for proven collaborators. In Hungary, the bill submitted to the floor by the government coalition became so harsh as a result of successive amendments that in the end it was repealed by the Constitutional Court. In East Germany, the federal bill on dealing with secret police files *(Stasi – Unterlagen-Gesetz)* of December 1991 left it up to individual *Länder* to determine how the files were to be used. Although the Unification Treaty stipulated that "evidence of secret police activity could constitute an important ground for disqualification," virtually all Eastern *Länder* interpreted this legislation as an effective lustration bill (McAdams 1997). Transcripts from 1992 parliamentary debates in Poland indicate that only two MPs resisted the lustration resolution.[17] Transcripts from the 1992

---

[17] Sprawozdanie z Obrad Sejmu, 28 Maja, 1992, Pos 16 Kad I.

debates in Czechoslovakia indicate that only members of the Communist Party protested against the law.[18]

Thus, the federal law, identical with the federal legislative median's ideal point, set the agenda.[19] Until 1996, when the federal bill was set to expire, there was a very limited set of viable lustration alternatives for Slovakia: the harsh federal bill (M_{CZ}), an even harsher bill from the interval (M_{CZ},1], or no transitional justice at all (0).

Although the 1991 Federal Assembly was the agenda setter, the Slovak executive (E_{SL}) had gate-keeping powers: It was up to this executive to determine whether a lustration agency would ever be proposed. Provided that the Slovak executive preferred the policy of "no transitional justice" to the federal median's ideal point ($\varepsilon > 0$ in Figure 7.11), the Slovak executive would keep the gates closed. As long as the Slovak median shared the preferences of the executive, opening the gates would not result in legislation implementing the federal law. However, if the Slovak median preferred the federal bill to no transitional justice (if $M_{CZ} - M_{SL} \leq M_{SL}$ in Figure 7.11), the Slovak executive could still avoid transitional justice by "keeping the gates closed."

The two theoretical insights of the model are as follows:

- Keeping the gates closed, resulting in the outcome of "no transitional justice" (0), is consistent with the Slovak executive preferring the Slovak median's ideal lustration bill (M_{SL}) to "no transitional justice" (0).
- Not implementing transitional justice is consistent with having a legislative median that would rather take a harsh federal lustration bill than deal with no bill implemented at all.

The obstacle to implementation was that the Slovak median's ideal policy (M_{SL}) was not a feasible choice. Also notice that if the Slovak executive could freely propose any legislation to the Slovak median, he could even propose his ideal policy, E_{SL}, which would be accepted by the Slovak median. What explains the lustration impasse is the non-zero status quo inherited from Slovakia's federal predecessor, the harsh federal lustration law.

---

[18] Transcript of Federal Assembly of ČSFR, 1991, 17th session.

[19] The federal bill is assumed to be identical with the federal median in the legislature, because evidence from literature as well as elite interviews indicate that the final version of the 1991 Lustration Law was to a large extent determined by amendments from the floor. See David (2003). Bills adopted in this way exemplify open rules of procedure in parliamentary decision making. See Gilligan and Krehbiel (1986).

Our theoretical model of Slovak legislative politics finds empirical support in data from Slovakia. Figure 7.12 illustrates Slovakia's legislative parties' relative seat shares as well as their positions on a pro- to anticommunist dimension, which can serve as an approximation of the transitional justice issue space. These positions were estimated on the basis of answers to questions asking experts about political parties' positions with respect to former communists' access to public office in the Party Policy in Modern Democracies (PPMD) survey (Benoit and Laver 2007). PPMD answers were measured on a 1-to-20 scale. I have normalized the scores to [0,1] by forcing the most lenient position to 0 and the harshest position to 1.

The median in both terms was Mečiar's HZDS with a position of .32, which is to the right of at least one other major legislative party (SDĽ). Using the PPMD data, one can see that during this time, both the median in the Slovak legislature and the Slovak executive preferred some form of lustration to a situation of "no transitional justice," but the preferences of both were far from the federal bill. Note that this model predicts the strategy of keeping the gates closed on lustration, irrespective of how close the Slovak median is to the federal bill. Therefore, even if one is unclear about how cohesive HZDS was under Mečiar, the prediction still holds.

Indeed, the PPMD data suggest considerable variance in attitudes to dealing with former communists among members of the HZDS.[20] It is controversial, however, whether these differences had the potential to translate into voting behavior. Petr Kopecký, in his work on Czech and Slovak republics, noted that in open-ended questions about "the most important tasks of an MP," 41 percent of parliamentarians in Slovakia indicated loyalty to one's party ("to fulfill the party's program") as the most important task (Kopecký 2001, 68–9). Irrespective of how one resolves the issue of HZDS cohesiveness, for the model to work, it is not necessary that the median be located *precisely* at .32 of the normalized transitional justice scale.[21]

---

[20] The standard error for HZDS's answers, at 3.7, is larger than for any of the remaining parties, save for SDĽ.

[21] In fact, one can even use one of the findings from the theory presented here as a test of the HZDS's cohesiveness. In the model, as long as the distance between the Slovak median (M_{SL}) and "no transitional justice" (0) is smaller than the distance between M_{SL} and the federal law (M_{CZ}), the median will not implement transitional justice legislation even when the gates are open. Indeed, prior to 1994, Mečiar's cabinet worked on empowering the Slovak Information Agency (SIS) to deal with the secret police files, but these efforts came to a standstill when it turned out that the SIS would have to implement the federal law.

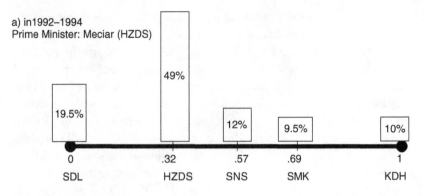

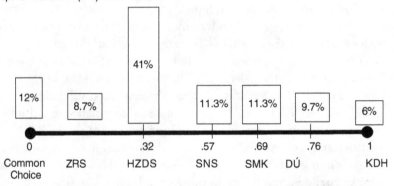

Figure 7.12. Positions of legislative parties in Slovakia and distribution of seats (%) in two Slovak parliaments: ordering from anti- to pro-lustration.
Note: Party positions were approximated with 2002 post-election data and were rescaled to place the leftmost and rightmost parties at 0 and 1, respectively. Common Choice was a coalition created prior to the 1994 elections comprising of SDĽ and minor leftist parties – its position is approximated with SDĽ's 2002 position. DÚ (Democratic Union) merged in 2000 with KDH to create the SDKÚ (Slovak Democratic and Christian Union) – its position is approximated by SDKÚ's 2002 position. ZRS (Revolutionary Socialist League) entered the parliament only in the 1994–8 term. Its exact position on how to deal with former communists could not be estimated, but it is plausible to assume that it was somewhere between that of SDĽ and Common Choice.

In 1994, Mečiar's cabinet lost a vote of confidence after a series of defections from HZDS, and until the early September 1994 elections it was temporarily replaced by a cabinet of Jozef Moravčík, leader of the Democratic Union (DÚ) of Slovakia, a party far right of HZDS.

Moravcik's government tried to implement the federal lustration bill, and Interior Minister Ladislav Pittner even attempted to prepare lustration certificates (Reuters, 1994). However, HZDS's electoral success brought Mečiar back into power in October 1994. He stalled the process and assumed the post of prime minister until the elections in 1998.

Lustration resurfaced again after the 1998 elections, when the coalition of four parties, headed by Mikuláš Dzurinda, formed a new cabinet. Although Prime Minister Dzurinda was a lustration skeptic, the coalition's appointment to the post of the minister of justice, Ján Čarnogurský, a member of the Slovak Democratic Coalition (SDK) and Mečiar's staunch opponent, brought lustration back to the political agenda. At this point, the federal law had expired, and the executive was free to propose any transitional justice law. However, Čarnogurský needed the support of all coalition partners to floor a lustration proposal, while two of the coalition partners – Slovak Party of the Democratic Left (SDĽ) and Slovak Party of Civic Understanding (SOP) – were categorically opposed to any form of dealing with the past, including opening files of the former secret police or lustration. Čarnogurský became isolated in his pursuit of dealing harshly with former collaborators, because preserving the coalition was a priority. When his proposal failed to gain approval of the coalition, he did not give up completely, although his hopes of establishing a full-fledged lustration agency faded. By an executive order, he created the Department for Documentation of the Crimes of Communism (ODKZ) within the Justice Ministry. With only two employees – including Marián Gula, former head of the Czech office for documenting communist crimes – the department collected documents and, in cases of suspected crimes that were not covered by the statute of limitations, launched complaints with the prosecutor's office. The special department was by no means equipped to carry out lustration. In 2000, Prime Minister Dzurinda told news reporters that "Slovakia [had] overcome the problem of lustration" (CTK, September 29, 2000). He could hardly have been more mistaken. In August 2002, Slovakia passed the Law on National Memory that created the Institute for National Memory (ÚPN), an institution resembling the Polish Institute for National Remembrance. One can attribute the ease with which lustration got passed to the fact that the electoral term was drawing to an end. This significantly reduced the costs of SDK's forcing a pro-lustration policy past its coalition partners. Since the coalition's tenure was drawing to an end anyway (neither SDĽ nor SOP stood much chance of winning in the upcoming elections), the threat that the coalition with SDĽ and SOP would break down as a result of a lustration proposal authorized by the cabinet was not important anymore. The Law on National Memory[22] was passed in 2002 at the last session of the parliament before the elections. This law chartered an agency responsible for collecting and publishing information on collaborators with the secret police. While the scope of such lustrations was not limited to a particular type of public servant and applied to virtually everybody, the law did not stipulate any legal sanctions against the implicated persons nor did it bar them from running for or remaining in public office.

Thus, in contrast to the Czech Republic, Slovakia refrained from transitional justice for over a dozen years. The timing of Slovakia's transitional justice regime presents a counterargument to popular theories in the transitional justice literature – namely, that procedures revealing the truth about past human rights violations and their perpetrators have the greatest chance of passing in the immediate aftermath of transition to democracy (Elster 1998; Nino 1996). However, the explanation for Slovakia's delay is more complicated than the explanation for late lustration in Poland and Hungary because of the atypical status quo.

7.5. Strategic Transitional Justice in the Baltics

Poland, Hungary, and Slovakia were not the only countries where postcommunists implemented lustration. Lithuania also did so, but its circumstances pose analytical challenges because of what Rein Taagepera has referred to as the problem of "radishes" in the former *nomenklatura*. A "radish" is white on the inside, but red on the outside. This term is used to describe some of the Lithuanians, Estonians, and Latvians who were members of their respective republics' communist parties, which were chapter organizations of the Soviet Union.[23] According to Taagepera, although many joined the *nomenklatura* to advance their careers, some did so for patriotic reasons – filling a position so as to deny it to a Russian colonist.

Taagepera argues that radishes outnumbered beets – those red inside and out – in the regional communist parties of pro-western republics of the Soviet Union, such as the Baltics, Moldova, and Ukraine. In Poland,

---

[22] Law No. 553/2002, dated 19 August 2002.
[23] Rein Taagepera (personal communication, December 2005).

Hungary, and the Czech Republic, radishes were less common than beets because party positions in satellite communist countries were not available to Russians. In East Central Europe, if an opportunistic radish resigned his or her seat, the worst that could happen would be that his or her position would go to a local ideologue, if such an ideologue were available.

The phenomenon of "strategic collaboration" created serious concerns when nearly every *nomenklatura* member claimed to have been a radish. Lithuania's first two lustration laws were passed when the Lithuanian communists were in power. Decree No. 418 of October 1991 required former KGB agents to resign from their posts if they worked in the ministerial departments, state services, or departments or as leading employees of cities and districts for a period of five years. Law No. I-2115 declared that deputies who were conscious collaborators of special agencies of the USSR (security, intelligence, or counterintelligence) would be required to have their mandates reconfirmed in their respective districts after voters had been informed about the deputies' past.[24]

In the 1990 elections, members of the Lithuanian Communist Party (LCP), the successor of the Communist Party of the Soviet Union (CPSU) chapter in Lithuania, won over 34 percent of the seats in the 1990 legislature. However, if Taagepera is correct and radishes constituted the core of the LCP, their sponsorship of lustration laws cannot be regarded as an instance of strategic transitional justice. While radishes would join the Lithuanian CPSU out of "patriotic motivations," they would not go so far as to serve as informants to the Moscow-based KGB. At the same time, ex-radishes had incentives to reveal who the KGB collaborators were because this would help draw a clear line between the Muscovite beets and the patriotic radishes. According to Taagepera's model, a decommunization law would hurt the LCP, but lustration would be to the party's advantage.

The implementation of lustration in Lithuania came to a halt when the KGB managed to remove its files from the country. Even though in advance of the October 1992 elections all candidates had to declare whether they had been connected with the KGB or other security services, there were no

---

[24] The ballot would state, "In view of the fact that deputy [name of deputy] collaborated with the KGB (or other special service), as shown in the facts which have become clear, I am in favor of the mandate of this deputy being 'confirmed' 'declared null' (cross out unnecessary word)."

documents to verify whether those declarations were truthful. Thus, for all practical purposes, following the 1992 elections, Lithuania had no lustration law in force.

The Lithuanian Democratic Labor Party (the actual post-communist party) won an absolute majority in 1992, implying that the median in the parliament was a post-communist. Since the early 1990s, the rules of procedure in the Lithuanian Assembly were open, with most bills subjected to floor amendments (Olson and Norton 1996). As a result, one would not expect lustration legislation to be implemented. Even though early in the legislative term it was quite obvious that anticommunists would win the elections and that they would start working on implementing harsh lustration, the ruling post-communists had no incentives to adopt lustration. This is because following the elections, the ideal lustration policy of the median would prevail. In 1996, the Homeland Union, the successor to Sajudis, the independence movement, almost won an absolute majority in the legislature. The even more hard-line KDS won another 12 percent. Thus, the median in 1996 became anticommunist. Consistent with predictions from Table 7.2, within two months of the elections, they began working toward effecting lustration. In October 1997 and again in June 1998, lustration statutes were passed. The 1998 legislation was vetoed by the president, but then passed anew the following month. Although this 1998 bill was challenged before the Lithuanian Constitutional Court, it was eventually upheld.

7.6. Conclusions

This chapter presented a strategic theory of adopting transitional justice that is consistent with the empirical phenomenon of post-communist parties passing bills that are different from their ideal lustration policies. There could be factors not accounted for in the Transitional Justice Bill game that possibly affected adopting transitional justice by post-communists. For instance, in Hungary, the MSzP may have adopted transitional justice as a bargaining chip with its coalition partner, the SzDSz, which felt more strongly about lustration and attempted to pass the first lustration law back in 1991. Finally, in Poland, the post-communist bill could have helped President Kwaśniewski to eliminate internal party competition for his office before his bid for reelection. I note that these alternative explanations are ad hoc and fit at most one case at a time. However, the data back my explanation that institutions, such as the rules of procedure and expectations about the election results, were critical.

A less idiosyncratic competing explanation of post-communist actions relies on transitional justice's saliency with the electorate: Post-communists may adopt lustration bills to show to the voters that they are clear of ties to the former enforcement apparatus. However, my analysis shows the limitations of this explanation: If it were true, post-communists would be adopting transitional justice bills irrespective of their expectations of losing power.

I have shown in previous chapters of this book that voters do not pay as much attention to lustration as politicians, for whom lustration can make the difference between gaining or losing office.

Another less idiosyncratic explanation is one attributing the passage of lustration by post-communists to generational differences within post-communist parties. Suppose younger members of post-communist parties see lustration as a means of rising to the top ranks of the party hierarchy without competing with communist veterans exposed as former collaborators. This explanation fails for two reasons. First, nothing in lustration laws prevents former collaborators from advancing careers in the party bureaucracy. In fact, party members ousted from legislative politics by lustration screenings frequently retreat to prominent positions within the party organization where lustration cannot reach. Furthermore, parties in East Central Europe have electoral incentives to maintain a cohesive team. Most electoral laws are closed-list proportional representation systems. This means that candidates compete in multimember districts and that party bosses design the lists of candidates and the ordering of party members on those lists. This reduces incentives for cultivating the personal vote, and consequentially, for intraparty competition because the reputation of being in a party of collaborators affects all party members. It dissuades voters sensitive to such information from voting on the party list. As a matter of fact, because the career prospects for junior members are longer than those of the senior members, lustration in closed-list PR systems is expected actually to hurt junior members *more* than it affects senior members. Finally, note that such intergenerational incentives should induce post-communists to adopt lustration in the middle of the electoral term or in the beginning of it and not toward the end of electoral terms, which is what one observes.

By no means is my argument about the strategic character of adopting lustration limited to Poland, Hungary, and Slovakia. The argument of the Transitional Justice Bill game can be extended to those countries of East Central Europe where post-communists have never been able to win office, such as Czechoslovakia, the Czech Republic, or Estonia. In these countries turnovers in power were among parties created after 1989. For instance, in Czechoslovakia (and later in the Czech Republic), lustration was adopted and renewed in periods preceding turnovers between the neoliberal ODS and the social democratic ČSSD. In Estonia, laws revealing collaboration with the KGB were passed within two months of elections that led to a turnover in power between the Pro Patria Union and the Coalition Party. Another law was passed within three months of elections that led to the turnover between the Coalition Party and the Estonian Center Party.

In other post-communist countries, such as East Germany, the post-Soviet and the post-Yugoslav republics, there was no lustration introduced by domestic actors. In the former Yugoslavia, the United Nations Security Council set up the International Tribunal for Former Yugoslavia (ICTY) and granted it authority over abuses of human rights committed during the civil conflict in the Balkans. There was no room for further domestic lustration. In Germany, the legislators from the West controlled the Stasi archives and the use of materials for lustration purposes. Finally, lustration in successor states of the former Soviet Union is rare, arguably because of the considerable influence of post-communist parties and politicians over politics. Detailed narratives, similar to those that I use in Chapter 8, could be presented for the remaining cases from Table 1.1. The upcoming elections around East and Central Europe may bring more transitional justice legislation, and there are strong reasons to believe that these processes will match the model's predictions. Importantly, however, the model of passing legislation prior to expected turnovers in power, such as I have presented in this chapter, is not restricted to the passage of transitional justice bills. Legislation on any issue over which the preferences of incumbents and challengers are significantly opposed could serve as an interpretation, provided that proposal power is shifting between incumbents and challengers and there is a veto player with policy preferences somewhere between the incumbent and challenger extremes. There are two important reasons for which, among many potential issue spaces, I chose transitional justice bills. First, lustration has critical consequences for politicians' ability to maintain office in East Central Europe. Stringent bills may (and have) ended careers of politicians who had collaborated in the past with the communist regime. Parties who have fewer ex-collaborators among their ranks than others may benefit from introducing lustration laws as a tool of political manipulation, to eliminate electoral competition. If politicians want to retain office and if they want to win larger representation of their parties in legislatures, they must be concerned about lustration.

Second, it can be argued that politicians are interested in how lustration laws get drafted even when the voters no longer see lustration as an important issue. A careful critic of my model could remark that it is unclear whether the preventive policy of the post-communists is an attempt to appease the legislative median or whether it is an attempt to appease the electoral median. Perhaps post-communist parties are passing transitional justice legislation because they want to present themselves to the electorate as a party unburdened with ties to the ancien régime. This would be a convincing argument if lustration and transitional justice were in fact a salient issue with voters. However, in East Central Europe this is no longer the case.[25] Furthermore, the electorate's preferences have had little significance in determining whether or not transitional justice gets passed. Contrary to predictions in the literature on coming to terms with the past, lustration laws were not implemented early after the transition, when public support for them was highest, but much later, in the late 1990s, when support for transitional justice was negligible. Finally, transitional justice legislation is rarely passed once and for all. Eastern European news reports and Human Rights agencies recorded a good deal of action in the transitional justice arena. Projects were put forward, amended, or rejected by succeeding decision makers in a way closely resembling the processes in Poland and Hungary. Rather than a matter of retribution or "coming to terms with the past and moving on," transitional justice legislation seems to be an arena of strategic interaction between actors devoted to maintaining their offices and prospective careers.

---

[25] As reported in Chapter 5, according to the TJS survey, on average, only 22 percent of respondents believe that former membership in the Communist Party is important in determining one's eligibility for legislative office. Other factors, such "talents and abilities," "representing voters' interests," and "being backed by powerful organizations" received 84, 84, and 59 percent, respectively. Also, as indicated by the Polish Election Survey 2000, Poles pay much more attention to politicians' attitudes toward the EU, church-state relationships, and the ways in which politicians deal with crime or corruption when making decisions about who to vote for (PGSW, ISP 2000).

8

Strategic Transitional Justice

BEYOND EAST CENTRAL EUROPE

In this book, I have demonstrated that issues of transitional justice – that is, procedures for dealing with members and collaborators of the ancien régime – are central to understanding the character, timing, and success of regime transitions. I have attempted to connect three influential bodies of literature that have largely been developing in isolation: the literature on regime transitions, the literature on transitional justice, and the new literature on authoritarianism and institutions.

An extensive body of scholarship uses the mode of transition to explain the types of transitional justice mechanisms that are adopted (Huntington 1991; Huyse 1995; Linz and Stepan 1996). Few scholars, however, have examined how former autocrats' anticipations of transitional justice may affect their willingness to democratize, and none has systematically linked the threat of retributive justice to the problem of amnesty for the old regime. Some scholars examining Latin American transitions have developed hypotheses about anticipating transitional justice (Geddes 1999, 2002; O'Donnell and Schmitter 1986). But those authors have argued that hypotheses about the effect of anticipating transitional justice on the feasibility of transitions to democracy cannot be extended to nonmilitary regimes of the fourth wave of democratization. They contend that single-party authoritarian regimes do not have access to the same coercive measures that outgoing military juntas do. Here, I demonstrate that the anticipation of punishment for past wrongdoings had a clear effect on the incentives of both outgoing autocrats and dissidents in East Central Europe, especially during the roundtable discussions in which the terms of transition were negotiated.

There is also a sizable literature on how transitional justice institutions contribute to the consolidation of democracy (Gibson 2002, 2006; McAdams 1997; Roht-Arriaza and Mariezcurrena 2006), but this research uses transitional justice to explain the period following the transition, assuming that the transition has already taken place. In this book, I place the dependent variable further in the past and ask how *expectations* of transitional justice affect the very possibility of transitions. Thus, I approach the dynamics of regime change as a political economist. To some extent, my line of inquiry follows scholars of international relations who have asked how creating international criminal tribunals affects peace (Gilligan 2006). My subject is domestic transitional justice, which is potentially more dangerous to the autocrats.

Finally, recent years have brought a slew of contributions to the field of authoritarian institutions. These contributions have been challenging the conventional wisdom that authoritarian regimes maintain legislatures and courts and hold regular democratic elections merely as a smokescreen to mislead outside observers (Friedrich and Brzezinski 1965). First, Jennifer Gandhi (Gandhi 2008; Gandhi and Przeworski 2006, 2007) has been arguing that particularly in countries that lack natural resources, autocrats in power must rely on cooperation from the broader public. One way of securing cooperation is by distributing rents widely. Another way to win over broader groups of society is by offering them policy concessions. However, to grant policy concessions, autocrats need to set up institutions for gauging the public's preferences. In the empirical part of their work, Gandhi and Adam Przeworski operationalize the degree of democratization of an authoritarian regime as the number of political parties (other than the authoritarian party) that the autocrats allow in the legislature. They find that as the need for cooperation on the part of the autocrats increases, so does the number of non-authoritarian legislative parties.

Institutions that are set up by autocrats also feature prominently in Jason Brownlee's work (Brownlee 2007), but instead of providing autocrats with access to information, institutions there serve to consolidate factions of opportunistic leaders by channeling collective benefits in their direction and marginalizing the opposition. The broader question that Brownlee seeks to answer is why only some of the authoritarian regimes that implemented liberalization in the twentieth century completed the full course to democratization. He challenges the conventional wisdom of the theoretical literature that liberalization not followed by democratization is unstable. Indeed, in countries such as Iran and the Philippines, multiparty elections have paved the way to further democratization by revealing the autocrats' vulnerability. But when autocrats concede to elections, their intention is to signal their strength and resilience rather than weakness. Ruling elites allow multiparty elections in hopes that their results will project their own con-solidation and expose how marginalized and isolated the opposition is. The ancien régime in Egypt and Malaysia successfully used this strategy to stay in power. In these countries, the autocrats maintained a stable degree of lib-eralization by letting the opposition run in elections, but preventing it from winning anything more than a minority of the representative seats. Brownlee summarizes this mechanism by saying that in such regimes, "elections tend to reveal political trends, not propel them" (Brownlee 2007, 9). While in Brownlee's model, as in Gandhi's, elections are conduits transmitting information, both the direction and the character of transmitted information are different. In Brownlee's work, elections broadcast to society how strong the dictatorship is. In Gandhi (2008), elections credibly transmit to the dictatorship the preferences of members in society.

Beatriz Magaloni (2006, 2008; Magaloni and Romero 2008) also investigates the role of elections in democratic transitions, but does so in the context of hegemonic party regimes, such as Mexico under the Institutional Revolutionary Party, known as PRI. Magaloni argues that hegemonic parties design electoral institutions when they are ready to concede to free elections. In those instances, they tailor electoral insti-tutions to their advantage by applying a "divide et impera" strategy to fragment the opposition. Hence, they cushion their descent from power and offer the opposition participation in the elections as part of a tran-sition pact. Magaloni notices that when Barry Weingast posited that, "to succeed, a pact must be self-enforcing," and that, "successful pacts create a focal solution that resolves the coordination dilemmas confronting elites and citizens" (Weingast 1997, 246), he left the mode by which pacts become self-enforcing unexplained. Magaloni proposes the following mechanism: "the ruling party must believe it can go on winning elections cleanly; and the opposition, under some particular circumstances, must credibly threaten to rebel against the election result, regardless of whether there is fraud or not, unless the ruling party finds a way to guarantee ex ante the transparency of the elections" (Magaloni 2006, 28). Magaloni's analysis, however, focuses on the persistence and peaceful resignation of hegemonic – not single-party – regimes. Hegemonic party regimes are different from single-party regimes in that in single-party regimes, electoral competition, if any, "takes place under the auspices of the single party and all candidates run on the ticket of that party" (Magaloni 2006, 32–3). It is not immediately clear how Magaloni's results would apply to single-party authoritarian regimes. For one, these autocrats may lack the information about popular support that is necessary to exploit electoral institutions strategically.[1] Furthermore, in single-party authoritarian regimes, the worst-case scenario for outgoing autocrats is much worse than losing elections: The outgoing autocrats may be punished with transitional justice. If autocrats cannot obtain immunity from transitional justice, they cannot pursue their political careers. Thus, whatever the autocrats want – be it rents, office, or policy – if they decide to share power with the former opposition, they need immunity from transitional justice to pursue these secondary goals.

The subject of this book is pacts exchanging election *for* this immunity from transitional justice (or, in short, amnesty). Specifically, I considered the credibility of political pacts that accompany transitions from authoritarian rule to democracy. Credible commitments in transitions from authoritarian rule have been investigated previously by Delia Boylan in Latin America in the context of central bank independence (Boylan 1998, 2001). Boylan questions the received wisdom that transitions challenge outgoing autocrats with uncertainty concerning their democratic future (O'Donnell and Schmitter 1986). She argues that autocrats will consent to democratization only if they have locked in economic institutions that protect their interests. While Boylan focuses on economic interests of outgoing autocrats and analyzes the degree to which they make central banks independent from democratic actors, I believe that focusing solely on economic interests of outgoing autocrats leaves an incomplete picture. This is not to say that economic outcomes are not relevant for autocrats' ability to maintain their privileged positions. For instance, Kenneth Greene (2007) makes a convincing argument that dominant parties such as the PRI in Mexico continued to accrue benefits of office without resorting to election rigging, because they could use their control over the economy to offer patronage in exchange for electoral support. However, amnesty commitments cannot be as easily institutionally entrenched as economic interests can.[2] My theory recognizes the political interests of outgoing autocrats and investigates how they ensure themselves immunity from transitional

---

[1] For an illustration of how misinformed ruling autocrats can be about their popular support, see Kaminski (1999); Kaminski and Nalepa (2004).

[2] For this reason, Boylan's argument might be more applicable to Mexico and hegemonic party regimes that do not need to fear transitional justice because their record of human rights abuses is considerably less sinister.

justice. Transitional justice policies are different from electoral institutions (such as the ones described by Magaloni in Mexico) or from macroeconomic policies (such as the ones described by Delia Boylan in Chile) that outgoing autocrats used in Latin America to entrench their preferred policies, because these promises have no "real guarantees" attached to them. The pre-democratic opposition has an incentive to break them, rendering commitments to amnesty incredible.

A final important difference that sets this book apart from those written on the subject of authoritarian institutions is that the variation it explains is not the persistence or downfall of authoritarianism (in contrast to Brownlee and Magaloni) but the variation in the timing of transitional justice. Thus, this book shares with the work of Gandhi, Brownlee, Magaloni, and Boylan the focus on two critical moments – the pre-transition stage and the transition stage – as well as the institutional approach. What it contributes to this scholarly tradition is the identification of a source of insurance for the autocrats that they will avoid prosecution with transitional justice.

In isolation, none of the current literature addresses the three puzzles associated with settling past accounts in East Central Europe. First, why did the opposition keep its promises of amnesty to communists at the round-table negotiations? Second, when and why were these promises eventually broken? And third, why did successors of former autocrats start adopting lustration laws? In this chapter, I summarize each of these three puzzles and how I have resolved them. Next, I explain how we can use the models described in this book to explain and predict other cases of successful conflict resolution. This may involve demobilization of illegal fighters – using Colombia as an example – or the longevity of power-sharing agreements that ensue in the aftermath of civil wars – using Northern Ireland as an example. I end the book with an epilogue describing the remarkable discoveries made by historians at the Polish Institute of National Remembrance that further corroborate the skeletons mechanism at work.

8.1. Summary of the Argument in Part I

The first puzzle is that of delayed transitional justice. After approximately half a century of communist rule frequently marked by political violence, there were many scores to settle.[3] But from June to December 1989, a series

---

[3] In some countries, the period of communist rule was a little longer than fifty years (as in the Baltic states); in others, such as Poland, it was a little less.

of communist countries in East Central Europe convened roundtable talks during which outgoing communist autocrats negotiated the terms of democratization with the former democratic opposition. The most remarkable feature of the ensuing democratic transitions was that, with the sole exception of Romania, all were peaceful.[4] The outgoing communists of East Central Europe had every reason to fear that, after stepping down from power, they would suffer transitional justice. Table 1.1 and the subsequent chapters discussing its patterns show that, although communists did suffer transitional justice in countries like the Czech Republic and East Germany, the vast majority of countries that avoided a sudden regime collapse refrained from transitional justice. The former communists found themselves in new democracies filled with political opportunities. The communist *nomenklatura* did not flea to nonpolitical spheres. Instead, in postcommunist Europe, the former communist parties transformed themselves into "social democratic parties," which by the mid-1990s became serious players in democratic elections (Grzymała-Busse 2002).

Chapters 2 and 3 interpreted this puzzle within a credible commitment framework. I proposed a dynamic game of incomplete information in which the uncertainty about infiltration of opposition elites with collaborators of the communist secret police plays the role of the "stick" that makes promises of amnesty credible. In the empirical chapter (Chapter 4), I used semi-structured interviews with elites on both sides who had participated in the negotiation as well as elites who did not want to negotiate the transition. After operationalizing the parameters of interest with detailed analytical narratives, I presented the data in an aggregate format. Poland and Hungary serve as cases in which the opposition's uncertainty about the degree to which it had been infiltrated curbed its retributive preferences. In these two countries, the post-communist parties flourished; by the mid-1990s, they had gained significant representations in parliament and even led democratic governments. On the other hand, Czechoslovakia presents an example of almost the opposite scenario: Toughened by the 1968 experience, the anticommunist opposition remained so deep underground that the secret police had difficulty recruiting its members. At the same time, the secret police was busy infiltrating the communist party to prevent resistance from within the

---

[4] Another exception would be the former Yugoslavia, but the violence in the form of civil wars within the succeeding republics accompanied the federal breakup rather than the communist overthrow.

party organization (which was how the Prague Spring movement had begun). Thus, by 1989, the opposition had few skeletons in its closet and both sides knew this quite well. The communists could not count on any guarantees for refraining from transitional justice. The communist party organization experienced harsh transitional justice consequences. Unlike its Polish and Hungarian counterparts, Czechoslovakia's communist party did not even bother to reform (Grzymała-Busse 2002) or change its name from "communist" to the less discredited "social-democratic." As a result, the party was marginalized on the sidelines of political life for years. The case study of Czechoslovakia – later the Czech Republic and Slovakia – provides an important variation that illustrates how the skeletons model operates.

8.2. Summary of the Argument in Part II

In the end of Part I, I returned to Table 1.1, noting that the skeletons model explains the lack of transitional justice in the early 1990s. However, the fact that eventually lustration laws were adopted in countries where the opposition, fearing infiltration, had pulled its transitional justice punches for so long, still demanded an explanation. The book's second puzzle was to explain why the roundtable promises of amnesty eventually broke down and why lustration escalated. I began Part II by evaluating the conventional wisdom that the timing of lustration is determined by the preference of voters to punish the former autocrats and their collaborators. I used available surveys that had been conducted since the beginning of the transition as well as original data from my own 2004 mass survey in Poland, Hungary, and the Czech Republic to evaluate this conventional wisdom. I found that although voters believe in the purpose of lustration, they consider other issues more salient for their voting decisions. Even though the ultimate laws that got adopted in the three countries varied to a great extent, there was little difference in voters' preferences across Poland, Hungary, and the Czech Republic. Finally, voter demand for lustration has been remarkably stable over time, despite the variation in the lustration laws actually adopted in these countries.

These three findings undermine the voter-demand–based theory of lustration timing. Thus, in Chapter 5, I turned to the supply-side explanations and explored the incentives of political actors for adopting lustration laws. Tracing the development of the party system in East Central Europe throughout the 1990s, I found that as the post-transition cleavage dividing parties into post-oppositionists and post-communists began to fade, new parties gradually entered the political scene. These newcomers had nothing to lose from lustration because they knew their ranks had few, if any, collaborators; yet, they had much to gain. If lustration eliminated political competition, more legislative seats would become available to the newcomers. New parties, in terms of organization, tenure, and youth of particular members, tended to favor lustration. The Law and Justice Party in Poland served as a good example of such young parties. FiDeSz in Hungary sets an example of reorganizing a party to capitalize on benefits (paid out in legislative seats) that can stem from lustration.

Remarkably, though, it was not the anticommunist parties that ended up adopting lustration laws. Instead, as shown in Figure 1.1, both in Poland and in Hungary, the first lustration laws to survive the legislative process were actually implemented when post-communist majorities led democratic governments. Polish and Hungarian post-communists adopted lustration laws when they were expecting to *lose* power to the new and young anticommunist lustration zealots. Adopting lustration was, therefore, a preemptive move to appease the median legislator in parliament with a moderate bill that this median preferred to the harsh proposal that would have been sponsored by anticommunists. Once this moderate bill was in force, the anticommunists' proposal had no appeal. Had the transitional justice status quo remained at null, however, the anticommunists would have had no problem with pushing through with their retributive agenda.

Before discussing how this book's transitional justice models may be extended, it is appropriate to observe a cautionary note about how *not* to interpret my findings. By employing the skeletons model, I am not passing judgment on the opposition that had participated in roundtable negotiations, even though the image that emerges from this analysis is less rosy compared to how it may have appeared from the West.[5] The formal models do not serve as subterfuge to advance normative judgments; the model's assumptions are clear up front. The assumption here is simply that the opposition could not, as it sat for the roundtable talks, know with certainty the extent to which it had been infiltrated with secret police agents. This is fully consistent with the possibility that the opposition was

---

[5] The epilogue of Chapter 9, which describes the recent discovery of Lech Wałęsa's collaboration with the secret police, is another departure from the romanticized vision of anticommunist dissidents.

not infiltrated *at all* as long as there remained either (a) considerable uncertainty (as in Poland and Hungary) or (b) no negotiation (as in Czechoslovakia).

One expected implication that emerges from the model is that the outgoing communists acted rationally and exercised strategic forethought in dealing with their circumstances. First, they did not hastily abandon their positions of control and leave themselves at the mercy of their vengeful opposition. Second, when they did punish themselves with lustration, they did it for rational reasons. In both circumstances, they acted carefully, making the best decisions given the information that was available to them at the time. In fact, this appreciation for the post-communists' ability to exploit their legislative and informational advantages strategically is consistent with Anna Grzymała-Busse's work on the communists' swift adaptation to democratic conditions (Grzymała-Busse 2002). These adaptive skills manifested themselves most clearly when Hungarian and Polish post-communist parties emerged victorious in democratic elections in the mid-1990s.

There are, however, indirect normative implications of the models I use. One is that involvement with the secret police is not something that falls neatly into one of the dichotomous categories of "collaboration with the ancien régime" or "anti-authoritarian dissent." Instead, there are meaningful shades of gray between these two ideal types. These shades of gray generate the uncertainty about collaboration within the dissident movement. Once more, this point is illustrated well in an episode from Krzysztof Kieslowski's *Blind Chance*. In the first version of the movie, while Witek's candidacy for communist party membership is being considered, he unintentionally reveals information about his girlfriend's samizdat publication facility. While she ends the romantic relationship, Witek's career as a communist apparatchik is also over. But it also makes him persona non grata among dissident circles. Was Witek a conscious collaborator? No. Would he be considered a collaborator for lustration purposes? By a stringent procedure, yes. The skeletons model's analytical force comes from the difficulty that post-opposition parties had in determining how many of their members had Witek-like pasts.

By incorporating important differences in the distribution of information between the two sides negotiating regime transition, the skeletons model explains the timing of lustration laws. It can also help us understand why so many of the East Central European democratizations occurred through peaceful transitions of power. If the communists knew that the opposition was uncertain about the extent of its infiltration, they could peacefully surrender control, knowing that they would not be persecuted with transitional justice. Thus, the model helps us understand why certain transitions take the form that they do. The remainder of this chapter is devoted to a discussion of how broad the model's applications are.

8.3. Broader Implications

It is tempting to use Barbara Geddes' typology and limit the model's range of applications to single-party regimes. I believe, however, that the limiting conditions on the model's applications are considerably broader. Within regime transitions, the skeletons model explains peaceful negotiations from any authoritarian regime to democracy provided that the authoritarian regime:

- lasted long enough to replace brute force as a tool of combating the opposition with a professional secret police that relied on networks of secret informers
- is succeeded with a democracy in which political actors are organized into groups (such as party organizations) so that the assumption about uncertainty concerning the innocence of members of one's group makes sense.

The skeletons model could apply, for instance, to South Africa, which before 1990 and during apartheid was not a not single-party regime. However, the controlling National Party had a long tenure and a powerful enforcement apparatus that relied on a network of secret police informers (Bell and Ntsebeza 2003; Boraine 2000). The Truth and Reconciliation Commission appointed to describe the pattern of abuses committed in the apartheid era uncovered atrocities that had been perpetrated on both sides of the conflict: by the African National Congress as well as the apartheid-supporting nationalist government. Eventually, this had a peace-building effect, as it made it easier for blacks and whites to reconcile their differences (Gibson 2006).

I believe that the model's applications extend beyond regime transitions and even beyond the field of comparative politics. According to Barry Weingast (1997), a pact has to be self-enforcing to be meaningful. In relationships between states, the enforcing power of pacts stems from their function as focal points (Schelling 1980). There is no sense, however, in which pacts regulating regime transitions or peace settlements in the aftermath of civil wars can act as focal points, at least not in the sense of guaranteeing the outgoing autocrats that they will not be persecuted with transitional justice for human rights violations or war crimes. Skeletons in the closet have the capacity to replace focal points in enforcing power-sharing agreements after conflict situations more generally. It makes sense here to distinguish between two classes of actors: the pre-settlement stronger side (which after the settlement becomes the weaker side) and the pre-settlement weaker side (which after the settlement becomes the advantaged side). The enabling power of skeletons comes from instilling confidence in the post-settlement weaker side – such as a demobilizing paramilitary group – that after surrendering arms, it will not be persecuted by the post-settlement advantaged side. Because of its general features, the skeletons model can also apply to the bargaining processes that terminates civil wars. Figure 8.1 illustrates this point.

Any authoritarian regime has at least two junctures at which a skeletons scenario could play out: (1) If the opposition has skeletons in the closet, the regime may peacefully transition to a democracy (because the autocrats are not afraid of transitional justice); or (2) if, instead of a peaceful transition, civil conflict breaks out, the insurgents can later be induced to demobilize if the government has skeletons in the closet. In other words, skeletons existing in the closet of the side that emerges as more powerful in the transition aftermath enable peaceful transitions as opposed to civil war. However, if a civil conflict is already under way, skeletons may enable peaceful demobilization as part of a peace settlement. The following illustration from Colombia is an example of (2).

8.3.1. An Application to Colombia

This section illustrates how the skeletons model can apply beyond East Central Europe, because it offers a mechanism through which governments can make promises of amnesty credible to paramilitary fighters in the aftermath of civil war.[6]

On July 25, 2005, Colombia passed the Justice and Peace Law (JPL). This statute, Law No. 975, offered demobilizing paramilitaries partial amnesty in exchange for testimony and surrendering weapons. This

---

[6] This section is an abbreviated version of Nalepa (2009).

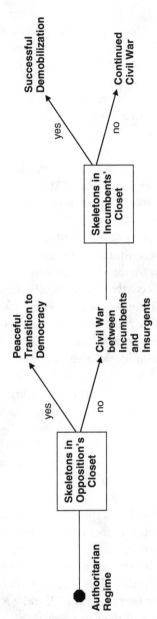

Figure 8.1. Skeletons scenarios in regime transitions and civil wars.

legislation resembles the promises of refraining from transitional justice in East Central Europe. Both pose a credible commitment problem.

Human rights organizations and the United Nations Human Rights Commission criticized Colombia's Justice and Peace Law, pointing out that paramilitaries should be held accountable for human rights violations and that the benefits extended to demobilizing paramilitaries are too generous. This pressure has made negotiating with other groups involved in the civil war, such as the National Liberation Army (Ejército de Liberación Nacional, ELN) or the Revolutionary Armed Forces (Fuerzas Armadas Revolucionarias de Colombia, FARC), difficult. How can the Colombian government make credible promises of amnesty or partial amnesty to these groups?

We can use the solution to the commitment problem developed in this book to illustrate how infiltration of negotiating elites may serve as an insurance mechanism to make credible promises of amnesty to demobilizing fighters.[7] Recently, the paramilitaries from the United Self-Defense Forces of Colombia (Autodefensas Unidas de Colombia, AUC) have been participating in the judicial procedures established by the JPL. They have testified that the current Colombian government is infiltrated with ties to paramilitaries and to violations of human rights. The skeletons model allows us to interpret these events as the fulfillment of the AUC paramilitaries' threat – that if the government reneged on its promise, the AUC would reveal the government's skeletons in the closet.

To illustrate this point more clearly, let me be specific about the players in the Colombian case. In the simple transitions game from Chapter 2, there were two players and two stages of the game. In the civil wars application, the players are the fighters, F, and the government, G. In the first stage, F decides whether to accept the offer of surrendering arms in exchange for amnesty or not. If F does not surrender, the game ends with the status quo payoffs of 0 to everyone. If F surrenders, in the next stage, G decides whether to honor the agreement about providing amnesty or not. If G decides to keep the promise, players get a payoff of 1 each. But if G reneges on the agreement, it gets a payoff of 2, while F gets a payoff of -1. The three possible outcomes of the game are:

---

[7] I use the term "amnesty" in a rather broad sense to incorporate benefits granted under the JPL.

- **Status quo (SQ)**: Fighters do not enter the settlement.
- **Demobilization with amnesty (A)**: Fighters enter the settlement and receive amnesty.
- **Demobilization without amnesty (NoA)**: Fighters enter the settlement but the government reneges on the promise of amnesty.

Applied to the context of civil war settlements, the simple model suggests that the government will not keep promises of amnesty given to fighters to induce disarmament. Thus, fighters should refrain from agreeing to such settlements. The structure of the game and payoffs are common knowledge. Because amnesty will be delivered *after* the fighters surrender their arms, how can the government ensure the fighters that it will keep its promise?

We can use the skeletons model to solve this credible commitment problem. The government can credibly commit to delivering amnesty to the surrendering fighters if the government has skeletons in its own closet that the fighters could divulge if the government reneges on its promise of amnesty. In this interpretation, Colombian paramilitaries would hold the government hostage for as long as it takes for the amnesty promise to be delivered. The skeletons could take the form of infiltration of governmental elites with members of the paramilitary. Since members of the paramilitary were involved in drug trafficking, such infiltration is particularly embarrassing for the government. However, any information embarrassing the reputation of the government elites that the paramilitaries are at liberty to release can play the role of skeletons.

In terms of the skeletons model, the fighters (F) are the Sender, while the Receiver is the government (G). The private information is the level of infiltration of the government, $i \in [0,1]$ where $i = 1$ represents the highest level of infiltration, while $i = 0$ represents the lowest level. The government prefers less infiltration to more, whereas the fighters prefer the opposite. The fighters have private information about the exact value of i, but the government is uncertain about i, although it does know that the parameter i is distributed according to some density function, f. The justification of the relations between parameters is straightforward: If amnesty is broken, and the government is sufficiently compromised by links to the fighters, the fighters begin to reveal information about the corrupt activity of government officials. This may involve naming army generals and politicians who "bankrolled paramilitary operations" and even "worked hand in hand with [paramilitary] fighters to help carry them out" (Forero 2007, A01).[8]

In the skeletons model, if the amnesty is broken, the more compromised the government is with links to the paramilitaries, the better it is for the fighters (their payoff in such a case is i). In this situation, the fighters would have an incentive to reveal the corrupt linkages. Why would the fighters choose this course of action? A possible justification runs as follows. After the fighters have surrendered their arms, they can no longer revert to violence. They are forced to seek political influence within the public arena – perhaps by organizing political parties or supporting existing ones and competing for legislative and executive seats within the existing government. Exposing the corruption of existing governmental elites makes it easier for the fighters to place their own representatives in positions of responsibility. The fighters already have a reputation as perpetrators of human rights violations. Consequently, by sharing this responsibility for human rights violations with some government officials, the fighters from the AUC can only gain. The costs of revealing embarrassing information are fully absorbed by government elites, and they can expect to suffer the electoral consequences of such revelation. Hence, F's payoff is increasing in i. When infiltration is extremely high (that is, i close to 1), revealing the government's infiltration might even be better for the fighters than an amnesty (thus $t_F \leq 1$).

On the other hand, for the government, revealed infiltration has electoral consequences and thus its payoff from reneging on the promise of amnesty (which implies the revealing of skeletons) is decreasing in i. The government prefers reneging when its level of infiltration is low (that is, when $t_G \leq 1-i$). In this case, the fighters bare the greater burden of responsibility for human rights violations and the government stands a better chance at staying in power and reaping the benefit of bringing human rights violators to justice. However, for greater levels of infiltration (that is, i close to 1), the government will prefer to keep its promise of amnesty over reneging. This is the case because circulating information about corrupt governmental elites shames members of the governmental elites and reduces their chances for reelection. The worst outcome for the government, however, is if the fighters refuse to give up their arms altogether ($N_G \leq t_G$).

---

[8] See Forero (2007) for an example of top paramilitary commanders revealing that governmental elites were involved in the killing of civilians and cocaine trafficking.

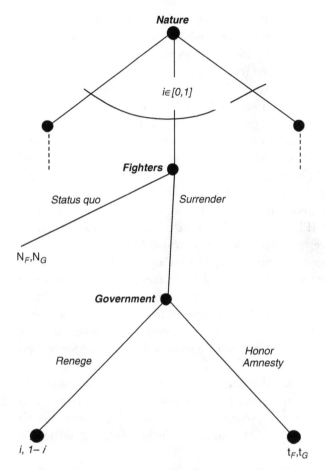

Figure 8.2. Skeletons in the closet in civil wars.

The Transition with Secret Information (TSI) game adapted to the Colombian case is presented in Figure 8.2.

The key insight from the skeletons model for Colombia is that potential infiltration makes the promises of amnesty credible and provides fighters with incentives to surrender arms. In this model, for promises of amnesty to be credible, the following conditions must be met:

- The government should suspect that members of its own elite have incriminating links, but should be uncertain about where precisely the links are.
- The fighters should be in a position to reveal this information if the government reneges on its promise of amnesty.

This means that the fighters must have both the access to information about the government's infiltration and an incentive to disclose that information. If embarrassing the government by exposing its links to human rights violations would further compromise the fighters, they lack incentives for revealing the secret. However, as a result of revealing these secrets to the public, the fighters would shed part of the responsibility for human rights violations. In doing so, they could weaken the political position of governmental officials. This in turn would increase the electoral chances of their political representatives. Thus, the ability to reveal the governments' skeletons to the public gives the fighters a threat they can use to make amnesty promises credible.

These observations are particularly important in light of recent events in Colombia. The JPL was to "facilitate the processes of peace and individual or collective reincorporation into civilian life of the members of illegal armed groups, guaranteeing the victims' rights to truth, justice, and reparation" (Congress of Colombia 2005, Chapter 1). In practice, it offered a three-tier transitional justice system that provides perpetrators with amnesty in exchange for the disclosure of truth and illegally acquired assets. The truth was used to induce additional perpetrators to come forward and demobilize; the assets were supposed to be used for reparations to victims.

By combining the three elements of truth, justice, and reparations into one system, the Justice and Peace Law presented itself as an advancement over incentives-based truth revelation procedures, such as South Africa's Truth and Reconciliation Commission, which combined justice in exchange for truth.

The JPL has provoked criticism for its leniency toward perpetrators from international human rights organizations and NGOs. There are also problematic aspects associated with monitoring what constitutes a full disclosure of weapons, illegally acquired assets, and the truth that the law requires for amnesty. Specifically, demobilizing fighters were expected to forfeit all ill-gotten assets, including land, to the National Reparation Fund. They also had to disclose their involvement in crimes as well as knowledge of paramilitary structures and financing sources.[9]

---

[9] It is unclear, though, how well equipped the National Prosecutorial Office is to confirm that no truth or assets have been withheld by a surrendering paramilitary (Pablo Kalmanovitz, personal communication).

In other words, paramilitaries may be demobilizing and avoiding harsh sentencing without fulfilling their end of the bargain. This may be disconcerting from the point of view of justice, but the paramilitary forces have been demobilizing in impressively large numbers, with more than 31,600 AUC members demobilized by October 2006 (International Crisis Group 2006). The numbers are so impressive that the government found it hard to provide them with "re-immersion [into society] benefits" promised to induce demobilization (Congress of Colombia 2005).[10]

If the government reneges on the terms of amnesty, the skeletons model predicts that paramilitaries would start revealing information that is embarrassing to governmental elites. Indeed, such revelations began in the fall of 2006. In May 2007, a top paramilitary commander, Salvatore Mancuso, revealed that over and above seventeen thousand armed fighters, the paramilitary controlled a network of more than ten thousand collaborators among the civilian population. Some were linked to the ruling elites. These revelations have led to charges against twenty-one congressmen, the head of the secret police, as well as many mayors and governors. The most embarrassing revelations concerned General Rito Alejo del Río, for whom President Álvaro Uribe had personally vouched when the United States rescinded his visa in July 1999. Mancuso's testimony also implicated two ministers from President Uribe's cabinet (Forero 2007). The skeletons model explains why paramilitaries had been so willing to disarm. Their infiltration of governmental elites provided them with sufficient insurance that the terms of amnesty would be met.

An important caveat to note here is that although the implementation of the JPL was far from what the paramilitaries had anticipated, this was not necessarily due to mistakes made by the Uribe government. In May 2006, a Constitutional Court ruling placed severe restrictions on the way paramilitaries would surrender arms under the JPL. It ruled that "reparation to victims not be limited to ill-gotten assets held by ex-paramilitaries, that all members of a paramilitary unit be held responsible for crimes committed by members of that block, that prison terms under the JPL be no less than 5 years (with time served in detention centers not counting towards the sentence) and that all JPL benefits be forfeited if the ex-paramilitary under consideration fails to confess the

---

[10] Among the benefits were a stipend and professional training.

whole truth" (International Crisis Group 2006). These restrictions resulted in a settlement that would have never fallen within the bounds of the bargaining range of the government and the paramilitary (the set of outcomes acceptable to both parties).[11]

Because the Constitutional Court's ruling made the full disclosure of truth mandatory for taking advantage of the JPL benefits, many paramilitaries changed their decision to disarm, disarmed only partially, or joined newly forming military groups (International Crisis Group 2007). Paramilitaries may well have feared that criticism targeting the JPL for leniency from foreign human rights activists, the EU, and to some extent the United States further jeopardized the guarantees of amnesty. Thus, the decision of some of the paramilitary leaders to start revealing linkages between the paramilitary and the government could have been motivated by these external pressures rather than the Uribe administration's mistakes. Importantly, revealing infiltration is part of an equilibrium strategy for the demobilized paramilitary.

To illustrate the generality of this model further – how it extends to pacted transitions as well as settlements in the aftermath of civil war – I present side by side the two applications of the Transitional Justice with Secret Information model in Table 8.1. The column on the right presents the interpretation from East Central Europe, whereas the column on the left presents the interpretation from Colombia.

8.3.2. Other Broader Applications

The skeletons model can also explain settlements in civil wars involving conflict between two sides and a third party that serves as a biased or unbiased mediator (Kydd 2006; Savun 2008, 2009). This case is exemplified by Northern Ireland. There, the political branch of the Loyalists (the Democratic Unionist Party, DÚP) entered into a power sharing agreement with the Sinn Fein in May 2007. This deal was secured by the British government, which for years was viewed as supporting the Protestant cause. It is puzzling that despite earlier breakdowns of similar power-

---

[11] There are reasons to suspect that the negotiations between the government and paramilitaries were extremely tight and therefore the bargaining range was never especially broad. An indication of this is the fact that many prominent parties to the agreement – such as Vicente Castano, a paramilitary leader – left the negotiation table.

Table 8.1. *Interpretation of the Simple Transition Game for civil war settlements and pacted transitions.*

Model	Civil war settlements	Pacted transitions
Autocrats	Illegally armed fighters, such as AUC, FARC, ENL	Outgoing communists in 1989
Opposition	Executive since implementation of JPL	Dissident opposition, e.g. Solidarity in Poland
NonTJ	Benefits awarded to paramilitaries demobilizing under the JPL	Refraining from transitional justice
TJ	Failure to deliver benefits under JPL to surrendering paramilitaries	Transitional justice
Status quo	Paramilitaries fail to demobilize (may result in prolonged civil war, associated with losses to both the government and paramilitaries)	Failure to invite dissident opposition to roundtable negotiations (may result in revolution or regime breakdown, which is undesirable to both communists and dissidents)

sharing agreements, the IRA chose to trust the British government and disarm yet again. Previously, the British government was never viewed as having a credible commitment to impartiality. Apparently, though, the government on Downing Street had skeletons in its closet and in August 2007, Sinn Fein initiated a massive spy revelation scandal. Over two days, *The Irish News* revealed documents showing that the Northern Ireland special police units (the Union Defense Regimen, UDR) had been, as early as 1973, supplying the UDA (the unionist death squads) with weapons. *The Irish News* also revealed that up to 15 percent of UDR's soldiers were involved in with loyalist paramilitary groups. Critically, the Irish daily published news that the British government knew about these links from its military intelligence.

This scandal, which came to be known as the "Collusion Affair," may fit into the skeletons model. That analysis would unfold along the following lines. The paramilitary unit of the Sinn Fein was obviously skeptical about demobilizing, concerned that following demobilization, it would lose all its bargaining power in Northern Ireland. Fortunately for the IRA, the

British government had skeletons in its closet: It had been aware of collusion between Northern Ireland police forces and the paramilitary units in the past but failed to act upon this information. When Sinn Fein felt disappointed in the British government's assistance in the peace process, it could resort to revealing the skeletons – which apparently it did. The story developed further over the summer of 2007 when a member of Ian Paisley's Democratic Unionist Party threatened to name a senior Sinn Fein politician who was allegedly involved in the killing of a police officer in 1979 but then became an informer for the British security forces. The member of the DÚP in question refused to release the name before October 2007, which could be interpreted as a signal to Sinn Fein to back off its allegations of collusion.[12]

8.4. Conclusions

Observers of the East Central European transition often attribute the peaceful nature of the transitions to the promises exchanged at the roundtable negotiations between outgoing communists and the incoming oppositions. Traditionally, such pacts present outgoing autocrats with the opportunity to extract guarantees of amnesty from the opposition. Hence, in Greece, Argentina, Uruguay, and Spain, the local autocrats traded control over political institutions for immunity from criminal investigations (Colomer 1991). In South Africa, members of the apartheid government were guaranteed the security of their property rights (Omar 1996). In Latin America, outgoing autocrats insulated their monetary policies from incoming democrats by granting autonomy to central banks (Boylan 1998, 2001). According to this account, the former communist leaders in Bulgaria, Czechoslovakia, Hungary, and Poland extended open and free elections to the dissident opposition parties in exchange for promises of amnesty. Jon Elster (2004), however, has identified a flaw in this reasoning applied to East Central Europe termed the "delivery problem": Once the ancien régime resigns from positions of control, the opposition has strong incentives to renege on any earlier promises, casting doubt on the credibility of such promises. The communists should therefore fear that their ability to protect themselves from the opposition's

---

[12] I am indebted to Christian Davenport and Paul Staniland for empirical data used in this section.

revenge will last only as long as they retain a monopoly over the institutions of government. Once negotiations are concluded and power is surrendered, the opposition can deal with the ancien régime as it likes, disregarding any promises of amnesty.

In East Central Europe, as a result of the free elections, the dissident opposition assumed power from the communists (Kaminski 1999; Benoit and Schieman 2001; Elster 1996). Soon after taking power, it could easily break any promises made to the former rulers now rendered powerless. Indeed, the opposition's incentives were to do exactly that. The opposition could open up further political opportunities for its members by holding the former autocrats responsible by, for example, implementing lustration.

The skeletons model that I have developed in this book resolved the dilemma of peaceful transitions to democracy in East Central Europe, followed by delayed lustrations. My argument models the incentives of former dissidents who, uncertain about the extent to which they are infiltrated with former secret police collaborators, prefer to refrain from lustration. As a result, these policies are not implemented until much later than the transition aftermath, when dissidents who are certain that they are not tainted by collaboration with the ancien régime become competitive in democratic elections. This is the solution to the first and second puzzles of the book: that transitional justice is not adopted directly following the transition, despite prevailing incentives to do so; and that these policies are adopted later, when popular support for their adoption has considerably dampened. The model from the second part of the book explains the final puzzle: why the specific timing of lustration falls in periods when successors of former communists are in power. I developed an agenda-setting model where the critical parameters are electoral turnover and restrictiveness of procedures for parliamentary decision making. I show how former communists who anticipate losing power to anticommunists are incentivized to pass mild lustration bills. The fundamental argument is that accepted lustration proposals in one legislative term form the status quo of the succeeding term. Consequently, rational proposers anticipate this and set the future status quo strategically. The party with proposal power before the elections – the post-communists – sets the status quo to reduce the winset of the future median party, and thus reduces the room for the new proposing party – the anticommunists – to shift policy in the extreme direction.[13]

The by-products of this research are two game theoretic models. The first is a signaling game that can be fruitfully used in other contexts where credible commitment problems arise. One could build skeletons models explaining why parties abide by international alliances when there is no external enforcement (Leeds 2003) as well as when there is such enforcement (Simmons and Steinberg 2006). The model may also help explain patterns of corruption and corporate governance (Tirole 2001) in political economy. The second model can be used to explain why politicians holding complete agenda control initiate legislation that seemingly hurts them. My analysis leads us to expect that incumbent proposers adopt seemingly self-hurting behavior when they expect to lose the upcoming elections to a challenger from the opposite side of the political scene who wants to punish them more harshly. To prevent this harsh legislation, the incumbents preemptively pass milder bills that appease a median legislator and make him or her reluctant to accept the challenger's proposals.

I have chosen to apply both models to the pacted transitions in East Central Europe for two reasons. First, twenty years after the pacted transitions had been negotiated, research on post-communism has no uniform explanation for how so many transitions could have occurred peacefully. Second, although the literature on communist successor parties explained the success of former autocrats in transforming their party organizations into players that could successfully compete in democratic elections (Grzymała-Busse 2002), we still lacked an understanding of why the former dissidents in East Central Europe did not try to prevent this transformation with transitional justice. I have shown how skeletons in the opposition's closet – the uncertainty about its infiltration with secret police informers – could have acted as the autocrats' insurance against possible retribution. At the onset of the roundtable negotiations, the autocrats had a distinctive informational advantage over the opposition. They knew to what extent the various dissident groups had been engaged in collaboration with the ancien régime and could successfully use this information to their advantage. The risk-averse opposition, afraid of possible skeletons in the closet, preferred to keep them there, even if these skeletons were fewer

---

[13] The win-set of alternative a is the set of all alternatives the median prefers to proposal a.

than the communists would have them believe. The metamorphosis of Lech Wałęsa from Solidarity hero to protagonist of reconciliation with former communists and "letting sleeping dogs lie" illustrates this mechanism but too well.

9

Epilogue

BETWEEN AGENTS AND HEROES

In the summer of 2008, the Polish Institute of National Remembrance published its best-selling but most controversial monograph, *The Secret Police and Lech Wałęsa: a Biographical Addendum,* by historians Slawomir Cenckiewicz and Piotr Gontarczyk. The eight hundred–page 'addendum' describes a six-year episode of Lech Wałęsa's secret life as an informer for the communist political police.

The western news media discovered Wałęsa in the early 1980s. In 1978, Wałęsa, a shipyard worker with a signature long mustache, had been laid off for soliciting strike activity. By the early 1980s, he had become the star leader of Solidarity, the first independent trade union in the Soviet bloc. Solidarity was also the first civil society organization that had stood up to the communist regime in the middle of the Leonid Brezhnev era. This accomplishment was largely attributed to Wałęsa's charismatic leadership. In 1980, he negotiated Solidarity's legalization with the communist government in the Gdańsk Shipyard. When he signed the accords, he proclaimed, "We now have the most important thing: an independent and autonomous trade union!" This was the first in a series of tears in the Iron Curtain. Within a few months, the trade union's membership was three times as great as that of the communist Polish United Workers' Party (PZPR). Eighteen months into Solidarity's existence, the communists reneged on the deal they struck in the Gdańsk Shipyard. General Wojciech Jaruzelski implemented martial law, banned Solidarity, and arrested most of its leaders, including Wałęsa. While most unionists were released within a few months, Wałęsa stayed in jail until 1983. He was still in jail when he was awarded the Nobel Peace Prize. Western media elevated him to nothing short of the Martin Luther King or Mahatma Gandhi of communist Europe. He maintained this celebrity status throughout the period of peaceful revolutions that swept through East Central Europe. In 1989–1990, the roundtable talks initiated in Poland and Hungary brought Solidarity back to center stage again. In 1988, during the preparatory stages of the roundtable negotiations, 95 percent of the population recognized Wałęsa's name, while other prominent dissidents were recognized by 5 percent or less.[1] In 1990, he was elected the first president in post-communist Poland. Conflicts divided the Solidarity leadership as the social movement splintered into multiple separate parties, but Wałęsa kept his position until 1995.

After being replaced by Aleksander Kwasniewski, a former communist technocrat, Wałęsa preoccupied himself with running his institute (the Lech Wałęsa Institute) and traveling to invited talks and lectures. His name returned to newspaper headlines in 2008 when S. Cenckiewicz and P. Gontarczyk published their monograph documenting Wałęsa's life as secret collaborator between 1970 and 1976.[2] The evidence showed that Wałęsa had spied on his coworkers at the Gdansk Shipyard, tipping off his leading officers about planned anticommunist demonstrations. This helped the secret police map underground dissident networks. According to Cenckiewicz and Gontarczyk, Wałęsa collaborated voluntarily; he was neither blackmailed nor threatened. The information he supplied allowed the secret police to track down more than twenty dissidents associated with the early trade union organizations that predated Solidarity.

In 1976, Wałęsa decided to end his collaboration. Since the intelligence he was providing to his leading officers was erratic and hardly useful, the secret police closed his file and sent it to the archives. It remained there for over ten years. Meanwhile, Wałęsa became the dissident hero the world knows today.

---

[1] These data come from a series of surveys conducted by a polling company established by the communist regime in the aftermath of martial law, Centrum Badania Opinii Społecznej (1988).

[2] The first historian to define the term "collaborator," Stanislaw Korbonski, described a collaborator as "someone who works with an invader to the detriment of his or her nation." After some modification, the definition can be used to denote informing for the communist secret police in communist Europe. While the Soviet Union was not perceived uniformly throughout East Central Europe as an invader, especially following the Yalta Treaty, even those who had once seen it as a liberator and ally would agree it had over-stayed its welcome (Leffler 1992; Trachtenberg 1999). The communist secret police was perceived as the extension of the KGB and working with it amounted to working with the representative of an occupying force.

The revelations of Wałęsa's pre-transition secret life as a communist police agent shocked most Poles. Poles were most appalled by the evidence that the former Solidarity leader tried to destroy the evidence of his collaboration. But because the secret police had terminated its relationship with Wałęsa long before the 1989 transitions, his file was closed and archived. In contrast to files of "active agents," Wałęsa's file was preserved intact. Recognizing this, he overextended his privilege of executive office and "checked out" his file from the archives. Wałęsa kept the file in his private safe while he destroyed much of the material that could identify him as an agent under the pseudonym Bolek.[3] Because of his role as a former dissident, the public expected him to hold former communist autocrats responsible for their history of human rights violations. But Wałęsa adopted a very restrained approach to transitional justice. He did not merely oppose opening archives of the former secret police to the public. When the Polish parliament passed a resolution requiring the minister of interior to create a list of politicians who had been secret collaborators, Wałęsa masterminded a coalition that brought down the entire government along with the unfortunate interior minister. Wałęsa was likely concerned about the skeletons in his closet and was therefore disinclined to risk having his reputation as freedom-fighting hero besmirched.

It is only coincidental that the publication of Cenckiewicz and Gontarczyk's historical research coincided with the preparation of this book. But the evidence supplied by archivists, especially when it concerns someone as high in the dissident hierarchy as Lech Wałęsa, directly corroborates my argument. My book uses methods of political science. It is not a work of history. Its goal is to offer a mechanism that links dissident activity prior to the transition with deals struck at the roundtable negotiations. Communist infiltration of dissident activity occasionally produced skeletons in the opposition's closet. The deals struck at roundtable negotiations between the outgoing communists and the opposition were sealed by those skeletons. This mechanism accounts for the delays in implementing transitional justice in the post-transition period. The disturbing revelations about Wałęsa's murky past, his attempts to hide it, and his ambiguous stance toward transitional justice are all consistent with the mechanism I present. However, my argument does not rely on the truth or falsehood of the most contentious part of their research: whether or not

---

[3] In the fall of 2008, the regional prosecutor's office initiated a formal investigation into Wałęsa's abusing his executive prerogatives by "checking out his files" (Gmyz 2008).

Wałęsa collaborated voluntarily or even knowingly. Wałęsa's story supports the skeletons argument because it demonstrates that dissident organizations were infiltrated with secret collaborators (Wałęsa's experience could have easily been that of someone else from the top echelons of Solidarity) and such information was embarrassing for the former opposition. Indeed it was so embarrassing that it incentivized the opposition not to open the archives of the former secret police to hold the former autocrats accountable for their communist past. To be sure, this book does not propose normative judgments about Lech Wałęsa or any other dissidents.

A

Mathematical Proofs to Chapter 3

Definition: Formally, the Transition with Secret Information (TSI) game is defined by $N = \{A,O\}$ the set of players, where O, the opposition, is the Receiver and A, the autocrats, are the Sender, who has private information about the parameter i affecting and O and A's payoffs;

$i \sim u[0,1]$ is A's private information about infiltration levels; O knows that i is uniformally distributed;

$E(i)$ is the expected value of i based on O's prior belief about the distribution of i

$\mu(i \mid m)$ is O's a posterior belief about i after having observed A's action, m

$M : [0,1] \rightarrow \{Negotiate, SQ\}$ is the set of A's strategies;

$R : \{Negotiate, SQ\} \rightarrow \{refuse, renege, honor\}$ is the set of O's strategies;

N_A, N_O represent payoffs to A and O, respectively, associated with the status quo;

n_A, n_O represent payoffs to A and O, respectively associated with A's action to negotiate and O's action to refuse;

t_A, t_O represent payoffs to A and O, respectively, associated with A's action to negotiate and O's action to honor;

$i, 1-i$ represent payoffs to A and O, respectively, associated with A's action to negotiate and O's action to renege;

I assume that the relationships between the parameters of the model are as follows:

$$1 \geq t_A > N_A > n_A > 0,$$
$$0 \leq N_O < n_O < t_O \leq 1$$

The appropriate solution concept for solving this game is Perfect Bayesian Equilibrium (PBE). To find the PBE $(r^*, m^*, \mu(i|m)^*)$, we need to characterize a best response of A, $BR_A(i, r^*(m^*))$, a best response of response of O, $BR_O(m(i, r^*))$, and O's a posterior beliefs $\mu(i|m)$, consistent with O and A's strategies. There are two general classes of equilibria in signaling games: pooling (in which the receiver cannot update beliefs) and separating (in which such updating is possible).

Proposition 1: If $t_O \geq \frac{1}{2}$, (μ'; *Negotiate always; honor*) is a PBE, where μ' are the opposition's beliefs defined by *Prob* $(i|Negotiate) \sim u[0,1]$ and *Prob* $(i|Status\ Quo) \sim u(1-t_O, 1]$.

Since this is a pooling equilibrium, the opposition's beliefs on the equilibrium path are such that i is uniformly distributed on the $[0,1]$ interval (*Prob* $(i|Negotiate) \sim u[0,1]$). In PBE, beliefs off the equilibrium path also ought to be specified. I have assumed above that *Prob*$(i|Status\ Quo) \sim u(0,1-t_O]$ are the opposition's beliefs about the distributiton of i if the autocrats do not step down.

Note that the assumption of $t_O > n_O$ ensures there are no pooling equilibria where the autocrats play SQ and the opposition plays refuse. Such an equilibrium would require that $n_O \geq \frac{1}{2} > t_O$. Note further that only in very unique circumstances is there a pooling equilibrium in which the autocrats negotiate and the opposition plays a mixed strategy. To see this, note that in this equilibrium O would not update its beliefs, so these would be identical with the priors, and, in expectation, $E(i) = \frac{1}{2}$, implying the expected payoff from reneging for the opposition is $\frac{1}{2}$. In order for it to be optimal for the opposition to mix between Honor and Renege, we would have to have, $u_O(honor) = u_O(renege) = \frac{1}{2}$. To find the probability with which the opposition can make the autocrats indifferent between Negotiate and SQ, we need $N_A = p\frac{1}{2} + (1-p)t_A \Leftrightarrow p = \frac{N_A - t_A}{\frac{1}{2} - t_A}$.

The probability p is defined whenever the following conditions are satisfied: $t_A > \frac{1}{2} \geq N_A$.

This leads to the corollary:

Corollary: If $t_O = \frac{1}{2}$ and $t_A > \frac{1}{2} \geq N_A$, then ($\mu^*$; *Negotiate always; p*) is PBE, where $p = \frac{N_A - t_A}{\frac{1}{2} - t_A}$ and μ' is defined as in Proposition 1.

Thus, apart from this generically nonexisting case, if the opposition plays a mixed strategy, this has to be in conjunction with a separating equilibrium, as described in Proposition 2.

Proposition 2: If $1-2t_O \leq N_A$, $(\mu^{**};$ *Negotiate if* $i \geq i^* = 1-2t_O;$ $q)$ is PBE, where $q = (t_A - N_A)/(2t_O + t_A - 1)$ is the probability with which the opposition reneges on the amnesty promise $1-q$ is the probability that O honors the promise μ^{**} defined by $Pr(i \mid Negotiate) \sim u[i^*, 1]$ and $Pr(i \mid SQ) \sim u[0, i^*]$ describes the opposition's posterior beliefs supporting this equilibrium.

If the opposition observes that the autocrats negotiate, it knows that their level of infiltraton is at least i^*; if it does not, it knows its infiltration is lower than $i.^{*1}$

A separating equilibrium in which A *negotiates* when $i \geq i^*$ requires that O play a mixed strategy q (where O plays *renege* with probability p and *honor* with probability $1-q$, keeping A indifferent between *Negotiate* and *SQ*:

$$m = \begin{cases} Negotiate & \text{if } i \geq i^* \\ SQ & \text{if } i < i^* \end{cases}, \text{when } i = i^*.$$

And i^* has to make O just indifferent between reneging and honoring, that is:

$$u_O(honor) = u_O(renege)$$
$$n_O < 1 - E(i \mid Negotiate) = t_O$$

$E(i \mid Negotiate)$ is O's expectation of the value of i conditional on having observed *Negotiate*. We can write this expectation as $E(i \mid Negotiate) = \frac{i^*+1}{2}$ and calculate i^* from indifference and write this as follows:

$$i^* = 1 - 2t_O$$

A posterior belief consistent with the preceding strategy requires that:

$$Prob(i \mid Negotiate) \sim u[i^*, 1]$$

$$Prob(i \mid SQ) \sim u[0, i^*).$$

O's best response must make A indifferent between *Negotiate* and *~Negotiate*. To prevent A from sending a cheap talk message (always *Negotiate*), O must

---

[1] Note that any separating equilibrium must involve the opposition playing a mixed strategy. To see this, note first that knowing that O will choose *honor*, A would have an incentive to choose *Negotiate* whenever $i < t_A$. But if this were the case, O can update its beliefs about the distribution of i and there no longer is a pooling equilibrium. Similarly, knowing that O will choose *renege*, A would have an incentive to choose *Negotiate* whenever $i > N_A$, in which case O can again update their beliefs about the distribution of i, and there no longer is a pooling equilibrium.

use a mixed strategy. Note that if O always reneged, A would never step down unless $N_A < i$. On the other hand, if O always honored, A would always step down, which would destroy the quality of the signal. The mixed strategy is defined by a parameter q (where O plays *renege* with probability q and *honor* with probability $1-q$) that satisfies $q(i^*) + (1-q)(t_A) = N_A$, that is,

$$t_A - qt_A + qi^*q = N_A$$

$$q(i^* - t_A) = N_A - t_A$$

$$q = \frac{N_A - t_A}{i^* - t_A}$$

Substituting for i^* from $i^* = 1 - 2t_O$,

$$q = \frac{t_A - N_A}{2t_O + t_A - 1}$$

Note that since q is a probability, it must be within 0 and 1. Given that $t_A > N_A$ by assumption, we only require that $i^* > N_A$. This condition ensures that $q < 1$ (directly) and indirectly that $q > 0$ (by $t_A > N_A$). Thus, we have shown that when $N_A \geq 1 - 2t_O$, the strategy profile and beliefs (μ^{**}, *Negotiate* if and only if $i \geq i^*$, q) constitute a separating PBE.

We conclude this section by conducting comparative statics on the parameters determining q:

$$\frac{\partial q}{\partial t_A} = \frac{N_A + t_A - 1}{(t_O + t_A - 1)^2} > 0$$

This is positive whenever the condition for mixing is satisfied.

$$\frac{\partial(q)}{\partial t_O} = 2\frac{N_A - t_A}{(t_A + 2t_O - 1)^2} < 0$$

$$\frac{\partial(q)}{\partial N_A} = -\frac{1}{t_A + 2t_O - 1} < 0$$

Hence, we have Proposition 2: Provided that the opposition's payoff from not adopting TJ is sufficiently high relative to the communists' payoff from not negotiating, the communists will offer negotiations whenever the level of infiltration, i, is not less than $i^* = 1 - 2t_O$. The opposition's best response is a mixed strategy that randomizes between reneging and honoring with probability q and $1-q$, respectively. A marginal increase in the communists' utility from amnesty, t_A, makes the opposition more likely to renege, while marginal increases in the opposition's utility from amnesty, t_O, or the communists' utility from not stepping down, N_A, make the opposition less likely to renege.

B

Answers of MPs and Their Constituents to "More Should Be Done to Punish People Who Were Responsible for the Injustices of the Communist Regime"

The scale in the following tables is from 1 to 5, where 1 represents "completely agree" and 5 represents "completely disagree."

Czech Republic	Sample	Obs	Mean	Se
ODS	MPs	27	1.851852	0.6015175
	Public	165	1.848485	1.192487
KDP	MPs	13	1.384615	0.5063697
	Public	11	2	1.095445
KCSM	MPs	4	2	0.8164966
	Public	13	3.615385	1.192928
ČSSD	MPs	7	1.857143	0.3779645
	Public	34	2.882353	1.249599
Liberal and Social Union	MPs	4	2	0.8164966
	Public	9	2.444444	1.236033
KDÚ	MPs	4	1.75	0.5
	Public	15	2.133333	1.125463
ODA	MPs	5	1.8	0.4472136
	Public	46	1.847826	1.34936
Movement for self-governing democracy	MPs	3	1.666667	0.5773503
	Public	20	2.45	1.050063
Assembly for the Republic	MPs	5	1	0
	Public	21	2.333333	1.197219

(continued)

Table *(continued)*

Czech Republic	Sample	Obs	Mean	Se
OF	MPs	1	4	
	Public	15	3.066667	2.016598
Mean MP		1.75548		
Mean public		2.238348		

Slovakia	Sample	Obs	Mean	Se
HZDS	Public	45	3.022222	1.802636
SDL'	Public	38	2.842105	1.103467
SNS	Public	33	2.909091	1.82626
KDH	Public	27	2.555556	1.625123
SMK	Public	18	2	0.9074852
Slovak Green Party	Public	46	2.413043	1.001689
Conservative Democratic Party	Public	9	2.111111	1.054093
Alliance of Democrats in Slovak Republic	Public	6	2	1.095445
Slovak Social Democratic Left Party	Public	27	2.62963	1.043225
DÚ	Public	9	2.111111	1.166667
Mean public		2.459387		

Hungary	Sample	Obs	Mean	Se
FiDeSz	MPs	6	2.333333	0.8164966
	Public	105	2.742857	1.59945
SzDSz	MPs	14	2.785714	0.8925824
	Public	42	2.833333	1.575989
MDF	MPs	6	2.5	1.048809
	Public	33	2.121212	1.96465
Smallholders	MPs	7	1.285714	0.48795
	Public	28	2.392857	1.749906
MSzP	MPs	32	2.90625	0.9954534
	Public	100	2.83	1.449869
KDMP	MPs	6	1.833333	1.32916
	Public	58	2.448276	1.708312
Mean MP		2.27		
Mean public		2.56		

Ukraine	Sample	Obs	Mean	Se
Communist Party of Ukraine	MPs	22	3.863636	1.457181
	Public	52	3.153846	1.419536

Answers of MPs and Their Constituents

Ukarine	Sample	Obs	Mean	Se
Socialist Party of Ukraine	MPs	20	3.6	1.602629
	Public	17	3.117647	1.536325
Rukh	MPs	6	1.666667	.5163978
	Public	52	2.403846	1.445203
Green Party of Ukraine	MPs	5	2.8	1.48324
	Public	62	3.064516	1.32900
Ukrainian Conservative	MPs	2	2.5	2.12132
Republican Party	Public	8	2.375	1.685018
Congress of National	MPs	3	1.666667	1.154701
Democratic Forces	Public	5	2.6	1.51657
Mean MPs			2.682828	
Mean Public			2.785809	

Russia	Sample	Obs	Mean	Se
Communist Party of	MPs	13	3.153846	1.068188
Russian Feder.	Public	80	3.475	1.2010023
Liberal Democratic Party	MPs	13	3.076923	1.037749
	Public	120	2.666667	1.1474
Russia's Choice	MPs	9	2.888889	1.054093
	Public	138	2.710145	1.215489
Party of Russia's Unity	MPs	3	3.666667	0.5773503
and Consent	Public	67	2.716418	1.40136367
Yavlinsky Block	MPs	5	3.4	1.341641
	Public	90	2.822222	1.277091
Mean MPs			3.237265	
Mean public			2.87809	

Source: Miller, White, and Heywood (1998).

C

Sampling Technique and Transitional Justice Survey Questionnaire

The Transitional Justice Survey (TJS) was written and administrated by the author. It was based on 3,057 face-to-face interviews conducted in December 2004 by the Pentor Survey Research Company in Poland, Hoffman Research International in Hungary, and the Opinion Window Research International in the Czech Republic. In this appendix, I use Poland to describe the specific sampling technique used in the Transitional Justice Survey. I use the Hungarian version of the questionnaire.

The Sampling Technique

The Polish part of the survey was conducted using the omnibus technique with direct, face-to-face interviews of 1,006 persons representative of a random sample of the population aged fifteen and older. As a result, only two-thirds of the samples included citizens who at the time of the survey were at least twenty years old. However, when the samples were split into those respondents who at the time of the survey were younger than thirty-five and those who were older than thirty-five, the between-group differences in the dependent variable and independent variables of interest were not sensitive to age (even in variables such as involvement in the secret police and opposition networks) and were insignificant at the 90 percent confidence intervals (CI). Furthermore, in Poland, the younger cohort showed a higher average number of persons known in both the secret police and opposition networks. In all three countries, average transitional justice (TJ) demand was higher among the younger cohort, although at the 90 percent level, insignificantly so.

Interviews were conducted at the respondents' homes during weekends (to increase the chance that the respondents would be present). The sampling procedure consisted of three steps:

1. In the first step of the sampling procedure, strata were defined using administrative regions (in Poland, there are eighteen such regions) and types of localities (e.g., villages, towns, cities with population size under twenty thousand, cities with population size between twenty thousand and fifty thousand, cities with population size between fifty thousand and two hundred thousand, and cities with population size over two hundred thousand). The number of sampling units was calculated for each such strata (for instance, the Mazowsze region, cities between fifty thousand and two hundred thousand), proportionally to the number of people aged fifteen and above within that strata. The total number of sampling points was 200. Each sampling unit was assigned five interviews. Hence the first stage of sampling involved distributing a layer of sampling units across strata proportional to the structure of the population.

2. The next step involved random sampling of localities where interviews would be conducted. The sampling was conducted separately for each stratum, with probabilities of drawing particular localities proportional to their size (for instance, if locality x is twice the size of locality y, x is twice as likely to be sampled than y). This ensured that every person living within a strata had exactly the same chance of being sampled. The sampling was conducted with returns, meaning that any locality could be sampled twice. This was essential, since the number of sampling units could exceed the number of localities in a given strata (for instance, in the Mazowsze region, there is only one city with a population greater than two hundred thousand, but ten sampling units were assigned to it in stage 1).

3. The third stage involved the PESEL Information Database (containing ID numbers similar to social security numbers in the United States). On the basis of the list of localities resulting from stages 1 and 2, specific persons were sampled based on their ID numbers along with their home addresses in the sampled localities. Half of the persons were women, the remaining half were men.

Each thus characterized person became a sampling unit. The interviewer conducted the first interview with the sampled person and the four following interviews in dwellings in close proximity to the sampled address. These dwellings were chosen using the random route method: After finishing the first interview, the interviewer followed a course described in his or her instructions (excluding arbitrariness) and conducted interviews in one in every five dwellings he or she passed.

Within each dwelling, the specific respondent was also randomly selected. It was the person who was at least fifteen and who had his or her birthday most recently. In addition, the respondents alternated between men and women.

The interviewers' calls were preceded with a letter announcing his or her visit. Further checks included mailing cards after the interview had been completed and telephone calls made randomly to 10 percent of the respondents.

This way, one thousand interviews were specified. The thus-constructed sample represents fully the structure of the population in terms of type of locality and administrative region and almost fully in terms of gender (the sample contains 50 percent women, although 52 percent of the Polish population are women). All remaining variables are distributed randomly, but with a sample of this size, one can assume that the distribution of these variables resembles the distribution in the population.

The only limitation of the randomness of the sample is the error associated with frequent refusals in some demographic groups and frequent absences from home of certain demographic groups. This is corrected by applying weights based on age, gender, and education, separately for rural and urban areas.

To estimate the magnitude of this error, we conducted an analysis comparing the structure of the obtained samples with the structure of the population. We detected only two systematic differences:

- An underrepresentation of teenagers relative to their participation in the population, most likely due to their larger mobility and decreased chances of finding them at home
- An overrepresentation of persons with college degrees combined with an underrepresentation of persons without high school degrees, most likely owing to differences in the readiness to share opinions between educated and uneducated persons

Both tendencies are corrected by applying weights to the obtained results.

The Questionnaire (based on the Hungarian survey)

I would like to start with asking you a few questions about your political views.

1) Which party did you vote for in the most recent (2002) parliamentary elections?
   1. MSzP
   2. SzDSz
   3. MDF
   4. FiDeSz
   5. MIEP

2) Which party do you intend to vote for in the upcoming (2006) elections?
   1. MSzP
   2. SzDSz
   3. MDF
   4. FiDeSz
   5. MIEP

In your opinion, how important are the following factors in determining whether a person is elected to parliament?

3) (ELECTC1 53.1) Their talents and abilities
   5. very important
   4. somewhat important
   3 uncertain
   2. somewhat unimportant
   1. very unimportant
   8. no answer/refused

4) (ELECTC1 53.2) Being backed by powerful organizations or people
   5. very important
   4. somewhat important
   3. uncertain
   2. somewhat unimportant
   1. very unimportant
   8. no answer/refused

5) (ELECTC1 53.3) Representing the interests of voters
   5. very important
   4. somewhat important
   3. uncertain
   2. somewhat unimportant
   1. very unimportant
   8. no answer/refused

6) (ELECTC1 53.4) Being members of the former communist leadership
   5. very important
   4. somewhat important
   3. uncertain
   2. somewhat unimportant
   1. very unimportant
   8. no answer/refused

7) (THREATC 72) How threatening to Hungary's way of life would you
   say fascists are?
   4. extremely threatening
   3. somewhat threatening
   2. not particularly threatening
   1. not at all threatening
   7. Don't know (DK)/no answer

8) (THREATC 73) How threatening to Hungary's way of life would you
   say communists are?
   4. extremely threatening
   3. somewhat threatening
   2. not particularly threatening
   1. not at all threatening
   7. DK/no answer

To what extent do you agree with the following statements:

9) (TOLCOM1 85) Communists should be banned from putting up
   candidates for public office.
   5. agree strongly
   4. agree
   3. uncertain
   2. disagree

1. disagree strongly
8. no answer/refused

10) (TOLCOM2 85) Communists should be allowed to hold public meetings in our town.
   5. agree strongly
   4. agree
   3. uncertain
   2. disagree
   1. disagree strongly
   8. no answer/refused

11) (CHG89) Since the changes in 1989 in Hungary do you think the political system in Hungary:[1]
   3. changed for the better
   2. stayed the same
   1. changed for the worse
   7. DK
   8. no answer/refused

Now I would like to talk to you about the ways in which Hungary has been dealing with its non-democratic past. Specifically, I would like to ask about your opinions on lustration (screening) laws, i.e., examining links of politicians with the communist secret political police. I would also like to learn your opinion about decommunization, i.e., preventing former communists from holding public office. I would now like to find out what is your opinion concerning these two institutions.

12) Do you believe that at this point in time lustration should be carried out, that is, links of politicians to the secret political police should be examined?
   5. agree strongly
   4. agree
   3. uncertain
   2. disagree
   1. strongly disagree
   6. no answer/refused

---

[1] The first eleven questions are identical with James Gibson's questions used in his Legal Values Survey in 1995.

13) What is your evaluation of the consequences of the lustration law so far?
    5. positive
    3. indifferent
    1. negative
    6. difficult to say

14) Do you know anyone who before 1989 had worked as an informer for the III/III agency?
    5. yes, I know ten such persons
    4. yes, but less than ten such persons
    3. yes, but less than five such persons
    2. I know perhaps one or two such persons
    1. I don't know anyone like that
    8. no answer/DK

15) Is there anyone you know personally who you suspect that before 1989 had been under investigation by the III/III agency?
    5. yes, I know ten such persons
    4. yes, but less than ten such persons
    3. yes, but less than five such persons
    2. I know perhaps one or two such persons
    1. I don't know anyone like that
    8. no answer/DK

(Ask the following question only if the respondent gave at least 3 in response to question 12)

16) Lustration should only apply to persons who worked for the secret police
    5. before 1956
    4. before 1968
    3. before 1981
    1. no one should be exempted from lustration
    8. DK/no answer

17) Decommunization should only apply to persons who were active:
    5. before 1956
    4. before 1968
    3. before 1981

1. no one should be exempted from lustration
8. DK/no answer

(Check all that apply.)

18) An ideal lustration or decommunization procedure would cover the following positions:
    1. communist (MSzMP) party membership
    2. leading role in the Central or Regional Committee of the MSzMP
    3. working full time for the III/III Department (secret police) or the AVH paramilitary militia units
    4. being an informer of the III/III secret communist police
    5. having conversations with the communist police officers
    6. working for military intelligence and counterintelligence
    7. pacifying anticommunist demonstrations as a draft soldier in the military forces
    8. pacifying anticommunist demonstrations as a professional officer in the military or militia forces

(Check all that apply.)

19) Ideally, lustration and decommunization should cover the following professions:
    1. university professors
    2. justices and prosecutors
    3. attorneys
    4. the police and military
    5. candidates running in national parliamentary elections
    6. candidates running in local parliamentary elections
    7. governors, mayors, and members of the city council
    8. bankers
    9. doctors
    10. priests

20) The problem with lustration is that files of the III/III Department (the secret police) were destroyed, so that many collaborators will not be uncovered anyway
    5. agree strongly
    4. agree
    3. uncertain/DK

2. disagree
1. disagree strongly
8. no answer/refused

21) The problem with lustration is that files of the III/III Department (the secret police) are not reliable as evidence of collaboration and using them in the lustration procedure may result in accusing innocent people.
   5. agree strongly
   4. agree
   3. uncertain/DK
   2. disagree
   1. disagree strongly
   8. no answer/refused

D

Birth and Death of Parliamentary Parties by Their Position Regarding Lustration

Country	Party acronym	PPMD score	Seatshare when in parliament for the first time	Seatshare when in parliament for the last time
Bulgaria	BSP	0.00	(1990) 52.75	(2005) 34.17
	EL	0.00	(1997) 5.83	
	NDSV	0.21	(2001) 50	(2005) 22.08
	BBB	0.32	(1991) 10	(2005) 14.17
	DPS	0.32	(1990) 5.75	(1997) 5
	G	0.38	(2005) 8.75	
	ODS	0.94	(1990) 36	(2005) 8.33
	DSB	0.94	(2005) 7.08	
	BZNS	1.00	(1994) 7.5	
Czech R.	LB	0	(1992) 14.1	
	KSČ	0	(1990) 13.2	
	CSCM	0	(1992) 17.5	(2006) 12.8
	ČSSD	0.34	(1992) 6.5	(2006) 32.33
	Green Party	0.49	(2006) 6.3	
	LSU	0.49	(1992) 6.5	
	ODA	0.75	(1992) 5.9	(1996) 6.36
	ODS	0.75	(1992) 38	(2006) 35.4
	ODS-KDS	0.75	(1992) 29.7	
	KDÚ	0.77	(1990) 8.4	
	KDÚ-ČSL	0.77	(1992) 6.3	(2006) 7.2
	US-KDÚ-ČSL	0.83	(2002) 14.27	
	US	0.89	(1998) 8.6	
	REP		(1992) 6	
	SPR-RSÈ (Union for the Republic)		(1996) 8.01	
	HSDSMS		(1990) 10	(1992) 5.9

(continued)

Table *(continued)*

Country	Party acronym	PPMD score	Seatshare when in parliament for the first time	Seatshare when in parliament for the last time
Estonia	EÜRP	0.07	(1999) 5.95	
	MKE	0.07	(1995) 5.95	(1999) 6.93
	KMU		(1995) 40.59	
	EME		(1999) 6.93	
	KK	0.11	(1992) 16.83	
	Kesk	0.15	(1992) 7.92	(2003) 27.72
	RL	0.18	(2003) 12.87	
	Ref	0.32	(1995) 18.81	(2003) 18.81
	SK	0.32	(1992) 7.92	
	Mõõd	0.50	(1992) 11.88	(2003) 5.94
	ResP	0.56	(2003) 27.72	
	R	0.56	(1992) 14.85	
	Isam	1.00	(1992) 28.72	(2003) 6.94
	ERSP		(1992) 9.9	
Hungary	MSzP	0.00	(1990) 8.55	(2006) 43.2
	SzDSz	0.31	(1994) 17.9	(2006) 6.5
	KDNP	0.37	(1990) 5.44	(1994) 5.7
	MDF	0.60	(1990) 42.49	(2006) 5
	FIDESz	0.75	(1990) 24.09	
	Fidesz-MPP	0.75	(1990) 5.7	(2002) 42.49
	FKgP	0.88	(1990) 11.4	(1998) 12
	Fidesz – KDNP		(2006) 42	
Latvia	PCTVL	0.00	(1990) 27.36	
	SP	0.00	(1995) 8	
	LSP	0.00	(1995) 18	
	S	0.00	(1995) 5	
	TSP	0.11	(1993) 13	(1998) 16
	ZZS	0.58	(1993) 12	(2002) 16.7
	LPP	0.77	(2002) 10	
	LKDS	0.77	(1993) 6	(1998) 14
	LTF	0.77	(1990) 65.17	
	LC	0.77	(1993) 36	(1998)21
	JL	0.81	(1998) 8	(2006) 16.4
	TP	0.82	(1995) 16	(2006) 19.5
	TB/LNNK	1.00	(1993) 21	(2006) 7
	Indep		(1990) 7.46	
	DCP		(1993) 5	
	LPP-LC		(2006) 8.6	
	SC		(2006) 14.42	

Parliamentary Parties and Lustration Position

Country	Party acronym	PPMD score	Seatshare when in parliament for the first time	Seatshare when in parliament for the last time
Lithuania	LKP	0.00	(1990) 34.07	
	LKD		(2004) 27.66	
	LDLP	0.00	(1990) 6.01	(2000) 18.44
	LSDP	0.00	(1992) 5.67	(2004) 14.18
	CPSU	0.00	(1990) 5.19	
	VNDPS	0.03	(2004) 7.09	
	CS	0.34	(1996) 9.49	
	NS	0.34	(2000) 19.86	
	LDP	0.50	(2004) 7.09	
	LTS	0.58	(2000) 23.40	
	LPKTS/ LKDP/LDP	0.66	(1992) 12.77	
	ODS	0.73	(1990) 30.88	(1992) 21.28
	TS(LK)	0.73	(1996) 51.09	(2004) 17.73
	KDS	1.00	(1996) 11.68	
	LiCS	1.00	(2004) 12.77	
	Independents		(1990) 17.19	
Poland	SLD	0.00	(1991) 13	(2005) 12.01
	PZPR	0.00	(1989) 37.6	
	SD	0.00	(1989) 13.7	
	UP	0.08	(1993) 8.9	
	PSL	0.26	(1991) 10.4	(2005) 5.46
	PL	0.26	(1991) 6.1	
	ZSL	0.26	(1989) 13.7	
	Self-Defense	0.32	(2001) 11.5	(2005) 12.23
	UW	0.40	(1997) 13	
	UD	0.40	(1991) 13.5	(1993) 16.1
	KLD	0.40	(1991) 8	
	PO	0.53	(2001) 14.1	(2005) 29.04
	AWS	0.70	(1997) 43.7	
	Solidarity	0.97	(1989) 35	(1991) 5.9
	KPN	0.98	(1991) 10	
	PiS	0.98	(2001) 9.6	(2005) 33.84
	ZChN	1.00	(1991) 10.7	
	LPR	1.00	(2001) 8.3	(2005) 7.42
Romania	PRM	0.00	(1996) 5.54	(2004) 15.29
	RSDP	0.00	(1996) 26.53	(2000) 47.4
	PSD	0.07	(2004) 35.99	
	FSN	0.07	(1990) 66.41	(1992) 13.11

(continued)

Table *(continued)*

Country	Party acronym	PPMD score	Seatshare when in parliament for the first time	Seatshare when in parliament for the last time
	PUNR	0.15	(1992) 9.15	(1996) 5.25
	PUR	0.23	(2004) 5.42	
	FDSN	0.30	(1992) 35.67	
	USD	0.56	(1996) 15.4	(2000) 47.4
	PD	0.56	(1990) 6	(2004) 15.29
	RMDS	0.75	(1990) 7.32	(2004) 7.01
	PNL	0.83	(1990) 7.32	(2004) 20.38
Slovakia	KSS	0.00	(1990) 16.33	(2002) 7.33
	SDĽ	0.14	(1992) 19.1	(1998) 15.33
	HZDS	0.57	(1992) 47.06	(2006) 8.79
	Smer	0.75	(2002) 16.67	(2006) 29.14
	SNS	0.61	(1992) 11.76	(2006) 11.73
	SMK	0.71	(1992) 9.8	(2006) 11.68
	ANO	0.75	(2002) 10	
	SKDÚ	0.76	(2002) 18.77	(2006) 18.36
	KDH	0.96	(1992) 11.76	(2006) 8.31

E

Mathematical Proofs to Chapter 7

Recall that:

$$EU_{PC}(y) = - \begin{cases} y(1-q) - (1-q)(2lp + 2r(1-p)) - \Delta & \text{for } y \in [2r-1, l) \\ y(1-q)(1-2p) - 2r(1-p)(1-q) - \Delta & \text{for } y \in [l, r] \\ y(q-1) - \Delta & \text{for } y = (r, 1] \end{cases}$$

where $\Delta = pql + (1-p)qr$

Taking the derivative of EU_P gives

$$\frac{\partial EU_{PC}}{\partial y} = \begin{cases} 1-q & \text{for } y \in [2r-1, l) \\ (1-q)(1-2p) & \text{for } y \in [l, r] \\ q-1 & \text{for } y = (r, 1] \end{cases}$$

$$\frac{\partial EU_{PC}}{\partial y} > 0 \Rightarrow y^* = \begin{cases} l - \varepsilon & \text{if } y \in [2r-1, l) \\ r & \text{if } y \in [l, r] \end{cases}$$

$$\frac{\partial EU_{PC}}{\partial y} < 0 \Rightarrow y^* = \begin{cases} l & \text{if } y \in [l, r] \\ r + \varepsilon & \text{if } y \in (r, 1) \end{cases}$$

and

$$\frac{\partial EU_{PC}}{\partial y} = 0 \Rightarrow y^* = \begin{cases} \text{any } y \in [2r-1, l) & \text{for } y \in [2r-1, l) \\ \text{any } y \in [l, r] & \text{for } y \in [l, r] \\ \text{any } y \in (r, 1) & \text{for } y \in (r, 1) \end{cases}$$

$$\frac{\partial EU_{PC}}{\partial y} > 0 \ \& \ y \in [2r-1, l) \Rightarrow q = 0$$

$$\frac{\partial EU_{PC}}{\partial y} > 0 \ \& \ y \in [l, r] \Rightarrow q = 0 \ \& \ p < \tfrac{1}{2}$$

$$\frac{\partial EU_{PC}}{\partial y} = 0 \ \& \ y \in [2r-1, l) \cup (r, 1] \Rightarrow q = 1$$

$$\frac{\partial EU_{PC}}{\partial y} = 0 \ \& \ y \in [l, r] \Rightarrow q = 1 \text{ or } p = \tfrac{1}{2}$$

$$\frac{\partial EU_{PC}}{\partial y} < 0 \ \& \ y \in [l, r] \Rightarrow q = 0 \ \& \ p > \tfrac{1}{2}$$

$$\frac{\partial EU_{PC}}{\partial y} < 0 \ \& \ y \in (r, 1] \Rightarrow q = 0$$

Notice that $y \in [l, r] \Rightarrow \frac{\partial EU_{PC}}{\partial y} \leq$, implying $y^* = l$

and $y \in (r, 1] \Rightarrow \frac{\partial EU_{PC}}{\partial y} \leq$, implying $y^* = r$

Thus, there are only three cases to consider:

1) $p < \tfrac{1}{2} \ \& \ q = 0$
2) $p > \tfrac{1}{2} \ \& \ q = 0$
3) $q = 1$ or $p = \tfrac{1}{2}$

1) $\arg \max_{\{y | y \in [2r-1, \, l)\}} EU_{PC}(y) = l - \varepsilon$

$\arg \max_{\{y | y \in [l, r]\}} EU_{PC}(y) = r$

I show that $EU_{PC}(l) < EU_P(r)$

$$\begin{aligned}
LHS &= EU_P(l) = (l - \varepsilon)(1 - q) - (1 - q)(2lp + 2r(1 - p)) - \Delta \\
&= (l - \varepsilon)(1 - q) - (1 - q)(2lp + 2r(1 - p)) - \Delta \\
RHS &= EU_P(r) = r(1 - q)(1 - 2p) - 2r(1 - p)(1 - q) - \Delta \\
LHS &< RHS \leftrightarrow l(1 - 2p) + 2p\varepsilon - \varepsilon - 2r(1 - p) < r(1 - p) - 2r(1 - p) \\
&\leftrightarrow l(1 - 2p) + 2p\varepsilon < r(1 - 2p) - \varepsilon
\end{aligned}$$

But by $p < \tfrac{1}{2}$, this is always the case. Thus, $EU_{PC}(l) < EU_{PC}(r)$ and $r = \arg \max_{\{y | y \in [0,1]\}} EU_{PC}$ for $p < \tfrac{1}{2} \ \& \ q = 0$

This concludes the proof that if $p < \tfrac{1}{2}$ and $q = 0$, PC's optimal strategy is $y^* = r$. from the proposition in section 7.2.2.2.

2) $\arg \max_{\{y | y \in (l, r]\}} EU_{PC}(y) = l$

$\arg \max_{\{y | y \in (l, r]\}} EU_{PC}(y) = r + \varepsilon$

I have to show that $EU_{PC}(l) > EU_{PC}(r + \varepsilon)$

$LHS = EU_{PC}(l) = l(1 - q)(1 - 2p) - 2r(1 - p)(1 - q) - \Delta$

$RHS = EU_{PC}(r + \varepsilon) = (r + \varepsilon)(q - 1) - \Delta$

$LHS > RHS \leftrightarrow (l)(1 - q)(1 - 2p) - 2r(1 - p)(1 - q) > -(r + \varepsilon)(1 - q)$

$\leftrightarrow l(1 - 2p) - 2r(1 - p) > -r - \varepsilon$

$\leftrightarrow l - 2lp + -2p - 2r + 2rp > -r - \varepsilon$

$\leftrightarrow 2p(r - l) + l > r - \varepsilon$

$\leftrightarrow 2p(r - l) > r - l - \varepsilon$

But by $p > \frac{1}{2}$ this is always the case. Thus, $EU_{PC}(l) > EU_{PC}(r + \varepsilon)$ and $l = \arg\max_{\{y|y \in [0,1]\}} EU_{PC}$ for $p > \frac{1}{2}$ & $q = 0$

This concludes the proof that if $p > \frac{1}{2}$ and $q = 0$, PC's optimal strategy is $y^* = l$ from the proposition in section 7.2.2.2.

3) It is easy to see that in the generically nonexistent case, when $p = \frac{1}{2}$, PC is indifferent to outcomes associated with the strategy $y = l$, $y = r$, and any $y \in [l, r]$. It remains to be proven that if $q = 1$, PC's optimal strategy is any $y \in [0, 1]$. Note that if $q = 1$, then by lemma 3, it is irrelevant which strategy the post-communists pick.

Thus, for $q = 1$, $EU_{PC}(y) = -pl - (1 - p)r$, for all $y \in [0, 1]$.

This concludes the proof of the proposition from section 7.2.2.2.

Sensitivity Analysis

In this section, I relax constraints placed upon the utility functions of the players in order to demonstrate that the results are robust with respect to different ways of representing preferences. I proceed in two steps:

1. Relaxing linearity: I assume that the preferences of all players *PC, R, L*, and *A* are single-peaked and symmetric but are represented by quadratic instead of linear utility functions.
2. Relaxing symmetry: I assume that the quadratic utility functions representing the preferences of players *R* and *L* are no longer symmetric around their ideal points (although their ideal points are still the same as before).

I focus on only the cases of closed rules of procedure, that is, cases where $q = 0$. In the case of open rules, the median always adopts his or her ideal policy in the final stage, so the outcome will be identical irrespective of the utility functions, as long as they are single-peaked.

1) Let b_i represent Player i's bliss point. Relaxing linearity and introducing symmetric quadratic preferences, assume:

$$u_M(a_M) = \begin{cases} -(x - b_M)^2 & \text{if } a_M = x \\ -(y - b_M)^2 & \text{if } a_M = y \end{cases}$$

$$u_{PC}(a_M) = \begin{cases} -x^2 & \text{if } a_M = x \\ -y^2 & \text{if } a_M = y \end{cases}$$

$$u_A(a_M) = \begin{cases} -(x - b_P)^2 & \text{if } a_M = x \\ -(y - b_P)^2 & \text{if } a_M = y \end{cases},$$

where a_M is M's action and $M \in \{R, L\}$.

Since the functions are single-peaked, the interaction between M and A will proceed in the same way as outlined in section 7.2.2.1. There are three cases to consider:

a) $0 < r \leq \frac{1}{2}$

b) $\frac{1}{2} < r \leq \frac{1+l}{2}$

c) $\frac{1+l}{2} < r < 1$

These cases are distinguished by the positioning of the possible medians (the moderate/left and moderate/right parties) with respect to each other and with respect to the 0, 1 extremes. The positions and the corresponding outcomes of the interaction between the median, M, and anticommunist proposer, A, are calculated similarly to the restricted case in section 7.2.2.1 and we obtain, as before, the formulas for PC's expected utility:

PC's utility function can be written in case a $(0 < r \leq \frac{1}{2})$ as:

$$EU_P(y) = \begin{cases} -p(2l - y)^2 - (1 - p)(2r - y)^2 & \text{for } y \in [0, l) \\ -py^2 - (1 - p)(2r - y)^2 & \text{for } y \in (l, r) \\ -y & \text{for } y = [r, 1] \end{cases}$$

In case b $(\frac{1}{2} < r \leq \frac{1+l}{2})$:

$$EU_{PC}(y) = \begin{cases} -p(2l - y)^2 - (1 - p)(2r - y)^2 & \text{for } y \in [2r - 1, l] \\ -py^2 - (1 - p)(2r - y)^2 & \text{for } y \in (l, r) \\ -y & \text{for } y = [r, 1] \end{cases}$$

Mathematical Proofs to Chapter 7

and in case c ($\frac{1+l}{2} < r \leq 1$):

$$EU_{PC}(y) = \begin{cases} -py^2 - (1-p) * (1)^2 & \text{for } y \in [l, 2r-1) \\ -py^2 - (1-p)(2r-y)^2 & \text{for } y \in (l, r) \\ -y^2 & \text{for } y = [r, 1] \end{cases}$$

Taking the derivative of EU_P gives:

a) $\frac{\partial EU_{PC}}{\partial y} = \begin{cases} 4pl + 4r - 4pr - 2y & \text{for } y \in [0, l] \\ 4r - 4pr - 2y & \text{for } y \in (l, r) \\ -2y & \text{for } y = [r, 1] \end{cases}$

b) $\frac{\partial EU_{PC}}{\partial y} = \begin{cases} 4pl + 4r - 4pr - 2y & \text{for } y \in [2r-1, l] \\ 4r - 4pr - 2y & \text{for } y \in (l, r) \\ -2y & \text{for } y = [r, 1] \end{cases}$

c) $\frac{\partial EU_{PC}}{\partial y} = \begin{cases} 2py & \text{for } y \in [l, 2r-1) \\ 4r - 4pr - 2y & \text{for } y \in (2r-1, r) \\ -2y & \text{for } y = [r, 1] \end{cases}$

The first-order conditions are:

a) $\frac{\partial EU_{PC}}{\partial y} = 0 \Rightarrow y^* = \begin{cases} 2(r - p(r-l)) & \text{for } y \in [0, l] \\ 2r(1-p) & \text{for } y \in (l, r) \\ 0 & \text{for } y \in [r, 1] \end{cases}$

b) $\frac{\partial EU_{PC}}{\partial y} = 0 \Rightarrow y^* = \begin{cases} 2(r - p(r-l)) & \text{for } y \in [2r-1, l] \\ 2r(1-p) & \text{for } y \in (l, r) \\ 0 & \text{for } y \in [r, 1] \end{cases}$

c) $\frac{\partial EU_{PC}}{\partial y} = 0 \Rightarrow y^* = \begin{cases} 0 & \text{for } y \in [l, 2r-1] \\ 2r(1-p) & \text{for } y \in (2r-, r) \\ 0 & \text{for } y \in [r, 1] \end{cases}$

It is necessary to verify for which parameter values the optimal y^* is in the required range, that is:

$0 \leq 2(r - p(r-l)) \leq l$

$l \leq 2r(1-p) < r$

$r \leq 0 \leq 1$

$2r(1 - p)$ is in the required range for $p \in (\frac{1}{2}, 1 - \frac{l}{2r})$, but the maxima of the utility functions in cases $y \in [0, l]$ and $y \in [r, 1]$ are outside of the specified range, so we have corner solutions, leading to the following:

a) if $y \in [0, l]$, then $\frac{\partial EU_p}{\partial y} > 0 \Rightarrow y^* = l$

if $y \in [r, 1]$, then $\frac{\partial EU_p}{\partial y} < 0 \Rightarrow y^* = r$

Taken together this yields:

a) $y* = \begin{cases} l & \text{if } p \geq 1 - \frac{l}{2r} \\ 2r(1 - p) & \text{if } p \in (1 - \frac{l}{2r}, \frac{1}{2}) \\ r & \text{if } p \leq \frac{1}{2} \end{cases}$

Conducting the same analysis for (b) and (c):

b) $y* = \begin{cases} l & \text{if } p \geq 1 - \frac{l}{2r} \\ 2r(1 - p) & \text{if } p \in (1 - \frac{l}{2r}, \frac{1}{2}) \\ r & \text{if } p \leq \frac{1}{2} \end{cases}$

c) $y* = \begin{cases} l & \text{if } p \geq \frac{l}{2r} \\ 2r(1 - p) & \text{if } p \in (\frac{l}{2r}, \frac{1}{2}) \\ r & \text{if } p \leq \frac{1}{2} \end{cases}$

2) In the case of PC and A, it is not significant whether the utility functions are symmetric or not, because their ideal points are at the boundaries of the transitional justice issue space. Assume that players L and R have the preferences:

$$u_M(x) = -(x - b_M - \Delta)^2$$

where b_M is M's bliss point and the parameter $\Delta > 0$ represents the extent to which M's preferences are skewed so that she is more sensitive toward transitional justice milder than her ideal point. Consider the interaction between the Proposer, A, and Median, $M \in \{R, L\}$. Suppose that PC proposed $y < m$, where $m \in \{r, l\}$. To make M at least as happy with x as with y, A has to propose x such that:

$$U_M(x) \geq U_M(y)$$
$$-(x - b_M - \Delta)^2 \leq -(y - b_M - \Delta)^2$$

where $x, y \in [0, 1]$

which simplifies to:

$$-x^2 + x(2m + 2\Delta) + y^2 - y(2m + 2\Delta) \leq 0$$

The optimal proposal under this constraint is found solving for x, giving

$$x_1 = \frac{-2(m+\Delta)+(2(m+\Delta)-2y)}{-2} = 2(m + \Delta) - y$$

$$x_2 = \frac{-2(m+\Delta)-(2(m+\Delta)-2y)}{-2} = y$$

Thus, depending on whether L or R gets chosen, PC's payoff from playing y is exactly the same as in case (1), except for the parameter Δ added to l or r. Collecting this together, as in (1), we get:

a) $0 < r \leq \frac{1}{2} - \Delta$

$$EU_{PC}(y) = \begin{cases} -p(2(l + \Delta) - y)^2 - (1 - p)((2r + \Delta) - y)^2 & \text{for } y \in [0, l) \\ -py^2 - (1 - p)(2(r + \Delta) - y)^2 & \text{for } y \in (l, r) \\ -y & \text{for } y = [r, 1] \end{cases}$$

b) $\frac{1}{2} - \Delta < r \leq \frac{1+l}{2} - \Delta$

$$EU_{PC}(y) = \begin{cases} -p(2l - y)^2 - (1 - p)(2r + \Delta) - y)^2 & \text{for } y \in [2r - 1, l] \\ -py^2 - (1 - p)(2(r + \Delta) - y)^2 & \text{for } y \in (l, r) \\ -y & \text{for } y = [r, 1] \end{cases}$$

c) $\frac{1+l+\Delta}{2} < r < \frac{1+l+\Delta}{2} - 1$

$$EU_P(y) = \begin{cases} -py^2 - (1 - p) * (1)^2 & \text{for } y \in [l, 2r - 1) \\ -py^2 - (1 - p)(2r + \Delta) - y)^2 & \text{for } y \in (l, r) \\ -y^2 & \text{for } y = [r, 1] \end{cases}$$

The solution for PC's optimal strategy is also analogous:

a) $y* = \begin{cases} l + \Delta & \text{if } p \geq 1 - \frac{l}{2r} \\ 2(r + \Delta)(1 - p) & \text{if } p \in (1 - \frac{l}{2r}, \frac{1}{2}) \\ r + \Delta & \text{if } p \leq \frac{1}{2} \end{cases}$

Conducting the same analysis for (b) and (c), I get the following results:

b) $y* = \begin{cases} l + \Delta & \text{if } p \geq 1 - \frac{l}{2r} \\ 2r(1-p) & \text{if } p \in (1 - \frac{l}{2r}, \frac{1}{2}) \\ r + \Delta & \text{if } p \leq \frac{1}{2} \end{cases}$

c) $y* = \begin{cases} l + \Delta & \text{if } p \geq \frac{l}{2r} \\ 2(r+\Delta)(1-p) & \text{if } p \in (\frac{l}{2r}, \frac{1}{2}) \\ r + \Delta & \text{if } p \leq \frac{1}{2} \end{cases}$

F

Lustration Laws by Target, Targeted Activity, and Sanction Type in Poland, Hungary, and the Czech Republic

Country	Targets (parameter X)	Targeted Activity (parameter y)	Sanction (parameter z)
Hungary	• Members of the national assembly • Members of the regional and county-level party presidiums (if the party is supported by a central budget) • Judges and prosecutors • President of the state • Members of the cabinet and state secretaries • President and vice presidents of State Audit Office, National Bank, Office of Economic Competition, Bank of Issue Board, and the Hungarian Public Television and Radio • Head manager of the Hungarian News Agency • Editors, reader-editors, columnists, and main staff of newspapers with nationwide, regional, or countywide circulation who have direct or indirect influence on public opinion • Editors of Internet news agencies registered in Hungary by the competent authority and with at least nationwide accessibility, and their assistants who have direct or indirect influence on public opinion	• Informers and officers of the III/III division of the secret police • Communist officials who prior to the transition had received briefs from the secret police	Revealing the fact of collaboration to voters

Country	Targets (parameter X)	Targeted Activity (parameter y)	Sanction (parameter z)
Poland	• Elected governmental officials in national and local elections (MPs, senators, president, cabinet members) • Members of the core executive (Central Bank, Central Controllers Office) • Officials of the central judicial system (justices of the supreme court, state prosecutor) • Top officials of the state health and social welfare systems • Chief editors of the public media • Administrators and the faculty of public and private universities (deans, presidents) • High school headmasters • Managerial personnel of the national postal service • CEOs of companies where the state is shareholder of over 50 percent of the stock	• Officers and informers of the secret police • Police units that were subject to the command of the secret police • Faculty and administrators of the police academy • Members of the border guard patrol • Officers working for military intelligence and counterintelligence • Employees of the communist Agency for Religious Beliefs • Employees of the Censorship Office	• Mandatory declarations revealing the extent of collaboration with secret police • In the event of a false declaration (as proven by the lustration agency), ban from running and holding public office for a period of 10 years • In the event of truthful declaration, the content of the declaration is revealed to the electorate
Czech Republic	• Non-elected politicians and civil servants at the national and local level (the criterion is receiving compensation out of the state budget and holding a managerial position)	• Secret police officers and informers • Communist party officials • Members of the Peoples' Militia • Members of the 1968 "Trojkas"	Permanent ban from public office

Bibliography

Surveys:

Center for Public Opinion Research (CBOS). 1988. Rozmowy Przy Okraglym Stole: Nadzieje i Sceptycyzm." Badanie 336/50/88.
1999. "Polacy o Lustracji" Komunikat 1999–2004.
2001. "Stosunek do Politykow w Sierpniu 2001," komunikat.
2002. "Polacy o Lustracji i Zmianach w Ustawie Lustracyjnej," komunikat.
Gibson, James L. 1998. Legal Values Survey. University of Houston.
Hungarian Gallup Institute Poll. June 19–20, 2002. Reported in *Nepszabadsag,* Budapest, June 24.
Miller, William, Stephen White, and Paul Heywood. 1998. "Values and Political Change in Post-communist Europe Survey," used in William Miller, *Values and Political Change in Post-Communist Europe.* New York: St. Martin's Press.
MVK Opinion Poll. 2005. March 29.
OBOP (Osrodek Badania Opinii Publicznej). 1997. *Preferencje partyjne Polakow w kwietniu 1997 r.* Available online at http://www.tns-global.pl/archive-report/ id/78.
PGSW, ISP. 2000. "Polski Generalny Sondaz Wyborczy" (Polish General Election Survey). Warsaw: Instytut Studiow Politycznych, PAN.
Szonda, Ipsos. 2006. "Preference for Parties." Budapest: Szonda Ipsos.

News sources:

Akl, Aida. 2007. "Former Liberian President Charles Taylor, Awaiting Justice." Voice of America (VOA) News, August 20, Washington, DC. Available online at http://www.ictj.org/en/news/coverage/article/1309.html.
Almond, Mark. 1992. *The Rise and Fall of Ceausescu.* London: Chapmans.
Associated Press. 1999. "Parliament Amends Controversial Law on Secret Files." LexisNexis Academic Universe, March 5.
Bachman, Klauss. 1996. "Cien Pastora Gaucka nad Polska." *Rzeczpospolita,* January 23.
BBC International Monitoring. 2002. "Hungarian Premier's Bill on Access to All Agents Files Detailed."(Source: Hungarian Radio, Budapest, text of report in Hungarian, June 19.)

Bertchi, C. Charles. 1994. "Lustration and the Transition to Democracy: the Cases of Poland and Bulgaria." *East European Quarterly* 28(4): 435–7.

Bohrer, Linda D. 1992. "Hungary Compensates Victims." *Wall Street Journal*, February 21, p. A6.

Boissevain, Benjamin. 1991. "Hungary Compensates Former Land Owners." *International Law Review* 10(10): 33.

Bollag, Burton. 1991. "In Czechoslovakia, Hunt for Villains." *New York Times*. February 3, p.19.

　　1996. "East Germans Purge Universities of Former Spies for Communist Secret Police." *Chronicle of Higher Education* 42(26): A39.

Boyes, Roger. 1990. "Disbanded Secret Police Swap Uniforms." *Times* (London), February 21.

Broadcasts, BBC Summary of World. 1991a. "Former Communist Party Assets Taken Over by the State."

　　1991b. "UDF Introduces BSP Property Bill as First Legislation in New Parliament."

Clark, Bruce. 1992. "Moscow Rivals Claim Victory in Verdict on Communist Party." *Times* (London), December 1.

Cohen, Tom. 1998. "Polish Legislators Override Veto on Secret Files Bill." Associated Press, December 18.

"Constitution Watch, September 4." 1992. *East European Constitutional Review*, Fall.

CTK, National News Wire. 1993. "Survey on Slovak Press." December 28.

　　1994a. "Czech Nobility Fares Best in Restitution." June 28.

　　1994b. "KSČ Property Was Taken Over by State." December 28.

　　1994c. "Lustration Law Should be Amended." May 23.

　　1997. "Nobody Told Prisoners They Had Been Rehabilitated." September 16.

　　2000. "Lustration Processes over in Slovakia." September 29.

Danko, I. 2008. *Prokurator: SB chciała zastraszyć Pyjasa i rozbić grupę. Interview with Krzysztof Urbaniak. Gazeta Wyborcza*. Warsaw: Agora.

Darski, Jozef. 1991–2. "Police Agents in Transition Period." *Uncaptive Minds* 4 (Winter): 19–21.

Darton, Robert. 1990. "Stasi Besieged." *New Republic* 202(7): 15.

Dempsey, Judy. 1994. "Germany Passes Law to Compensate Property Owners." *Financial Times*, May 27, p.16.

Dempsey, Judy, et al. 1991. "Haunted by the Ghosts of the Past," *Financial Times*, November 11.

Deutsche Presse-Agentur. 1999. "Poles to Be Given Access to Personal Secret Files," August 10.

Dobson, Christopher. 1990. "Red Baron Plucked from His Nest." *Sunday Telegraph*, June 17, p.13.

Dornbach, A. 1992. "Retroactivity Law Overturned in Hungary." East European Constitutional Review (Spring): 7–8.

Easton, Adam. 2006. "Poland Moves against Former Spics." BBC News Online, July 21. Available online at http://news.bbc.co.uk/2/hi/europe/5205280.stm.

Bibliography

Elon, Amos. 1992. "East Germany: Crime and Punishment." *New York Review of Books* 39(9): 6.

Engel, Matthew. 1990. "Stasi Informer Buries Past in Future." *Guardian* (London), October 4, p.20.

Eyal, Jonathan. 1990. "Front Takes the Fast Lane to Privatization." *Guardian* (London) January 2.

Finn, Peter. 2000. "Poles May Bar Payments for Postwar Acts: Panel Narrows Definition of Who May Be Compensated." *Washington Post*, January 8.

Forero, Juan. 2007. "Paramilitary Ties to Elite in Colombia Are Detailed; Commanders Cite Complicity in Violent Movement." *Washington Post*, May 22.

Franklin, David. 1991. "A Velvet Purge in Prague." *Guardian* (Manchester) January 5, p.21.

Gedmin, Jeffrey. 1991. "European Documents." *American Spectator* 24(10): 26.

"German Professors Appeal Their Dismissal in Purge of Thousand." 1992. *Nature* 359(6398): 762.

Gmyz, C. 2008. "Sledza teczke TW 'Bolka' Prokuratura Okregowa w Warszawie wszczela postepowanie w sprawie zaginionych w latach 1992–1994 dokumentow SB o Lechu Walesie." *Rzeczpospolita* (Warsaw).

Guy, Martin. 1991. "Old Nazis, New Nazis." *Esquire* 115(1): 70.

Harris, David. 1997. "Romania to Return Jewish Assets." *Jerusalem Post*, April 11, p.20.

Hejma, Ondrej. 1990a. "Government Demands Expropriation of Communist Property." Associated Press, October 11.

1990b. "Symbolic Mass Strike Demands Confiscation of Communist Property." Associated Press, April 12.

Holman, Robert, et al. 1990. "Transformation of a Post-Communist Economy: Czechoslovakia." *Journal of World Business* 25(4): 5.

International Crisis Group. 2006. "Tougher Challenges ahead for Colombia's Uribe." *Latin America Briefing*, No. 11, October 20.

2007. "Colombia's New Armed Groups." Latin America Report, No. 20, May 10. Available online at http://www.crisisgroup.org/home/index.cfm?id=4824.

Johnston, Philip. 1997. "New Evidence of Swiss Holocaust Plunder." *Daily Telegraph*. January 25, p.4.

Kadlecek, Jiri. 1998. "From the Zoo to the Jungle: A Brief Look at the Czech Information Market." *Business Information Review* 15(2): 111–17.

Kauba, Krzysztof. 1996. "Historia i Sprawiedliwosc. Czlonkowie Reakcyjnych Band stali sie dzialaczami niepodleglosciowymi" (History and Justice. Members of Reactionist Gangs Become Contributors to Polish Sovereignty). *Rzeczpospolita* (Warsaw). September 46, p.199.

Keresztes, Peter. 1990. "Darker Forces behind Romania's Front." *Wall Street Journal*. May 18, p. A10.

Kiefer, Francine. 1991. "Germans to Sell East's Lands to Investors Who Will Create Jobs." *Christian Science Monitor*. March 14.

Kinzer, Stephen. 1992. East Germans Face Their Accusers. *New York Times Magazine*. April 12, p.24.

Koenig, Richard E. 1992. "The Churches and the Stasi." *Christian Century* 109 (13): 396.

Kosobudzki, T. 1990. "Skubi's Salon." *Polish News Bulletin.*

Kumermann, Daniel. 1994. "Discrimination against Émigrés Has Deep Roots." *Prague Post*, July 20.

Laan, Nanette van der. 1998. "Securitate Files Stay under Wraps in Romania." *Daily Telegraph*, June 26, p.19.

Lane, Charles. 1995. "The Undead." *New Republic* 213(24): 10.

Laszlo, Erika. 1993. "President Signs Bill to Prosecute Crimes during 1956 Revolution." Budapest, United Press International, October 22.

Lawson, Maggie Ledford. 1996. "A Parliamentary Pariah Is Finally Allowed to Come in from the Cold." *Prague Post*, January 24.

Maass, Peter. 1992. "Hungary Blocks Trials for Ex-Leaders; President, Once Imprisoned by Communists, Challenged Law." *Washington Post*, March 3, p.20.

Mallet, Victor. 1990. "Clearing Up the Debris of Ceausescu." *Financial Times*, February 2.

Marsh, Virginia. 1992. "Romanian Farmers Wait to See How Land Lies – A Vast Majority Has Not Received Titles to Redistributed Property." *Financial Times*, July 10, p.28.

1994. "Romania Moves on New Law to Return Property." *Financial Times*, June 21, p.3.

1996. "Loose Alliance" Section Survey – Hungary." *Financial Times*, December 16, p.3.

Martin, Edward. 1992. "In the Stasi Cesspit." *Times Literary Supplement* (4638): 13.

McAdams, A. James, ed. 1997. *Transitional Justice and the Rule of Law in New Democracies*. Notre Dame: University of Notre Dame Press.

McKinsey, Kitty. 1992. "Debate Grows over Revenge on Former Communists." *Ottawa Citizen*, June 28, p. B5.

Menaker, Drusilla. 1992. "Poland, after Hesitation, Starts Prosecutions." Associated Press, October 8.

Meurs, Mieke. 1996. "The Persistence of Collectivism: Response to Land Restitution in Romania." In *Reconstructing the Balkans. A Geography of the New Southeast Europe*, eds. Derek Hall and Darrick Danta. New York: John Wiley & Sons: 169–78.

Milewicz, E. 1999. "Tadeusz Mazowiecki: Po dziesiecu latach" (interview with Tadeusz Mazowiecki). *Gazeta Wyborcza*, September 11–12.

Molnar, G. 2002. "Hungary to Open Communist Era Files." LexisNexis Academic Universe.

Mora, Imre. 1994. "Screening Targets Secret Informants." *Budapest Business Journal*, May 20, p.12.

MTI Hungarian News Agency. 2002. "Dispute on Disclosures Continues on Conference on Communist Past." September 9.

Nemeth Mary, and John Holland. 1992. "A House of Horrors." *Maclean's* 105(4): 22.

Newsfile, Press Association. 1994. "Priest Murder Generals Cleared." LexisNexis Academic Universe.

Nowacki, Pawel. 2007 "Biskup Dąbrowski nagrywał obrady episkopatu dla SB." *Wprost*, July 1.

Osiatynski, Wiktor. 2007. "Poland Makes Witch Hunting Easier." *New York Times*, January 22. Available online at //www.nytimes.com/2007/01/22/opinion/22osiatynski.html?_r=1&oref=slogin.

Paradowska, Janina. 1999a. "Bermudzki Trojkat Lustracji." *Polityka* 6(February 6).

1999b. "Trafiony Teczka," *Polityka* 37(September 9).

Parks, Michael, and Carey Goldberg. 1991. "Gorbachev Ends Party Rule; He Seizes Communist Assets, Disbands Cells." *Los Angeles Times*, August 25.

Pasek, Beata. 1998. "Poland's Screening Law Gets Go-Ahead from the Constitutional Tribunal." LexisNexis Academic Universe.

Polish News Bulletin. 1992. "Army Purge Proposals Discussed." LexisNexis Academic Universe, September 16.

1997a. "Commission Agrees on Screening Bill." LexisNexis Academic Universe, January 31.

1997b. "Senate Committee on Screening Bill." LexisNexis Academic Universe, April 24.

1997c. "Senators Propose Changes to Screening Bill." LexisNexis Academic Universe, May 14.

1997d. "Screening Bill Takes Effect." LexisNexis Academic Universe, August 4.

Polish Press Agency News Wire. 1992a. "Senate Examines Draft Law on De-communization." LexisNexis Academic Universe, July 24.

1992b. "Six Versions of De-communization Drafts Sent to Committees." LexisNexis Academic Universe, September 5.

1999. "Poland to Open Communist Files." LexisNexis Academic Universe, August 10.

Program Trzeci Polskiego Radia 2007. "Debata o Deubekizacji." Available via podcast at http://www.polskieradio.pl/_repository/_folders/f_99_890/7795.mp3.

Pross, Christian. 1998. *Paying for the Past: The Struggle over Reparations for Surviving Victims of the Nazi Terror*. Baltimore: Johns Hopkins University Press.

Remias, Ivan. 1999. "Crime Time Limit Almost Up." *Prague Post*, October 27.

Reuters. 1994. "Premier Is Ousted in the Slovak Republic." *New York Times*, March 11, p.4.

Riddel, Peter. 1993. "Putting Their House in Order." *Times* (London), December 27.

Rothschield, Hannah. 1994. "Coming Home." *Daily Telegraph* (London), March 12, p.38.

"Rozkaz: Zniszczyc Protokoly" (Order: Destroy Transcripts). 2001. *Rzeczpospolita*, January 11.

Rzeplinski, Andrzej. 1992. "A Lesser Evil. Attempting to Design a Fair Lustration Procedure." *East European Constitutional Review* 1(3): 33–5.

Sa'adah, Anne. 1998. *Germany's Second Chance: Trust, Justice, and Democratization*. Cambridge, MA: Harvard University Press.

Scharlak, Ulrich. 1995. "Victims of Communism Lose Out Again in Unified Germany." Deutsche Presse-Agentur.

Schoettler, Carl. 1993. "Arsonists Burn East German Property Records." *Gazette* (Montreal), April 23, p. A14

"Senate on Screening Resolution." 1992. *Gazeta Wyborcza* 143, June 19, p. 2.

Sietman, Richard. 1991. "Communist Academics Refuse to Fade Away." *Science* 253(5017): 261.

Simmons, Michael. 1991. "Hungarians Demand Trials of Communist Officials." *Guardian* (London), November 20.

Staff of Commission on Security and Cooperation in Europe. 1993. Human Rights and Democratization in Bulgaria. Washington: Commission on Security and Cooperation in Europe.

"Stasier Than Thou." 1991. *Economist*, November 23, p. 102.

Szamado, Eszter. 1991. "Emotions Running High over Plans to Punish Ex-Communists." Agence France Press, November 17.

1997. "Victims of Communist Secret Police Disappointed about Slim Files." Agence France Presse.

"Tainted Vestments. The Catholic Clergy's Hidden Collaboration with Communist Rule." 2007. *Economist*, January 11. Available online at http://rss.economist.com/research/articlesbysubject/displaystory.cfm?subjectid=1198560&story_id=E1_RVNVRPT.

Tomford, Anna. 1989a. "Only Obeying Orders – Forty Years On." *Guardian* (Manchester), December 13, p. 6.

1989b. "Stasi Secret Police to Disband." *Guardian* (Manchester), December 18, p. 6.

1990. "Leaders 'Cleared' of Informing the Stasi." *Guardian* (London), March 31.

1991. "Stasi Victims to Hear Who Spied on Them: Decision to Open Secret Files Could Split German Society." *Guardian* (London), December 30.

Tuffs, Annette. 1992a. "Germany: Doctor Spies." *Lancet* 339(8789): 356.

1992b. "Germany: Doctors' Links with Stasi Investigated." *Lancet* 340(8812): 168.

Tzvetkov, Plamen S. 1992. "The Politics of Transition in Bulgaria: Back to the Future?" *Problems of Communism* XLI(May–June): 34–43.

U.S. Congress, Commission on Security and Cooperation in Europe. 1999. "The Long Road Home: Struggling for Property Rights in Post-Communist Europe." Hearing before the Commission on Security and Cooperation in Europe, 106th Congress, First Session, March 25.

U.S. Department of State. 1992. *1991 Human Rights Report: Bulgaria*. Washington: U.S. Department of State.

"Ustawa o Instytucie Pamięci Narodowej-Komisja ścigania Zbrodni Przeciwko Narodowi Polskiemu." 1999. *Rzeczpospolita*, May 11, pp. I–VI.

"UW, UP, PSL: New Screening Bill?" February 2, 1996, *Rzeczpospolita*, No. 42. Warsaw.

Weschler, Lawrence. 1992. "From Kafka to Dreyfus." *New Yorker* 68: 62.

Woodard, Colin. 1997. "Universities in Romania Hope for Improvements with an Ex-Rector as the Nation's President." *Chronicle of Higher Education* 43 (26): A43–44.

Wyzan, Michael. 1992. "The Revised Bulgarian Land Law: Restitution Speeded Up." *Survey of Eastern European Law* 3(4): 6–8.

Bibliography

Zhelyazkov, Vladimir. 1992. "Bulgarian Parliament Adopts Agricultural Reform." United Press International, March 20.

1995a. "Bulgarians Protest Landownership Reform." United Press International, March 23.

1995b. "Bulgarian President Contests Land Law." United Press International, April 27.

Cited works:

Ackerman, B.A. 1992. *The Future of Liberal Revolution*. New Haven, Yale University Press.

Ágh, Attila. 1999. "The Parliamentarization of the East Central European Parties: Party Discipline in the Hungarian Parliament, 1990–1996." In *Party Discipline and Parliamentary Government*, eds. Shaun Bowler, David Farrell, and Richard Katz. Columbus: Ohio State University Press, pp.167–88.

Ágh, Atilla, and Sandor Kurtan. 1995. *Democratization and Europeanization in Hungary: The First Parliament, 1990–1994*. Budapest: Hungarian Center for Democracy Studies.

Alivizatos, Nicos C., and Nikoforos P. Diamanouros. 1997. "Politics and the Judiciary in Greece." In *Transitional Justice and the Rule of Law*, ed. J. McAdams. Notre Dame: University of Notre Dame Press.

Alt, James E., David Dreyer Lassen, and Shanna Rose. 2007. *The Causes of Fiscal Transparency: Evidence from the American States*. International Monetary Fund Staff Papers.

Appel, Hillary. 2005. "Anti-Communist Justice and Founding the Post-Communist Order: Lustration and Restitution in Central Europe." *East European Politics and Societies* 19 (Fall): 379–405.

Backer, David. 2006. "Comparing the Attitudes of Victims and the General Public towards South Africa's Truth and Reconciliation Commission Process." Paper read at the Annual Meeting of the American Political Science Association, Philadelphia, PA, September 3.

Baron, David P. 2000. "Legislative Organization with Informational Committees." *American Journal of Political Science* 44(3): 485–505.

Baron, David P., and John A. Ferejohn. 1989. "Bargaining in Legislatures." *American Political Science Review* 83(4): 1181–1206.

Barrett, Elizabeth, Peter Hack, and Agnes Munkàcsy. 2007. "Vetting in Hungary." In *Justice as Prevention: Vetting Public Employees in Transitional Societies*, eds. Alexander Mayer Rieckh and Pablo de Greiff. New York: Social Science Research Council.

Barro, R.J., and R.M. McCleary. 2003. "Religion and Economic Growth across Countries." *American Sociological Review* 68(5): 760–81.

2005. "Which Countries Have State Religions?" *Quarterly Journal of Economics* 120(4): 1331–70.

Bartlet, David L. 1996. "Democracy, Institutional Change, and Stabilisation Policy in Hungary." *Europe-Asia Studies* 48(1): 47–83.

Bawn, Kathleen. 1999. "Money and Majorities in the Federal Republic of Germany: Evidence for a Veto Players Model of Government Spending." *American Journal of Political Science* 43: 707–36.

Beke, Laszlo. 1957. *A Student's Diary: Budapest October 16–November 1, 1956.* Translated by L. Kossar and R.M. Zoltan. New York: Viking Press.

Bell, T., and D.B. Ntsebeza. 2003. *Unfinished Business: South Africa, Apartheid, and Truth.* London, New York: Verso.

Benoit, Kenneth, and Jacqueline Hayden. 2004. "Institutional Change and Persistence: Origins and Evolution of Poland's Electoral System 1989–2001." *Journal of Politics* 66(2): 396.

Benoit, Kenneth, and Michael Laver. 2007. *Party Policy in Modern Democracies.* London, New York: Routledge.

Benoit, Kenneth, and John W. Schieman. 2001. "Institutional Choice in New Democracies: Bargaining over Hungary's Electoral Law." *Journal of Politics* 13(2): 153–82.

Boraine, Alex. 2000. *A Country Unmasked.* London: Oxford University Press.

Boylan, D.M. 1998. "Preemptive Strike: Central Bank Reform in Chile's Transition from Authoritarian Rule." *Comparative Politics* 30(4): 443–62.

2001. *Defusing Democracy: Central Bank Autonomy and the Transition from Authoritarian Rule.* Ann Arbor: University of Michigan Press.

Bozóki, A. 2002. *The Roundtable Talks of 1989. The Genesis of Hungarian Democracy. Analysis and Documents.* Budapest: CEU Press.

Bozóki, András, and Márta Elbert. 1999. *A Rendszerváltás forgatókönyve: kerekasztal-tárgyalások 1989-ben.* Budapest: Magveto.

Brambor, Thomas, William Roberts Clark, and Matt Golder. 2007. "Understanding Interaction Models: Improving Empirical Analysis." *Political Analysis* (14): 63–82.

Braumoeller, Bear F. 2004. "Hypothesis Testing and Multiplicative Interaction Terms." *International Organization* 58(4): 807–20.

Brownlee, J. 2007. "Authoritarianism in an Age of Democratization." Cambridge, UK; New York: Cambridge University Press.

Bruce, S. 1992. *Religion and Modernization: Sociologists and Historians Debate the Secularization Thesis.* Oxford, New York: Oxford University Press.

Bruszt, Laszlo. 1990. "1989: The Negotiated Revolution in Hungary." *Social Research* 57(2): 365–87.

Budge, Ian. 2001. *Mapping Policy Preferences: Estimates for Parties, Electors, and Governments, 1945–1998.* Oxford, New York: Oxford University Press.

Bunce, Valerie. 1999. *Subversive Institutions: The Design and the Destruction of Socialism and the State.* Cambridge, UK; New York: Cambridge University Press.

Calda, Milos. 1996. "The Roundtable Talks in Czechoslovakia." In *The Roundtable Talks and the Breakdown of Communism,* ed. J. Elster. Chicago: University of Chicago Press.

Cassel, C.A., and Lee Sigelman. 2001. "Misreporters in Candidate Choice Models. *Political Research Quarterly* 54(3): 643–55.

Cassel, Douglass. 1998. Review of *Transitional Justice and the Rule of Law in New Democracies,* ed. A. James McAdams. *American Journal of International Law* 92 (3): 601–4.

Bibliography

Cenckiewicz, S. a. 2004. *Oczami bezpieki: szkice i materiały z dziejów aparatu bezpieczenstwa PRL*. Krakow. ARCANA.

Cenckiewicz, S., and P. Gontarczyk. 2008. *SB a Lech Wałęsa. Przyczynek do Biografii.* (The Secret Police and Lech Wałęsa: An Addendum to a Biography.) Warsaw: Instytut Pamieci Narodowej.

Choi, Suzanne, and Roman David. 2006. "Forgiveness and Transitional Justice in the Czech Republic." *Journal of Conflict Resolution* 50(3): 339–67.

Chun, Rodney M. 1997. *Compensation Vouchers and Equity Markets: Evidence from Hungary*. Hong Kong: Chinese University of Hong Kong, Department of Economics, manuscript.

Clark, Heather T. 1998. "Lustration in the Czech Republic: 'Purification of Manipulation?'" University of Washington Law School.

Colomer, Josep M. 1991. "Transitions by Agreement: Modeling the Spanish Way." *American Political Science Review* 85(4): 1283–1302.

1995. *Game Theory and the Transition to Democracy: the Spanish Model*. Aldershot, Hants, UK; Brookfield, VT: Edward Elgar.

2000. *Strategic Transitions. Game Theory and Democratization*. Baltimore: Johns Hopkins University Press.

Committee, Special Parliamentary. 1992. *Report on the Minister of Interior's Execution of Resolution from May 28*. Warsaw: Sejm, Lower House of Parliament.

Congress of Colombia. 2005. "Issuing Provision for the Reincorporation of Members of Illegal Armed Groups Who Effectively Contribute to the Attainment of National Peace" (Justice and Peace Law). Law No. 975, July 25. Available online at http://www.coljuristas.org/justicia/Law%20975.pdf.

Crawford, Vincent P., and Joel Sobel. 1982. "Strategic Information Transmission." *Econometrica* 50(6): 1431–51.

Darton, Robert. 1990. "Stasi Besieged." *New Republic* 202(7): 15.

David, Roman. 2003. "Lustration Laws in Action: The Motives and Evaluation of Lustration Policy in the Czech Republic and Poland (1989–2001)." *Law and Social Inquiry* 28(Spring 2003): 387–439.

Diamond, Larry J. 1997. *Consolidating the Third Wave Democracies: Regional Challenges*. Baltimore: Johns Hopkins University Press.

Druckman, James, and Andrew Roberts. 2005. "Communist Successor Parties and Coalition Formation in Eastern Europe." Paper read at the Annual Meeting of the Midwest Political Science Association, Chicago, April 7.

Dubinski, Krzysztof, Lech Wałęsa, and Czeslaw Kiszczak. 1990. *Magdalenka, transakcja epoki: notatki z poufnych spotkań Kiszczak-Wałęsa. Wyd. 1. ed.* (Magdalenka: the transaction of an era: secret notes from meetings between Kiszczak and *Wałęsa*).Warsaw: Sylwa.

Dudek, Antoni. 2004. *Reglamentowana Rewolucja* (A Rationed Revolution). Warsaw: Arcana.

Dudek, A., and R. Gryz. 2003. *Komuniści i Kościół w Polsce (1945–1989)* (The Communists and the Catholic Church in Poland). Kraków: Znak.

Dziennik Ustaw. 2002. *Ustawa o ujawnieniu pracy lub służby w organach bezpieczenstwa panstwa lub wspólpracy z nimi w latach 1944–1990 osób pelniacych funkcje publiczne* (Lustration Law extending to members and collaborators of the secret police from 1944 to 1990). Warsaw: Sejm Rzeczypospolitej.

Dziewulski, Jerzy. 1998. *Pierwsze czytanie (1) przedstawionego przez prezydenta Rzeczypospolitej Polskiej projektu ustawy o zmianie ustawy o ujawnieniu pracy lub służby w organach bezpieczeństwa państwa lub współpracy z nimi w latach 1944–1990 osób pełniących funkcje publiczne (druk nr 29)* (First reading of presidential proposal for law revealing work and collaboration with secret political police in 1944–1990). Parliamentary speech. Available online at www.sejm.gov.pl.

Ekiert, Grzegorz. 1996. *The State against Society: Political Crises and Their Aftermath in East Central Europe.* Princeton, NJ: Princeton University Press.

Elster, Jon. 1996. *The Roundtable Talks and the Breakdown of Communism: Constitutionalism in Eastern Europe.* Chicago: University of Chicago Press.

1998. "Coming to Terms with the Past." *European Journal of Sociology* 39: 7–48.

1999. *Alchemies of the Mind: Rationality and the Emotions.* Cambridge, UK; New York: Cambridge University Press.

2004. Closing the Books: Transitional Justice in Historical Perspective. Cambridge, UK; New York: Cambridge University Press.

Fearon, J. 1998. "Commitment Problems and the Spread of Ethnic Conflict." In *The International Spread of Ethnic Conflict*, eds. D.A. Lake and D. Rothchild. Princeton, NJ: Princeton University Press. 52: 269–305.

Finke, R., et al. 1996. "Mobilizing Local Religious Markets: Religious Pluralism in the Empire State, 1855 to 1865." *American Sociological Review* 61(2): 203–18.

Finke, R., and L.R. Iannaccone. 1993. "Supply-Side Explanations for Religious Change." *Annals of the American Academy of Political and Social Science* 527: 27–39.

Finke, R., and R. Stark. 1998. "Religious Choice and Competition." *American Sociological Review* 63(5): 761–6.

Friedrich, C.J., and Z. Brzezinski. 1965. *Totalitarian Dictatorship and Autocracy.* Cambridge, MA: Harvard University Press.

Gandhi, J. 2008. *Political Institutions under Dictatorship.* New York: Cambridge University Press.

Gandhi, J., and A. Przeworski. 2006. "Cooperation, Cooptation, and Rebellion under Dictatorships." *Economics and Politics*: 26.

2007. "Authoritarian Institutions and the Survival of Autocrats." *Comparative Political Studies* 40(11): 1279–1301.

Garlicki, Andrzej. 2003. *Karuzela. Rzecz o Okrągłym Stole* (Roundabout. A Book on Roundtable Negotiations). Warsaw: Czytelnik.

Garton Ash, Timothy. 1983. *The Polish Revolution: Solidarity 1980–82.* London: Jonathan Cape.

1999. "Authoritarian Breakdown: Empirical Test of a Game Theoretic Argument." Paper read at the American Political Science Association Meeting, Atlanta, September 2–5.

2002. "The Great Transformation in the Study of Politics in Developing Countries." In *Political Science: The State of the Discipline*, eds. I. Katznelson and H.V. Milner. New York; Washington: W.W. Norton and American Political Science Association.

Bibliography

Gibson, James. 2004. *Overcoming Apartheid: Can Truth Reconcile a Divided Nation?* New York: Russell Sage Foundation.

2006. "The Contribution of Truth to Reconciliation: Lessons from South Africa." *Journal of Conflict Resolution* 50(3): 409–32.

Gibson, James L. 2002. "Truth, Justice and Reconciliation: Judging the Fairness of Amnesty in South Africa." *American Journal of Political Science* 46(3): 540–56.

Gibson, James L., and Amanda Gouws. 2003. *Overcoming Intolerance in South Africa: Experiments in Democratic Persuasion.* Cambridge, UK; New York: Cambridge University Press.

Gilligan, Michael. 2006. "The International Criminal Court: Benign, Malign or Futile? A Formal Analysis." *International Organization* 60: 935–67.

Gilligan, T.W., and Keith Krehbiel. 1986. "Collective Decision-Making and Standing Committees: An Informational Rationale for Restrictive Amendment Procedures." *Journal of Law, Economics, and Organization* 3: 287–335.

Głowinski, Michal. 2001. *Magdalenka z razowego chleba* (Magdalenka out of rye bread). Edited by Wyd. 1. Krakow: Wydawn. Literackie.

Golder, Sona. N. 2006. *The Logic of Pre-electoral Coalition Formation.* Columbus: Ohio State University Press.

González Enríquez, Carmen, Alexandra Barahona de Brito, and Paloma Aguilar Fernández. 2001. *The Politics of Memory: Transitional Justice in Democratizing Societies.* Oxford, UK; New York: Oxford University Press.

Grabowska, M. a., and A. Sulek. 1993. *Polska 1989–1992: fragmenty pejzazu* (Poland 1989–1992: Pieces of a landscape). Warsaw: Wydawn. Instytutu Filozofii i Socjologii PAN.

Greene, Kenneth F. 2007. *Why Dominant Parties Lose: Mexico's Democratization in Comparative Perspective.* New York: Cambridge University Press.

Grzymała-Busse, Anna. 2002. *Redeeming the Communist Past: The Regeneration of Communist Parties in East Central Europe.* New York: Cambridge University Press.

Halmai, Gabor, and Kim Lane Scheppele. 1997. "Living Well Is the Best Revenge: The Hungarian Approach to Judging the Past." In *Transitional Justice and the Rule of Law in New Democracies*, ed. A.J. McAdams. Notre Dame: University o f Notre Dame Press.

Hayner, Priscilla. 2001. *Unspeakable Truths. Confronting State Terror and Atrocity.* New York, London: Routledge.

Holmes, Stephen. 1994. "The End of Decommunization." *East European Constitutional Review* 31(Summer/Fall): 33–6.

Horne, Cynthia, and Margaret Levi. 2004. "Does Lustration Promote Trustworthy Government? An Exploration of the Experience of Central and Eastern Europe." In *Problems of Post Socialist Transition: Building a Trustworthy State*, Vol. I., eds. Janos Kornai and Susan Rose-Ackerman. New York: Palgrave Macmillan.

Howard-Hassmann, Rhoda E. 1995. *Human Rights and the Search for Community.* Boulder: Westview Press.

Huber, J.D. 1996. "The Vote of Confidence in Parliamentary Democracies." *American Political Science Review* 90(2): 269–82.

Huckfeldt, R., and J. Sprague. 1987. "Networks in Context: The Social Flow of Political Information." *American Political Science Review* 81(4): 1197–1216.

Huntington, Samuel. 1991. *The Third Wave: Democratization in the Late Twentieth Century*. Norman: University of Oklahoma Press.

Huyse, Luc. 1995. "Justice after Transition: On the Choices Successor Elites Make in Dealing with the Past." *Law and Social Inquiry-Journal of the American Bar Foundation*: 20(1): 51–78.

Iannaccone, L., et al. 1998. "Rationality and the 'Religious Mind.'" *Economic Inquiry* 36(3): 373–89.

Ishiyama, John T. 1999. *Communist Successor Parties in Post-Communist Politics*. Commack, NY: Nova Science.

Iyengar, H., L. Novak, R. Sinn, and J. Zils. 1998. "Framing a Work of Art." *Civil Engineering* 68(3): 44–7.

Iyengar, S., and A. Simon. 1993. "News Coverage of the Gulf Crisis and Public Opinion: A Study of Agenda-Setting, Priming, and Framing." *Communication Research* 20(3): 365–83.

Jaruzelski, Wojciech. 1993. *Okowy i schronienie autobiografia (Bonds and Shelter: An Autobiography)*. Warsaw: BGW.

2008. *Być może to ostatnie słowo:(wyjaśnienia złożone przed sądem* (Maybe this is the last word: testimony in front of the court). Warsaw: "Comandor."

Jasiewicz, K. 1993. "Polish Politics on the Eve of the 1993 Elections towards Fragmentation of Pluralism?" *Communist and Post-Communist Studies* 26: 387–411.

2000. "Dead Ends and New Beginnings: The Quest for a Procedural Republic in Poland." *Communist and Post-Communist Studies* 53(1): 101–22.

Kaczyński, Jarosław, Micha Bichniewicz, and Piotr M. Rudnicki. 1993. *Czas na zmiany: z Jarosławem Kaczyńskim rozmawiają Michał Bichniewicz i Piotr M. Rudnicki* (Time for change: Michał Bichniewicz speaks with Jarosław Kaczyński). Warsaw: Editions Spotkania.

Kalmanovitz, Pablo. 2009. "Introduction: Law and Politics in the Colombia Negotiations with Paramilitary Groups." In *Law in Peace Negotiations*, eds. Morten Bergsmo and Pablo Kalmanovitz. Forum for International Criminal and Humanitarian Law (FICHL) No. 5, Oslo: Peace Research Institute, pp.7–21.

Kaminski, Bartlomiej. 1991. "Systemic Underpinnings of the Transition in Poland: The Shadow of the Roundtable Agreement." *Studies in Comparative Communism* 24: 173–90.

Kaminski, Marek, Grzegorz Lissowski, and Piotr Swistak. 1998. "The 'Revival of Communism' or the Effect of Institutions?: The 1993 Polish Parliamentary Elections." *Public Choice* 97(3): 429.

Kaminski, Marek, and Monika Nalepa. 2004. "Learning to Manipulate Electoral Rules." In *Handbook of Electoral System Choice*, ed. J. Colomer. London: Palgrave-Macmillan.

2006. "Judging Transitional Justice: A New Criterion for Evaluating Truth Revelation Procedures." *Journal of Conflict Resolution* 50: 383–408.

Bibliography

Kaminski, Marek M. 1999. "How Communism Could Have Been Saved: Formal Analysis of Electoral Bargaining in Poland in 1989." *Public Choice* 98(1–2): 83–109.

——— 2001. "Coalitional Stability in Multi-Party Systems: Evidence from Poland." *American Journal of Political Science* 45(2): 294–312.

——— 2004. *Games Prisoners Play: The Tragicomic Worlds of Polish Prison*. Princeton, NJ: Princeton University Press.

Karpiński, Jakub. 1988. *Polska, Komunizm, Opozycja: Słownik* (Poland, Communism, and Oppositon. A Dictionary). Warsaw: Most–samizdat publisher.

Kavan, J. 2002. "McCarthyism Has a New Name – Lustration: A Personal Recount of Political Events. In *Transition to Democracy in Eastern Europe and Russia: Impact on Politics, Economy, and Culture*, ed. B. Wejnert. Westport, CT: Praeger, x, 369.

Kenney, Padraic. 2003. *A Carnival of Revolution. Central Europe 1989*. Princeton, NJ: Princeton University Press.

Kieslowski, Krzysztof (director). 1981. *Przypadek*. (Blind Chance). Zaspół filmowy "TOR." Łódź, Poland.

Kitschelt, Herbert. 1999. *Post-Communist Party Systems*. Cambridge, UK: Cambridge University Press.

Klingemann, Hans-Dieter. 2006. *Mapping Policy Preferences II: Estimates for Parties, Electors, and Governments in Eastern Europe, European Union, and OECD 1990–2003*. Oxford, New York: Oxford University Press.

Knight, Jack. 1992. *Institutions and Social Conflict:, Political Economy of Institutions and Decisions*. Cambridge, UK; New York: Cambridge University Press.

Kopecký, Petr. 2001. *Parliaments in the Czech and Slovak Republics: Party Competition and Parliamentary Institutionalization*. Aldershot, UK; Burlington, VT: Ashgate.

Kritz, N.J., ed. 1995. *Transitional Justice: How Emerging Democracies Reckon with Former Regimes. General Considerations*. Vol. I. 3 vols. Washington: United States Institute of Peace Press.

Kunicova, Jana, and Monika Nalepa. 2006. "Explaining Late Lustration in Slovakia: Limited Choices and Limiting Coalitions." Paper read at the Midwest Political Science Association Meeting, Chicago, April 21.

Kwaśniewski, Aleksander. 1997. Prezydencki Projekt Ustawy. "Ø utworzeniu Archiwum Obywatelskiego oraz Powszechnym udostępnianiu dokumentacji wytworzonej w latach 1944–1990 przez organy bezpieczeństwa państwa." Sejm Rzeczpospolitej Polskiej, III kadencja. (Presidential proposal of a statute: a citizens archive for releasing secret police files from the archives to citizens, submitted to the Polish parliament in its third term.)

Kydd, Andrew. H. 2005. *Trust and Mistrust in International Relations*. Princeton, NJ: Princeton University Press.

Leeds, B.A. 2003. "Alliance Reliability in Times of War: Explaining State Decisions to Violate Treaties." *International Organization* 57(4): 801–27.

Leffler, M.P. 1992. *A Preponderance of Power: National Security, the Truman Administration, and the Cold War*. Stanford: Stanford University Press.

Letki, Natalia. 2002. "Lustration and Democratization in East-Central Europe." *Europe-Asia Studies* 54(4): 529–52.

Linz, Juan J., and Alfred Stepan. 1996. *Problems of Democratic Transition and Consolidation: Southern Europe, South America and Post-Communist Europe.* Baltimore and London: Johns Hopkins University Press.

Lipset, S.M. 1981. *Political Man: The Social Bases of Politics.* Baltimore: Johns Hopkins University Press.

Litynski, Jan. 1998. *Pierwsze czytanie (1) przedstawionego przez prezydenta Rzeczypospolitej Polskiej projektu ustawy o zmianie ustawy o ujawnieniu pracy lub sluzby w organach bezpieczeństwa państwa lub wspólpracy z nimi w latach 1944–1990 osób pelniących funkcje publiczne (druk nr 29)* (First Reading of Presidential Proposal for Law Revelaing work and collaboration with secret political police in 1944–1990). Parliamentary speech available online at www.sejm.gov.pl.

Los, M. 2003. "Crime in Transition: The Post-Communist State, Markets and Crime." *Crime, Law, and Social Change* 40: 145–69.

Luzzatto, Sergio. 2005. *The Body of Il Duce : Mussolini's Corpse and the Fortunes of Italy.* Translated by Frederika Randall. 1st. American ed. New York: Metropolitan.

Magaloni, B. 2006. *Voting for Autocracy: Hegemonic Party Survival and Its Demise in Mexico.* Cambridge, New York: Cambridge University Press.

2008. "Credible Power-Sharing and the Longevity of Authoritarian Rule." *Comparative Political Studies* 41(4–5): 715–41.

Magaloni, B., and V. Romero. 2008. "Partisan Cleavages, State Retrenchment, and Free Trade: Latin America in the 1990s." *Latin American Research Review* 43(2): 107–35.

Markowski, Radoslaw, and Joshua Tucker. 2005. "Pocketbooks, Politics, and Parties: The 2003 Polish Referendum on EU Membership." *Electoral Studies* 24(3): 409–33.

2008. *Euroskepticism and the Emergence of Political Parties in Poland.* Unpublished manuscript. Available online at http://homepages.nyu.edu/~jat7/MarkowskI_Tucker_Euroskep_2006.pdf.

McAdams, A. James, ed. 1997. *Transitional Justice and the Rule of Law in New Democracies.* Notre Dame: University of Notre Dame Press.

ed. 2001. *Judging the Past in Unified Germany.* New York: Cambridge University Press.

McBride, M. 2005. "Why Hasn't Economic Growth Killed Religion?" Paper read at the Meetings of the Association for the Study of Religion, Economics and Culture, Rochester, NY, November 4–5.

McCleary, R.M., and R.J. Barro. 2006a. "Religion and Economy." *Journal of Economic Perspectives* 20(2): 49–72.

2006b. "Religion and Political Economy in an International Panel." *Journal for the Scientific Study of Religion* 45(2): 149–75.

McManus-Czubinska, C., et al. 2004. "When Does Turnout Matter? The Case of Poland." *Europe-Asia Studies* 56(3): 401–20.

Bibliography

Miller, R.F., and F. Fehér. 1984. *Khrushchev and the Communist World*. London; Sydney; Croom Helm/Totowa, NJ: Barnes and Noble Books.

Moore, Barrington. 1966. *Social Origins of Dictatorship and Democracy: Lord and Peasant in the Making of the Modern World*. Boston: Beacon Press.

Nalepa, Monika. 2005. *The Power of Secret Information*. Dissertation defended at the Political Science Department of Columbia University.

2008a. "Procedural Fairness and Demand for Transitional Justice: Evidence from East Central Europe." Paper read at ISA's Forty-Ninth Annual Convention, "Bridging Multiple Divides," San Francisco, March 26.

2008b. "Punish the Guilty and Protect the Innocent: Comparing Truth Revelation Procedures." *Journal of Theoretical Politics* 20(2): 221–45.

2009. *Infiltration as Insurance: Committing to Democratization and Committing Peace*. In *Law in Peace Negotiations*, Morten Bergsmo and Pablo Kalmanovitz, eds., Forum for International Criminal and Humanitarian Law (FICHL) No. 5. Oslo: Peace Research Institute, pp.77–98.

Nino, Carlos. 1996. *Radical Evil on Trial*. New Haven: Yale University Press.

North, Douglass Cecil. 1990. *Institutions, Institutional Change, and Economic Performance: The Political Economy of Institutions and Decisions*. Cambridge, UK; New York: Cambridge University Press.

O'Donnell, Guillermo A., and Philippe C. Schmitter. 1986. *Tentative Conclusions about Uncertain Democracies*. Baltimore: Johns Hopkins University Press.

O'Dwyer, C. 2006. *Runaway State-Building: Patronage Politics and Democratic Development*. Baltimore: Johns Hopkins University Press.

Offe, Claus, and Ullrike Poppe. 2006. *"Transitional Justice in the Democratic Republic and in Unified Germany."* In *Retribution and Reparation in Tranistion to Democracy*, ed. Jon Elster. Cambridge: Cambridge University Press.

Okolicsanyi, Karoly. 1992. "Hungarian Compensation Law Proposal Covering the 1939–1949 Period." *Survey of East European Law* 3(1): 5, 8, 11–12.

1993. "Hungarian Compensation Programs off to a Slow Start." *Survey of East European Law* 2(11): 49.

Olson, David M., and William E. Crowther. 2002. *Committees in Post-Communist Democratic Parliaments: Comparative Institutionalization*. Columbus: Ohio State University Press.

Olson, David M., and Philip Norton. 1996. *The New Parliaments of Central and Eastern Europe*. London: Frank Cass.

Olson, Mancur. 1971. *The Logic of Collective Action; Public Goods and the Theory of Groups*. Cambridge, MA: Harvard University Press.

Omar, A.M. 1996. Foreword. In *Approaches to Amnesty, Punishment, Reparation and Restitution in South Africa*, ed. M.R. Rwelamira and G. Werle. Durban: Butterworths.

Oppenheim, A.N. 1992. *Questionnaire Design, Interviewing, and Attitude Measurement*. New ed. London; New York: Pinter.

Osiatyński, Wiktor. 1996. "The Roundtable Talks in Poland." In *The Roundtable Talks and the Breakdown of Communism*, ed. J. Elster. Chicago: University of Chicago Press.

Ost, David. 2005. *The Defeat of Solidarity: Anger and Politics in Post-Communist Europe*. Ithaca: Cornell University Press.

Paczkowski, Andrzej. 2000. *Aparat Bezpieczenstwa w Polsce. Taktyka Strategie, Metody. Vol. II Lata 1950–1952*. (The Polish secret service: tactics, strategies, methods, vol. II, 1950–1952). Warsaw: Instytut Studiow Politycznych PAN.

Pęk, Bogdan. 1998. *Pierwsze czytanie (1) przedstawionego przez prezydenta Rzeczypospolitej Polskiej projektu ustawy o zmianie ustawy o ujawnieniu pracy lub służby w organach bezpieczeństwa państwa lub współpracy z nimi w latach 1944–1990 osób pełniacych funkcje publiczne (druk nr 29)* (First reading of the presidential proposal for a law revealing work and collaboration with the secret political police in 1944–1990). Parliamentary speech available at www.sejm.gov.pl.

Persson, Torsten, and Guido Enrico Tabellini. 2000. *Political Economics: Explaining Economic Policy*. Cambridge, MA: MIT Press.

Petersen, Roger Dale. 2001. *Resistance and Rebellion: Lessons from Eastern Europe*. Cambridge, UK; New York: Cambridge University Press.

2002. *Understanding Ethnic Violence: Fear, Hatred, and Resentment in Twentieth-Century Eastern Europe*. Cambridge, UK; New York: Cambridge University Press.

Poganyi, Istvan. 1997. *Righting Wrongs in Eastern Europe*. Edited by E. Kirchner. Manchester, UK; New York: Manchester University Press.

Posner, Erik, and Adrian Vermuele. 2004. "Transitional Justice as Ordinary Justice." *Harvard Law Review* 117: 761–825.

Prezes, Rady Ministrow. 1998. Rzadowy Projekt Ustawy o Instytucie Pamieci Narodówej – Komisji Scigania Zbrodni Przeciwko Narodowi Polskiemu: Sejm Raczpospolitej Polskiej, III-a kadencja (Cabinet proposal of bill establishing the Institute of National Remembrance, submitted to the Third Polish Sejm).

Przeworski. A. 1991. *Democracy and the Market: Political and Economic Reforms in Eastern Europe and Latin America*. New York: Cambridge University Press.

1992. "The Games of Transition." In *Issues in Democratic Consolidation*, eds. S. Mainwaring, G. O'Donnell, and J.S. Valenzuela. Notre Dame: University of Notre Dame Press.

1999. "Minimalist Conception of Democracy: A Defense." In *Democracy's Value*, eds. I. Shapiro and Hacker-Cordon. Cambridge, UK: Cambridge University Press.

Putnam, Robert D., Robert Leonardi, and Raffaella Nanetti. 1993. *Making Democracy Work: Civic Traditions in Modern Italy*. Princeton, NJ: Princeton University Press.

Quint, P.E. 1997. *The Imperfect Union: Constitutional Structures of German Unification*. Princeton, NJ: Princeton University Press.

Raina, Peter K. 1997. *Wizyty Apostolskie Jana Pawła II w Polsce: rozmowy przygotowawcze Watykan-PRL-Episkopat* (The visits of John Paul II in Poland, preparatory talks between the Vatican, the PRL and Polish Episcopat). Warsaw: Wydawn. Ksiazka Polska.

Bibliography

Roht-Arriaza, Naomi, and Javier Mariezcurrena. 2006. *Transitional Justice in the Twenty-First Century: Beyond Truth versus Justice*. Cambridge, UK; New York: Cambridge University Press.

Romer, Thomas, and Howard Rosenthal. 1978. "Political Resource Allocation, Controlled Agendas, and the Status Quo." *Public Choice* 33: 27–44.

1979. "Bureaucrats vs. Voters: On the Political Economy of Resource Allocation by Direct Democracy." *Quarterly Journal of Economics* 93: 563–87.

Rose, Richard, and Neil Munro. 2006. *Project on Political Transformation and the Electoral Process in Post-Communist Europe at the University of Essex: Elections*. Center for the Study of Public Policy. University of Aberdeen, February. Available online at http://www.cspp.strath.ac.uk/.

Rosenberg, Tina. 1995. *The Haunted Land. Europe's Ghosts after Communism*. New York: Random House.

Roszkowski, Wojciech. 2000. *Historia Polski: 1914–2004* (History of Poland 1914–2004). Wyd 10., rozsz. ed. Warsaw: Wydawn. Naukowe PWN.

Sa'adah, Anne. 1998. *Germany's Second Chance: Trust, Justice, and Democratization*. Cambridge, MA: Harvard University Press.

Sajó, Andras. 1996. "The Roundtable Talks in Hungary." In *The Roundtable Talks and the Breakdown of Communism*, ed. J. Elster. Chicago: University of Chicago Press.

Savun, Burcu. 2008. "Information, Bias, and Mediation Success." *International Studies Quarterly* 52: 25–47.

2009. "Mediator Types and the Effectiveness of Information Provision Strategies in the Resolution of International Conflict." In *New Approaches to Mediation*, eds. Jacob Bercovitch and Scott Gartner. London, New York: Routledge.

Schelling, Thomas C. 1980. *The Strategy of Conflict*. Cambridge, MA: Harvard University Press.

Schwartz, Herman. 1995. "Lustration in Eastern Europe." In *Transitional Justice: How Emerging Democracies Reckon with Former Regimes: General Considerations*, ed. N.J. Kritz. Washington: United States Institute of Peace Press.

Sejm, Rzeczpospolitej Polskiej. 1992. *Sprawozdanie z Obrad Sejmu*, Pos 16 Kad I. 28 Maja, 1992 (Transcript of Parliamentary Proceedings, sixteenth session of the first term, May 28).

Sikkink, Kathryn. 2004. *Mixed Signals: U.S. Human Rights Policy and Latin America*. Ithaca: Cornell University Press.

Simmons, Beth A., and Richard H. Steinberg. 2006. *International Law and International Relations*. Cambridge, UK; New York: Cambridge University Press.

Staniszkis, J., and J.T. Gross. 1984. *Poland's Self-Limiting Revolution*. Princeton, NJ: Princeton University Press.

Stark, D.C., and L. Bruszt. 1998. *Postsocialist Pathways: Transforming Politics and Property in East Central Europe*. Cambridge, UK; New York: Cambridge University Press.

Stark, R., and W.S. Bainbridge. 1996. *A Theory of Religion*. New Brunswick: Rutgers University Press.

Stark, R., and R. Finke. 2004. "Religions in Context: The Response of Non-Mormon Faiths in Utah." *Review of Religious Research* 45(3): 293–8.

Suk, Jiri. 2003. *Labyrintem Revoluce: Akteri, zapletky a krizovatky jedne politicke krize.* (Labyrinths of the revolution: actors, events, and puzzles of a political crisis). Prague: Prostor.

Sutter, D. 1995. "Settling Old Scores: Potholes along the Transition from Authoritarian Rule." *Journal of Conflict Resolution* 39(1): 110–28.

Teitel, Ruti. 2000. *Transitional Justice.* New York: Oxford University Press.

Tirole, J. 2001. "Corporate Governance." *Econometrica* 69(1): 1–35.

Tokes, R.L. 1996. *Hungary's Negotiated Revolution: Economic Reform, Social Change, and Political Succession, 1957–1990.* New York: Cambridge University Press.

Tolley, H. 1998. Review of *Transitional Justice and the Rule of Law in New Democracies. Choice* 35(8): 1451.

Torpey, John C. 2003. *Politics and the Past: On Repairing Historical Injustices.* Lanham, MD: Rowman & Littlefield.

Trachtenberg, M. 1999. *A Constructed Peace: The Making of the European Settlement, 1945–1963.* Princeton, NJ: Princeton University Press.

Transkriptý Federálneho shromáždení ČSSR 1991, 17 pos. (Transcript of the Federal Assembly of the Czechoslovak Federal Republic, ČSFR, seventeenth session.)

Tucker, Aviezer. 2000. *The Philosophy and Czech Dissidence: From Patocka to Havel.* Pittsburgh: University of Pittsburgh Press.

2004. "Rough Justice. Rectification in Post-Authoritarian and Post-Totalitarian Regimes." In *Restitution and Retribution*, ed. J. Elster. New York: Columbia University Press.

Tucker, Joshua A. 2006. *Regional Economic Voting: Russia, Poland, Hungary, Slovakia and the Czech Republic, 1990–1999.* Cambridge, UK; New York: Cambridge University Press.

Ustavny Soud Ceske. Republiky. 2002. *selected Decisions/ The Constitutional Court of the Czech Republic.* Prague: Linde Praha.

Ustawa Lustracyjna. 2004. o ujawnieniu pracy lub służby w organach bezpieczeństwa państwa lub współpracy z nimi w latach 1944–1990 osób pełniacych funkcje publiczne. Z dnia 11 kwietnia 1997 roku. 2004. (Polish Lustration Law from April 11, 1997, updated version from 2004.)

Vanberg, Georg. 2000. "Establishing Judicial Independence in West Germany: The Impact of Opinion Leadership and the Separation of Powers." *Comparative Politics* 32(3): 333–53.

Walicki, Andrzej. 1997. "Justice and the Political Struggles of Post-Communist Poland." In *Transitional Justice and the Rule of Law in New Democracies*, ed. A.J. McAdams. Notre Dame: University of Notre Dame Press.

Weingast, Barry R. 1989. "Floor Behavior in the United States Congress: Committee Power under the Open Rule." *American Political Science Review* 83(3): 795–815.

1997. "The Political Foundations of Democracy and the Rule of Law." *American Political Science Review* 91(2): 245–63.

Welsh, Helga. 1994. "Political Transition Processes in Eastern Europe." *Comparative Politics* 26(4): 379–94.

1996. "Dealing with the Communist Past: Central and East European Experiences after 1990." *Europe-Asia Studies* 48(3): 413–28.

Wittenberg, Jason. 2006. *Crucibles of Political Loyalty: Church Institutions and Electoral Continuity in Hungary.* New York: Cambridge University Press.

Zemke, Janusz. 1998. *Pierwsze czytanie (1) przedstawionego przez prezydenta Rzeczypospolitej Polskiej projektu ustawy o zmianie ustawy o ujawnieniu pracy lub służby w organach bezpieczeństwa państwa lub współpracy z nimi w latach 1944–1990 osób pełniących funkcje publiczne (druk nr 29)* (First reading of the presidential proposal for a law revealing work and collaboration with the secret political police in 1944–1990). Parliamentary speech available online at www.sejm.gov.pl.

Zielinski, Jakub. 1999. "Transitions from Authoritarian Rule and the Problem of Violence." *Journal of Conflict Resolution* 43(2): 213–28.

Zybertowicz, A., and M. Los. 2000. *Privatizing the Police State: The Case of Poland.* London: Macmillan.

Archival Materials from Secret Police Files and Samizdat Collections (Accessed in Archiwum Osrodka Fundacji KARTA in Warsaw)

Anonymous. After 1981. *Mały Konspirator,* Ciąg Dalszy Nastąpi (a Samizdat Publication) (manual for conspiring members of the underground Solidarity network; contains instructions regarding how to behave in case of searches, arrests, etc.).

Anonymous. 1993. Taka Służba. Wspomnienia oficera SB. cz 1., cz 2. *Nowe Podkarpackie.* (That kind of service. Memoirs of a secret police officer.)

Beim, J. 1981a. Do kierownictwa sztabu komendy wojewodzkiej MO (Memo to the regional chiefs of communist police).

1981b. Informacja na temat odbioru "przesyłek specjanych" (Memo on technique for intersecting packages with Samizdat Publications).

Bielecki, Z. 1981. Plan dot. przeprowadzenia rozmów profilaktycznych z niektórymi figurantami wydz. II "A" KSMO. (Guidelines concerning conducting pre-emptive interviews with candidates for informers. Candidates for informers referred to persons "whose antisocialist activity had recently weakened, who had not been chosen to the leadership of Solidarity, although previously they had distinguished themselves as particularly aggressive in their antisocialist activity, and who were known for their antiregime attitudes, but usually activate in 'favorable' circumstances." The guidelines anticipated that those interviewed would sign declarations of loyalty *[lojalki]* at the end of the interview. All interviews were to be conducted either at police headquarters or in private apartments rented out for this purpose. The last pages of this file contain a plan for arresting Zbigniew Janas, Solidarity leader at large [as of 1985].)

Borodziej, W., and J. Kochanowski. 1995. *PRL w oczach Stasi,* Fakt. (Polish People's Republic in the eyes of Stasi.)

Jakimczyk, J. 1997. *Piłsudczycy, kiedyś w SB. Życie.* Warszawa: 5. (Pilsudzki supporters, once in the secret police.)

Gabinski, Z. 1980. Informacja w sprawie realizacji wytycznych Komendanta Glownego MO "Lad i Porzadek." Warszawa, Komenda Glowna MO. (Information about the implementation of operation "Law and Order.") (The report concerned the repeated conscription of retired police officers. It also contained information about the capture of one hundred anticommunist propaganda leaflets from twenty-four distributors.)

Jaruzelski, W. 1981. Wystąpienia na telekonferencji. Warszawa, Urzad Rady Ministrów. (Jaruzelski' teleconference with members of the cabinet; in which he advised participants of the teleconference to maintain positions [assumed during the implementation of martial law], because they are at a "point of no return." He advised them to prevent power being squandered, and said, "We are patient, but the government must remain the government." He also added that contrary to conventional wisdom, sternness does not aim at confrontation. "We would risk confrontation if we began to withdraw.")

1982. wypowiedź na posiedzeniu Wojskowej Rady Ocalenia Narodowego. (Speech of Jaruzelski given during a meeting of the Military Council for National Salvation.) Jaruzelski said, among other things: "We believe that martial law is our obligation to our homeland. We must use our own resources to untie this knot." He continued to talk about forces in the United States that have vested interests in the events in Poland leading to a shift in the balance of power in the world, the balance that gave Poles secure borders. "We have done everything in our power to strengthen the state. Just look at what has been happening in Chile, El Salvador, Turkey, and Ireland.")

Katowice, K. 1981. Informacja o przebiegu działań w KWK "Wujek"w dniu 16.12.1981 r. Warszawa, Archiwum Osrodka Fundacji KARTA. (Information about the pacification of the Wujek coalmine.)

Milewski. 1980. Telekonferencja z Kierownikami Sztabów Wojewodzkich "Lato 80" oraz komendantami Wojewodzkimi MO pozostalych jednostek KWMO na terenie kraju. Warszawa, Osrodek Fundacji "KARTA" (teleconference with regional chiefs of operation Summer '80 and regional chiefs of the People's Militia).

Ministerstwo Spraw Wewnętrznych. Sztab operacji "Lato '80." (Ministry of Internal Affairs, Headquarters of Operation Summer '80. The file describes the preparation of a list of 7,249 persons who were to receive training and permission for firearms for self-protection. The list included members of the prosecutors office, the judiciary, and social organizations whose health and livelihood may be threatened [if the confrontation with Solidarity were to escalate].)

MON. 1982. Zasadnicze Kierunki Działania oraz Zadania Realizowane przez WRON /Siły Zbrojne, MSW / w okresie stanu wojennego. Warszawa, Archiwum Osrodka Fundacji KARTA. (General Directives for the Realization Tasks by the Military Council of Nationa Salvation [WRON]).

MSW. 1981. Meldunek nr w zakresie internowania osób i w zakresie przeprowadzania rozmów profilaktycznych. (Report recruitment activity among interned Solidarity leaders; an estimated 56.9 percent were successfully prepared for being recruited by December 16, 1981.)

1982. Informacja dot. działan Ministerstwa Spraw Wewnetrznych i Ministerstwa Obrony Narodowej w okresie stanu wojennego. (Information about completion of operations Jodła [the internment of Solidarity leaders) and Klon (the media takeover); reports on the successful recruitment of 1,597 persons for collaboration.)

Okraj, J. 1981. Plan działan Wydziału III AKSMO w przypadku akcji krypt. 'KLON.' Warszawa, Archiwum Fundacji Osrodek "KARTA." (Plan of action for regional Peoples' Militia units in the event that operation "KLON" is initiated.)

"S." 1981. Tezy w sprawie przygotowania resortu spraw wewnetrznych do wprowadzenia stanu "W" na posiedzenie Komendantów Okręgu Katowickiego (Theses on preparing the Department of Internal Affairs to Introducing State "W" [martial law]), Warsaw, 1981.

Stachura, B. 1980. Telekonferencja z Kierownikami Sztabow Wojewodzkich "Lato 80"oraz komendantami Wojewodzkimi MO pozostałych jednostek KWMO na terenie kraju. (Teleconference with regional police chiefs regarding Operation Summer '80 and with commanders of police headquarters throughout Poland. The participants learned that around 1 million people were striking in 750 plants. They expressed concern about the engagement of students in the strike activity once the academic year started. They also estimated that the Catholic Church would not support the strikes.)

1981. Szyfrogram w sprawie sporządzenia listy osob, którym ma być wydana broń palna (do obrony własnej). (Coded instruction to prepare a list of secret police officers who were to receive firearms for personal protection.)

Tomaszewski, A. 1982. Scenariusz Działan Operacyjnych w przypadku zastosowania akcji "KLON"i "WRZOS" w obiektach CIECH, pp "METALEXPORT i POLIMEX-CEKOP. (Scenario for infiltrating Solidarity cells in foreign trade cooperatives: METALEXPORT and POLIMEX-CEKOP according to operations Klon and Wrzos. The plan anticipated helping someone "friendly" to the secret police become one of the Solidarity leaders. The "friendly" person would be known to be sympathetic to the secret police's cause either by coming from abroad or from the internment of current leaders of Solidarity. Recruitment for collaboration with the secret police would frequently follow a target assuming a leadership position in Solidarity. In case a target refused cooperation, follow-up conversations were sometimes scheduled. In the case of the POLIMEX cooperative, the Solidarity leader had already been elected. The secret police planned to interview him, intimidate him with questions about what he had been doing in the United States, and why he returned to Poland, and eventually pressure him to resign his position. The secret police had already selected a cooperative candidate to assume the leadership position. The plan outlined the creating of a coalition of workers, affiliated with the communist party, who would support the election of the new leader. Furthermore, the plan outlined the recruitment of members of the foreign service who had family in the West for collaboration. The secret police would contact the target by telephone first and outline the tasks of collaboration abroad in conjunction with working abroad. If this was not effective, the target would be summoned to appear at police headquarters. There he would be induced to collaboration by a combination of bribes, but where necessary, threats – explaining, for instance, that by virtue of having family in the United States he was not qualified to go on business trips to the United States unless he cooperated with the secret police [these threats were usually effective, because the target was anxious about losing his passport]. An attachment contained names of persons who had been selected as candidates for recruitment.)

WB, J. 1997. Raport z Drugiej Strony: historia: tajne raporty SB z okresu stanu wojennego. (Report from the other side: Secret reports of SB from martial law.) *Gazeta w Lublinie*. (Lublin), nr 290: 4–8.

Zaczkowski, Jacek. 1981. Telekonferencja gen. Żaczkowskiego. Warszawa, Ministerstwo Spraw Wewnetrznych Sztab operacji "Lato '80." (Teleconference transcript from meeting with General Zaczkowski, Ministry of Internal Affairs, Headquarters of Operation Summer '80. Participants admitted that the situation had considerably worsened and called for "a demonstration of force, more focused activity and maneuvers." Finally, participants were advised not to call Solidarity activists for military conscription, but they agreed not to create written lists of Solidarity activists, but just go by word of mouth.)

Zielinski, Z. 1981. Protokół z posiedzenia Wojskowej Rady Ocalenia Narodowego. (Report from a meeting of WRON in which the participants admitted that martial law preempted the confrontation of "internal and external forces that would have resulted in the internationalization of the Polish case." The report also postulated helping soldiers who had distinguished themselves by going to college and finding jobs. Finally, the report anticipated selecting thirty laborers for a meeting with the WRON during which they would be informed that martial law had been implemented as the government's strategy of last resort. The selected laborers would be cautioned about the "sabotage and diversion activities conducted by the western secret service.")

1982. Protokół z posiedzenia Wojskowej Rady Ocalenia Narodowego. (Report from a meeting of WRON with Bishop Glemp, during which the latter was supposed to have said that "Solidarity had become increasingly confrontational since the events in Radom" [the decision to organize a general strike in response to a new price hike]. The report also stated that Glemp had tried to come up with excuses for the Catholic Church's declaration toward Sejm [the lower house of parliament] and students. The file also contained a request issued to the chief of the Polish army to "prevent the creation of the myth of Solidarity.")

Index

Index

Jefferey M. Sellers, *Governing from Below: Urban Regions and the Global Economy*

Yossi Shain and Juan Linz, eds., *Interim Governments and Democratic Transitions*

Beverly Silver, *Forces of Labor: Workers' Movements and Globalization since 1870*

Theda Skocpol, *Social Revolutions in the Modern World*

Regina Smyth, *Candidate Strategies and Electoral Competition in the Russian Federation: Democracy without Foundation*

Richard Snyder, *Politics after Neoliberalism: Reregulation in Mexico*

David Stark and László Bruszt, *Postsocialist Pathways: Transforming Politics and Property in East Central Europe*

Sven Steinmo, Kathleen Thelen, and Frank Longstreth, eds., *Structuring Politics: Historical Institutionalism in Comparative Analysis*

Susan C. Stokes, *Mandates and Democracy: Neoliberalism by Surprise in Latin America*

Susan C. Stokes, ed., *Public Support for Market Reforms in New Democracies*

Duane Swank, *Global Capital, Political Institutions, and Policy Change in Developed Welfare States*

Sidney Tarrow, *Power in Movement: Social Movements and Contentious Politics*

Kathleen Thelen, *How Institutions Evolve: The Political Economy of Skills in Germany, Britain, the United States, and Japan*

Charles Tilly, *Trust and Rule*

Daniel Treisman, *The Architecture of Government: Rethinking Political Decentralization*

Lily Lee Tsai, *Accountability without Democracy: How Solidary Groups Provide Public Goods in Rural China*

Joshua Tucker, *Regional Economic Voting: Russia, Poland, Hungary, Slovakia, and the Czech Republic, 1990–1999*

Ashutosh Varshney, *Democracy, Development, and the Countryside*

Jeremy M. Weinstein, *Inside Rebellion: The Politics of Insurgent Violence*

Stephen I. Wilkinson, *Votes and Violence: Electoral Competition and Ethnic Riots in India*

Jason Wittenberg, *Crucibles of Political Loyalty: Church Institutions and Electoral Continuity in Hungary*

Elisabeth J. Wood, *Forging Democracy from Below: Insurgent Transitions in South Africa and El Salvador*

Elisabeth J. Wood, *Insurgent Collective Action and Civil War in El Salvador*

CPSIA information can be obtained
at www.ICGtesting.com
Printed in the USA
LVHW031534030321
680484LV00002B/235